Gender, Governance and International Security

The United Nations Security Council, in 2000, unanimously passed a resolution calling for women's increased participation in conflict prevention and peace-building, as well as their protection during conflict. This marked the first time that the UN Security Council explicitly addressed gender issues in 'conflict' and 'post-conflict' situations. But what difference has this international agenda on 'Women, Peace and Security' made to women's lives on the ground and to the governance of international peace and security?

This volume provides a critical evaluation of the mainstreaming of gender issues in matters of international peace and security resulting from the passage of Resolution 1325 in 2000. It considers how this agenda actually plays out in different contexts, and the implications for women's activism and for peace and security.

The picture that emerges is not uniform, obliging us to reconsider the links between gender, conflict, different visions of peace and, consequently, different projects of peacebuilding. Thus, the book poses new questions for transnational feminist scholars and activists.

This book is based on a special issue of the *International Feminist Journal of Politics*.

Nicola Pratt is Reader in the International Politics of the Middle East at the University of Warwick, UK. She researches and writes about gender, civil society and security in the Middle East. She is also joint leader of the 'Reconceptualising Gender' research network between Warwick and Birzeit University (Palestine).

Sophie Richter-Devroe is Lecturer in Gender and Middle East Studies at the Institute of Arab and Islamic Studies, Exeter University, UK. She is the author of several prize-winning articles on Palestinian women's activism against Israeli occupation. More recently her research focuses on Palestinian refugees and the Naqab Bedouins.

The Women, Peace and Security agenda began in the United Nations Security Council with Resolution 1325 but has since fanned out across the world to UN peacekeeping missions conflict, post conflict and non-conflict member states. It portends to make the participation of women in peace processes, the prevention of conflict and protection against gender-based and sexual violence central to international security policymaking. That has not happened even after a decade of 'gender mainstreaming' efforts. Gender, Governance and International Security explains why – interrogating the assumptions and the practices promoted by UNSCR 1325 at the highest level and on the ground in conflict and post conflict settings. It demonstrates that feminist research and transnational activism are needed more than ever not just to hold states to account but to transform a problematic Resolution into a critical engagement with the gendered nature of security politics.

Professor Jacqui True, School of Political and Social Inquiry, Monash University, Australia

This remarkable collection offers a timely opportunity to engage and reflect upon the impact of SC Resolution 1325 some 10+ years after its adoption. Lauded as one of the most important accomplishments concerning women, peace and security at the UN while simultaneously drawing sharp criticisms from feminist activists and academics alike, this volume captures the contours of that debate with nuance and sophistication in both theoretical and empirical terms. It is a must read for anyone interested in questions of gender, governance and security.

Sandra Whitworth, Professor of Political Science, York University, Canada

Gender, Governance and Security offers a timely and ethically relevant collection of essays that all critically engage with the virtues and shortcomings of United Nations (UN) Resolution 1325 on Women, Peace and Security. Pratt and Richter-Devroe and their contributors raise very important ethical questions regarding the universal applicability of 1325 and critically take on board the essential discourses and practices that surround the resolution and, as such, help to deconstruct the protection myth that underpins so much of international relations scholarship. The book is an indispensable contribution to debates about the lack of intersectional awareness among policy-makers charged with the task of furthering women's peace and security in international society. It offers telling feminist insights into the misuse of 1325 to justify, among other things, military intervention and brute force more generally.

Annika Bergman Rosamond, Senior Lecturer in International Relations, Lund University, Sweden.

Gender, Governance and International Security

Edited by
Nicola Pratt and Sophie Richter-Devroe

Routledge
Taylor & Francis Group

LONDON AND NEW YORK

First published 2014 by Routledge

2 Park Square, Milton Park, Abingdon, Oxfordshire OX14 4RN
711 Third Avenue, New York, NY 10017

Routledge is an imprint of the Taylor & Francis Group, an informa business

First issued in paperback 2018

British Library Cataloguing in Publication Data
A catalogue record for this book is available from the British Library

ISBN 13: 978-0-415-82915-1 (hbk)
ISBN 13: 978-1-138-38329-6 (pbk)

Typeset in Sabon
by Taylor & Francis Books

Publisher's Note
The publisher would like to make readers aware that the chapters in this book may be referred to as articles as they are identical to the articles published in the special issue. The publisher accepts responsibility for any inconsistencies that may have arisen in the course of preparing this volume for print.

Contents

CONTENTS

Citation Information

The following chapters were originally published in the *International Feminist Journal of Politics*, volume 13, issue 4 (December 2011), volume 14, issue 3 (September 2012)and volume 15, issue 1(March 2013). When citing this material, please use the original page numbering for each article, as follows:

Chapter 1
 Introduction: Critically Examining UNSCR 1325 on Women, Peace and Security
 Nicola Pratt and Sophie Richter-Devroe
 International Feminist Journal of Politics, volume 13, issue 4
 (December 2011) pp. 489–503

Chapter 2
 Sex, Security and Superhero(in)es: From 1325 to 1820 and Beyond
 Laura J. Shepherd
 International Feminist Journal of Politics, volume 13, issue 4
 (December 2011) pp. 504–521

Chapter 3
 No Angry Women at the United Nations: Political Dreams and the Cultural Politics of United Nations Security Council Resolution 1325
 Sheri Lynn Gibbings
 International Feminist Journal of Politics, volume 13, issue 4
 (December 2011) pp. 522–538

Chapter 4
 UNSCR 1325 and Women's Peace Activism in the Occupied Palestinian Territory
 Vanessa Farr
 International Feminist Journal of Politics, volume 13, issue 4
 (December 2011) pp. 539–556

Chapter 5

Resolution 1325 and Post-Cold War Feminist Politics
Carol Harrington
International Feminist Journal of Politics, volume 13, issue 4
(December 2011) pp. 557–575

Chapter 6

'Women, Peace and Security': Addressing Accountability for
Wartime Sexual Violence
Sahla Aroussi
International Feminist Journal of Politics, volume 13, issue 4
(December 2011) pp. 576–593

Chapter 7

Configurations of Post-Conflict: Impacts of Representations of
Conflict and Post-Conflict upon the (Political) Translations of
Gender Security within UNSCR 1325
Laura McLeod
International Feminist Journal of Politics, volume 13, issue 4
(December 2011) pp. 594–611

Chapter 8

Feminist Knowledge and Emerging Governmentality in UN
Peacekeeping: Patterns of Co-optation and Empowerment
Audrey Reeve
International Feminist Journal of Politics, volume 14, issue 3
(September 2012) pp. 348–369

Chapter 9

Leveraging Change: Women's Organizations and the
Implementation of UNSCR 1325 in the Balkans
Jill A. Irvine
International Feminist Journal of Politics, volume 15, issue 1
(March 2013) pp. 20–38

Notes on Contributors*

SAHLA AROUSSI has an MA in Human Rights from the University of Malta and has an LLM in Human Rights Law and Transitional Justice from the University of Ulster. She has just completed a PhD in politics at the University of Ulster. Her PhD thesis concerned the implementation of Security Council Resolution 1325 in peace agreements. Sahla is currently employed as a researcher in the faculty of law at the University of Antwerp in Belgium working on a project entitled 'Law, Power Sharing and Human Rights'.

VANESSA FARR holds a PhD from York University, Toronto, and is the Social Development and Gender Advisor at UNDP's Programme of Assistance to the Palestinian People where she focuses on how gender impacts individual experiences of the intra-Palestinian and Palestinian–Israeli conflicts. She is an expert on gendered experiences of armed conflict, including the demobilization, disarmament and reintegration (DDR) of women and men combatants after war, the impacts on men and women of prolific small arms and light weapons (SALW), and women's coalition-building in conflict-torn societies. During the past 10 years, she has worked on gender mainstreaming in weapon collection programmes and DDR processes, undertaken research on the gendered impact of SALW and co-edited a book entitled 'Sexed Pistols: The Gendered Impacts of Small Arms and Light Weapons' (UNU Press, 2009).

SHERI LYNN GIBBINGS is a Social Science and Humanities Research Council of Canada (SSHRC) Postdoctoral Fellow at the Institute of Asian Research, University of British Columbia. Gibbings received her BSc degree from McGill University, her MA from York University, and her Ph.D. from the University of Toronto. Her MA research is entitled 'Governing Women, Governing Security: Governmentality, Gender Mainstreaming and Women's Activism at the UN.' Her doctoral research focuses on Indonesia, where she has examined the growing number of street vendors as they confront the problems of urbanization, state violence and government regulations while also encountering new political and social imaginaries related to ideas of democracy and transparency. In 2012, Gibbings will start as an Assistant Professor in the Global Studies Department at Wilfrid Laurier University.

CAROL HARRINGTON lectures in sociology and social policy at Victoria University of Wellington, New Zealand. She is the author of 'Politicization of Sexual Violence from Abolitionism to Peacekeeping' (London: Ashgate 2010) and a number of articles concerned with gender and peacekeeping. Her current research interests focus upon questions related to gender, militarism and feminist activism.

LAURA McLEOD is a lecturer in International Politics at the University of Manchester, UK. She completed her PhD thesis 'Gender Politics and Security Discourse: Feminist and Women's Organizing in "Post-conflict" Serbia' at the University of Sheffield in March 2011.

NICOLA PRATT is an Associate Professor of the International Politics of the Middle East at the University of Warwick, UK. She is the co-author, with Nadje Al-Ali, of *What Kind of Liberation? Women and the Occupation of Iraq* (University of California Press, 2009) and co-editor, also with Nadje Al-Ali, of *Women and War in the Middle East* (Zed Press, 2009). She has also written on human rights, civil society and democratization in the Arab world, including *Democracy and Authoritarianism in the Arab World* (Lynne Rienner, 2007). Her current research is on gendering the politics of in/security in the Middle East, with a focus on Egypt, Jordan, Lebanon and Palestine. She is a joint leader of the Reconceptualizing Gender research network between Warwick and Birzeit University (Palestine). She tries to be an active member of the Stop the War Coalition, Palestine Solidarity Campaign and Women's International League for Peace and Freedom.

SOPHIE RICHTER-DEVROE is a lecturer in Gender and Middle East Studies at the Institute of Arab and Islamic Studies, Exeter University, with a broad research interest in gender theory and women's activism in the Middle East. Her PhD dissertation research (supervised by Prof. Gerd Nonneman and Dr Ruba Salih) focused on gender and conflict transformation in the Palestinian Occupied Territories, looking at women's participation in dialogue-based conflict resolution programmes as well as in various forms of formal and informal resistance activism after 2000. She is an advanced student of the Arabic and Persian languages and has published translations and reviews of Arabic literary works as well as journal articles and book chapters on Palestinian and Iranian women's activism.

LAURA J. SHEPHERD is a senior lecturer in International Relations at the University of New South Wales, Australia. She currently works at the intersection of gendered global politics, critical approaches to security and International Relations theory. Laura is the editor of *Gender Matters in Global Politics: A Feminist Introduction to International Relations* (London: Routledge, 2010) and the author of *Gender, Violence and Security: Discourse as*

Practice (London: Zed, 2008), as well as of many scholarly articles in peer-reviewed journals, including International Studies Quarterly, International Feminist Journal of Politics, Review of International Studies and Journal of Gender Studies.

*The contributor information for AUDREY REEVES and JILL A. IRVINE can be found on pages 140 and 161 respectively.

Preface

This volume is based on a special issue of the *International Feminist Journal of Politics* (IFJP), first published in December 2011 and entitled 'Critically Examining UN Security Council Resolution 1325 on Women, Peace and Security'. UNSCR 1325 was passed in 2000 with the aim of mainstreaming gender into matters of conflict, conflict prevention and peace building. It constituted the first time that the UN Security Council recognised the gender dimensions of international security. The tenth anniversary of its passage was the impetus for taking time to reflect on the Resolution, its achievements, its limitations as well as the challenges to its implementation. The contributions to the special issue critically examined 1325, both in terms of its conceptual foundations as well as in relation to policy-related and practical dimensions.

This edited volume includes the original introduction and all the full length articles that appeared in the special issue of IFJP. It also includes two further articles, by Audrey Reeves and Jill Irvine, which we were unable to include in the original special issue due to space constraints and which were subsequently published by IFJP. Both articles examine the potentialities and the constraints of 1325 in terms of promoting gender equality and women's participation in conflict resolution and peace building.

The article by Reeves explores the ways in which gender mainstreaming in peace operations, in line with 1325, has enabled the growth in gender experts within peacekeeping missions, who help to redefine the meanings of security (for example, highlighting peacekeeper sexual violence and abuse). However, the integration of feminist knowledge into peacekeeping has also depended upon the construction of particular gender and racial identities that may create new marginalities within peacekeeping contexts. Reeves's arguments echo those of Sheri Gibbings in this volume, whose article illustrates how gender advocates at the UN essentialise gender (women as "peaceful", men as "obstacles to peace") in order to persuade member states to implement 1325. Both articles highlight the need to monitor the longer term implications of 1325, particularly concerning the interactions between international institutions and women and men living in conflict zones, which may be guided by and rely upon these essentialised conceptualisations of gender (and race).

Irvine argues that women's groups in Serbia, Bosnia-Herzegovina and Kosovo have used 1325 to mobilise local support to pressure the UN and other international agencies to include women in post-conflict decision-making and to address issues of violence against women and of transitional justice. However, women activists have been unable to use 1325 to promote more sustainable transformations of structural inequalities. Irvine's conclusions, like those of Laura Shepherd and Vanessa Farr in this volume, point to the tensions within 1325 between the emphasis on women's agency in peace and security and the failure to address structural factors that may constrain women's agency in general, as well as structural inequalities that undermine peace and security.

Despite the limitations of 1325 highlighted by this volume, the Women, Peace and Security agenda continues to expand, perhaps a confirmation that feminist knowledge has become an integral part of governmentality (Reeves, this volume). Since the publication of the special issue in December 2011, the US administration and Australian government (amongst others) have launched their first National Action Plans to implement 1325 and the UK government has revised its National Action Plan to include implementation of 1325 in the Middle East and North Africa (in response to the uprisings, mass protests and political transitions taking place across the region). The expansion of the 1325 agenda into new areas makes it even more essential that we critically examine the resolution and monitor its effects.

Finally, we would like to acknowledge and thank the individuals who have played a part in the development of the ideas that led to the publishing of this volume. The basis for this volume first emerged from a series of panels that Nicola Pratt organized at the ABRI-ISA conference in Brazil in 2009, entitled, 'Critically Evaluating UNSCR 1325'. Present at those panels were: Sahla Aroussi (who has written one of the articles in this volume), Elena Grillenzoni, Ilja Luciak, Isis Nusair, Sophie Richter-Devroe (co-editor of this volume) and Rita Santos. The ideas emerging from these panels stimulated Nicola Pratt to propose a special issue of IFJP on 1325. We thank the then editor of IFJP, Sandra Whitworth, for all her help and support in making the idea of the special issue into a reality. Finally we thank Laura Sjoberg, a current editor of IFJP, and Steve Thompson and Sophia Levine of Routledge for their support in the publication of the special issue as this edited volume.

Nicola Pratt
Sophie Richter-Devroe
April 2013

i n t r o d u c t i o n

Critically Examining UNSCR 1325 on Women, Peace and Security

NICOLA PRATT AND SOPHIE RICHTER-DEVROE
University of Warwick, Coventry, UK and University of Exeter, Exeter, UK

Abstract

Here, we introduce the articles that comprise this special issue of *IFJP*, entitled, 'Critically Examining UNSCR 1325'. The aim of this special issue is to examine the implementation of UNSCR 1325 and its implications for women's activism and for peace and security. Given that the articles in this volume approach UNSCR 1325 from various perspectives and in different contexts, our aim in this introduction is to point out a number of conceptual, policy and practical issues that are crucial in the debates around UNSCR 1325 specifically, and women, peace and security more broadly. We do this in four parts: first, problematizing the resolution in relation to changes in global governance; second, examining the Resolution's assumptions about (gendered) agency and structure; third, examining the Resolution's assumptions about the links between conflict and gender; and, fourth, comparing different contexts in which 1325 is implemented. To some degree, differences between contributors may be accounted for by different understandings of feminism(s) as a political project. Different feminisms may underpin different visions of peace and, consequently, different projects of peacebuilding. Ultimately, this volume, while answering the questions that we originally posed, throws up new questions about transnational feminist praxis.

INTRODUCTION

On 31 October 2000, the United Nations Security Council unanimously passed Resolution 1325 on Women, Peace and Security (or, '1325' for short), calling for women's increased participation in conflict prevention and resolution initiatives, as well as their protection during conflict. The UN has heralded

1325 as a landmark document that promises to protect women's rights and guarantee their equal participation in peace processes (for example, United Nation Secretary General. (UNSG) 2008). The Resolution's adoption is considered by many to be an historic milestone since it marked the first time that the UN Security Council dealt specifically with gender issues and women's experiences in 'conflict' and 'post-conflict' situations and their contribution to conflict resolution and prevention (Cohn 2008). Previous UN resolutions had treated women as victims of war, in need of protection. However, 1325 also recognized women as agents in building peace and guaranteeing security.

Many feminist scholars and activists have lauded 1325 as highly significant for women's anti-war and peace activism.[1] The Resolution appears to build on a significant body of feminist scholarship highlighting men's and women's differential experiences of war, conflict and post-conflict,[2] redefining sexual violence as a weapon of war, rather than an 'unfortunate byproduct' (Chinkin 1994; Seifert 1994; and others), and recognizing the significant role played by women at the grassroots level in rebuilding the lives of their communities after conflict (Sorensen 1998). UNSC Resolution 1325 also seems to draw on feminist literature documenting the historic role of women's/feminist groups around the world in mobilizing against war, violence and militarism (Cockburn 1998, 2007; Waller and Rycenga 2001; among others).

The Resolution constructs a link between social (gender) change and political (conflict) transformation in mainstream international policy and has paved the way for new programs and measures at the international, governmental and non-governmental level. At the time of writing, the Resolution has been translated into more than 100 languages and 25 National Action Plans have been drafted to assist implementation at the country level.[3]

Yet, the ways in which this link between social and political dynamics is conceptualized, and whether and how this is applicable to widely diverging conflict scenarios needs to be interrogated. Several authors have urged a more critical engagement with UNSCR 1325, both in terms of its conceptual foundations as well as policy-related practical impacts.[4]

The contributions to this volume (by academics, practitioners and activists) critically examine UNSCR 1325 in terms of its implementation and relevance to women's activism in different parts of the world as well as its conceptualizations of approaches to gender, peacebuilding and conflict resolution.[5] They provide both theoretical/analytical critiques of the resolution, as well as examining the policy and implementation levels. More specifically, this volume addresses the following questions:

- To what degree is Resolution 1325 actually being translated into programs and measures on the ground and with what outcome for women's lives and for peace and security?
- What are the implications of the Resolution's focus on armed conflict, as opposed to other forms of structural violence, for peace and security?

- How do women activists in conflict areas use UNSCR 1325? How do they reconcile, if at all, the universality of the resolution with the particularity of different conflict situations?
- Is the privileging of a universal gender identity in understanding women's experiences and responses to conflict, above other social categories – such as, nationality, class, ethnicity or religion, among others – a useful tool or an obstacle to women's activism?
- What does the formulation, adoption and/or implementation of 1325 tell us about the nature of post-Cold War global governance?

Given that the articles in this volume approach UNSCR 1325 from various perspectives and in different contexts, our aim in this introduction is not to present a coherent theoretical framework. Rather we would like to point out a number of conceptual, policy and practical issues that are crucial in the debates around UNSCR 1325 specifically, and women, peace and security more broadly. We attempt to summarize some of the answers to the above research questions as presented by our contributors in four parts: first, problematizing the resolution in relation to changes in global governance; second, examining the Resolution's assumptions about (gendered) agency and structure; third, examining the Resolution's assumptions about the links between conflict and gender; and, fourth, comparing different contexts in which 1325 is implemented.

THE PATH TO UNSCR 1325 AND CHANGES IN GLOBAL GOVERNANCE

The origins of 1325 lie in the UN world conferences on women and long-term lobbying by women's and civil society organizations concerned with gender, development and conflict. The issue of women, conflict and peace received intense debate at the Third World Conference on Women in Nairobi in 1985 (Cockburn 2007: 139). It was, however, only once Boutros Ghali's Agenda for Peace in 1992 had introduced a bottom-up approach of peace*building* to mainstream conflict resolution (to complement the dominant state-centric, top-down approach of peace*making*) that women achieved a major breakthrough with the Beijing Platform for Action adopted at the Fourth World Conference on Women in 1995. The Platform emphasized the importance of a gender perspective and women's contributions for sustainable peacebuilding and identified '[t]he effects of armed or other kinds of conflict on women, including those living under foreign occupation' (United Nations [UN] 1995) as one of its 12 major areas of concern and urging governments, international organizations and civil society to take strategic actions.

A review of the implementation of the Beijing Platform for Action at the 23rd special session of the General Assembly on 'Women 2000: gender equality, development and peace for the twenty-first century' (Beijing +5) found that the critical area of concern 'Women and Armed Conflict' had not been sufficiently addressed, let alone implemented. As a result, the NGO Working

Group on Women and Armed Conflict (NGOWG) was founded to lobby the UN for the passage of a UN security council resolution that would help ensure that the issue of women, peace and security would be properly addressed. In October 2000, Namibia, which had earlier that same year passed the Windhoek Declaration and the Namibia Plan of Action on Mainstreaming a Gender Perspective in Multidimensional Peace Support Operations, took up the presidency of the UN Security Council. It responded to the NGO Working Group's lobbying by agreeing to sponsor a session on Women, Peace and Security. In preparation for this session, an Arria Formula meeting was held on 23 October 2000 giving civil society organizations and representatives the opportunity to present their experiences and raise their concerns to Security Council members. A week later, on 31 October 2000, UNSCR 1325 was passed unanimously.[6]

The increasing concern among activists for the impacts of conflict on women and women's participation in peacebuilding and conflict resolution was mirrored in the theoretical shift in international relations (IR) theory away from the (neo-)realist state-centerd to a more holistic, agent-centerd conceptualization of security, proposed particularly in the field of critical security studies (see e.g. Booth 2005) and feminist IR (e.g. Peterson 1992; Tickner 1992). The need to take into consideration the *human* dimension of security, and for rethinking security from a feminist perspective, was famously called for by Ann Tickner already in the early 1990s:

> Not until the hierarchical social relations, including gender relations, that have been hidden by realism's frequently depersonalised discourse are brought to light can we begin to construct a language of national security that speaks out of the multiple experiences of both women and men. (Tickner 1992: 66)

UNSCR Resolution 1325 opens with 10 pre-ambular paragraphs referring to broad normative standards embraced by the international community through legal principles, human rights and humanitarian law, as well as previous UN resolutions, declarations and documents, such as the Beijing Platform for Action, the United Nations Charter, the Windhoek Declaration and the Namibia Plan of Action. Its 18 operational paragraphs cover 3 main themes. First, the resolution recognizes women's contribution to peacebuilding and conflict resolution and calls for their increased *participation* at all decision-making levels in national, regional and international conflict prevention and resolution initiatives. Second, it highlights the gendered aspects of war and armed conflict demanding the *protection* of women's rights, including shielding women and girls from gender-based violence and other violations of international law. Finally, the resolution calls upon local actors, member states, but also the UN system itself, to adopt a *gender perspective* in peace operations, negotiations and agreements.

In terms of its recognition of women's role in peacebuilding and conflict resolution and women's differentiated experiences of war, 1325 appears to build on feminist scholarship and activism. However, Carol Harrington's article in this volume questions celebratory accounts that view feminist/women's activist lobbying inside and outside the UN as the main initiators of this shift in conceptualizations of peace and security for

> fail[ing] to analyze how the collapse of the Soviet Union transformed discourse on both 'women' and 'human rights' as problems for international government. In the post-Cold War order the US poses as leader of the democratic world and defender of women and children against brutal men who instigate 'new wars' characterised by mass rape.

Yet, the increase in peacekeeping in response to these 'new wars' 'creates environments in which sexual violence, abuse and exploitation flourish'. Resolution 1325, Harrington argues, 'speaks to these tensions within contemporary peacekeeping operations, proposing the technical solution of gender mainstreaming' (Harrington this volume). What her article suggests is that 1325 constitutes a tool for dealing with the new realities of post-Cold War international security rather than transforming them. This raises two questions about the link between 1325 and feminism: (a) does feminist activism and research really challenge the international security architecture? Or (b) does 1325 really build on feminist activism and research?

Sheri Gibbings's article, based on ethnographic research among gender advocates at the UN, including the Women's International League for Peace and Freedom (WILPF), demonstrates how 1325 and the discourses in support of it have omitted some significant feminist aims. She finds that '[p]rior to the passage of UNSCR 1325, WILPF-UN often portrayed women as agents of peace, but also provided an explicit critique of militarism and masculinity'. Discursive speech norms at the UN, however, later curtailed feminist critiques of militarization and militarized masculinities in conflict, instead requiring a unique focus on the positive, 'utopian' representation of women as 'bridge-builders' and 'peacemakers' (Gibbings this volume). One of the least studied aspects of the resolution (including within this volume) is the tracing of what sort of feminism is represented in 1325 and, consequently, with what implications. One could argue that, rather than transforming international security agendas, 1325 marginalizes anti-militarist feminism in advocating for international peace and security. The innovative conceptualizations of human security and the inter-relationship between gender and war dynamics advanced in critical and feminist IR scholarship thus have yet to be fully embraced by the mainstream international agenda on women, peace and security (see also Väyrynen 2004).

CRITICALLY EXAMINING UNSCR 1325: GENDER, STRUCTURE AND AGENCY

Several articles in this volume point to the tensions in the Resolution between highlighting the significance of women's agency in peace and security and failing to address structural factors that may constrain women's agency.

Laura Shepherd's contribution argues that a positive shift has taken place in the Council's language with regard to the 'women, peace and security' agenda: while 1325 portrays women mainly as victims, the later Resolutions add a discursive representation of women as actors, agents or even 'superheroines'. Although these developments may give rise to optimism, Shepherd also points out that structural causes (such as poverty) that inhibit women acting as agents with truly transformative potential are still not included in the mainstream international organizations' analytical framework. She critiques the way in which discourses around the 'women, peace and security' agenda equate women's agency with women's capacity to act, warning that 'this agency is both a rupture in the familiar representation of women-as-victim and an additional burden for (some) women to bear' (Shepherd this volume). Nevertheless, she concludes that the move away from victimization to a more plural (yet fragmented) representation of female subjectivity in conflict offers possibilities for feminist critical engagement and perhaps even transformation. Indeed, Margaret Owen of Widows for Peace for Democracy argues persuasively that 1325 and its subsequent resolutions have the potential to support a particularly vulnerable subset of women in post/conflict, that of widows. However, feminist and other activists must lobby to ensure that widowhood issues are included within the remit of the 'women, peace and security' agenda (Owen this volume).

This optimistic analysis is not necessarily shared by other contributors to this volume. In the case of Palestinian women's organizing (Farr this volume), the overall structure of the so-called peace process marginalizes women and civil society actors in general. This is despite a long history of Palestinian women's activism in resistance to Israeli occupation. As Vanessa Farr argues, 'Put starkly, no matter what instruments they use to help them position their peacebuilding arguments, Palestinian women are trying to organise a response to a process that clearly does not prioritize or value women's voices for peace' (Farr this volume).

Although the earlier essentialist representations of women as victims or peacebuilders might have been fragmented by later resolutions on 'women, peace and security', nevertheless, women continue to be represented in UNSCR 1325 and related mainstream policy documents solely in gendered terms. An articulation of the intersections between gender and other social categories and structures along which oppression, marginalization and violence occur (including nationality, class, ethnicity, religion, sexuality and age) is completely absent and even actively prevented in such representations. This has particular consequences for how women's agency is perceived, as Sheri Gibbings illustrates in her contribution to this volume. She describes a visit of two Iraqi women activists to the UN in 2003, where they addressed an informal group of gender advisers, NGOs and government representatives. Rather than speaking about 'gender concerns', the women condemned the US- and UK-led invasion of Iraq and the lack of support from the UN. Despite 1325 calling for more women's participation in peacebuilding and conflict resolution initiatives, the 1325 advocates attending this meeting were embarrassed by the 'angry comments' made by the Iraqi women. The event 'illustrated that powerful norms exist around the Women, Peace and Security agenda, and that certain performances could be anticipated and expected, while others were discouraged' (Gibbings, this volume). Gibbings's conclusion thus is less optimistic than that of Shepherd: as long as UN language continues to work with 'utopian visions' (of women as peacemakers), transformative agency might remain impossible. This suggests that the lack of recognition of structures of global capitalism, imperialism and (neo-) colonialism (structures within which the permanent UN Security Council members are deeply implicated) by advocates of 1325 may contain women's agency with regards to ending war and conflict.

CRITICALLY EXAMINING UNSCR 1325: DECONSTRUCTING THE LINKS BETWEEN GENDER AND CONFLICT

Despite the fact that 1325 does not condemn war and conflict (Cohn 2008), nonetheless, it does construct a link between gender violence and international security (Shepherd 2008). Several contributions to this volume examine this purported link and its implications for gender security and gender justice. Laura McLeod's contribution emphasizes the need to investigate the ways in which different actors understand the interlinkages between (post-)conflict and gender dynamics. Analysing the Serbian context (a case study generally considered a 'post-conflict' scenario) she argues that '"post-conflict" is a discourse with contested temporal and spatial aspects [and, just as "conflict",] a state of existence crafted in particular highly politicized ways, where certain ways are thrown into focus and others downplayed' (see also Vaughan-Williams 2006; Zalewski 2006; McLeod this volume). She examines the 'post-conflict' and/or 'gender security' discourses offered by three different actors in Serbia: the UN, the government and Women in Black. She finds that the conceptualizations of the interlinkages between gender and (post-)conflict among these three actors differ and have different political and policy implications: from controlling small arms to critiquing militarism. Ultimately, McLeod argues that this diversity of conceptualisations are productive 'in opening up spaces and choices for a variety of perceptions about what the achievement of gender security means' (McLeod this volume).

Sahla Aroussi's analysis of gender justice and accountability for wartime sexual violence problematizes the ways in which gender violence is conceptualized and instrumentalized in the UN's 'women, peace and security' agenda. Finding that 'a very narrow concept of justice focused on criminal prosecution is employed', which not only creates hierarchies of victims, but also glosses over the links between (structural) inequality and vulnerability/insecurity, she calls for 'broaden[ing] the way we think about accountability and drawing on non-legal remedies that deliver real justice for victims'. Moreover, she cautions us 'to be careful that dispensing justice for women victims does not become a political cover up for interventionist policies that have nothing to do with women's well being' (Aroussi this volume). A mission to eradicate gender-based violence and 'empower' women may end up being a justification for foreign (military) intervention, thereby maintaining global hierarchies (see also Harrington, this volume). We must therefore continue to ask how gender-discriminatory prac- tices (and more importantly their linkages with structural factors) in war-torn countries can be addressed without falling into the traps of 'colonial feminism' (Ahmed 1992; Orford 2002; Al-Ali and Pratt 2009).

A critical feminist approach thus should not only demand that gender (rather than women) becomes an integral part of conflict analysis and conflict resol- ution, but also remain wary as to *how* 'gender' is used and with what political implications. We might ask, for example, if – as has been the case in recent developments in IR literature – the focus of study becomes 'identity' (such as, 'ethnopolitics'), what role does a gender analysis play? Studies arguing that 'states characterized by gender inequality are more likely to experience intras- tate conflict' (Caprioli 2005: 161) or finding that 'domestic gender equality has a pacifying effect on state behavior on the international level' (Caprioli 2000: 51) put gender at the center of their analyses while sidelining global structural causes of war and/or the ways in which gender-discriminatory norms and prac- tices may be a symptom, rather than a cause, of war and violence. As Yuval- Davis and Anthias (1989) have shown, gender identity is often essentialized and instrumentalized to demarcate ethnic (or other) boundaries and construct conflict dynamics. There is a risk that conflict and peacebuilding analysis and practice fall victim to neo-colonial, civilizationary stances claiming the need to liberate women in other parts of the world from – what are often dubbed 'cul- tural' or 'traditional' – gender-discriminatory norms and practices. With this argument we do not want to downplay the crucial role that identity-related factors play in conflict, but rather call for the need to look carefully at the ways in which gender identities are constructed and politicized, and which role these play in comparison with (and in intersection with) more structural, material causes of war. This, of course, depends on context.

CRITICALLY EXAMINING UNSCR 1325 IN DIFFERENT CONTEXTS

Since its passing, the NGO Working Group on Women, Peace and Security and international, governmental and local organization have striven to develop strategies to implement 1325 (see, for example, Anderlini 2007).[7] Several empirical studies have been prepared by the UN and independent experts (e.g. Rehn and Sirleaf 2002; UN 2002); the UN has drafted a System-wide Action Plan (see UNSG 2008); a Peace Commission has been established in 2005 raising hopes it could support 1325 (see NGOWG/UNIFEM 2005; Ekiyor 2006); and subsequent resolutions dealing with gender and conflict have been drafted (UNSCR 1820 [2008], 1888 [2009], 1889 [2009]).[8] Nevertheless, evaluations have largely criticised slow advances in the implementation of 1325 at country and UN levels.[9]

Contributions in this issue consider the implementation and usage of UNSCR 1325 as well as the outcomes that such political translations have for women's lives and for peace and security in different contexts. They look at different policy levels, ranging from grassroots, to non-governmental, governmental and supra-national actors, as well as different geographical areas, covering Serbia, Palestine, Iraq, the UK and cross-country comparative cases.

McLeod's study on Serbia, Farr's study on Palestine and the interview with Sundus Abass about Iraq, draw attention to the different contexts in which local women activists use UNSCR 1325, with different implications. McLeod analyses how Women in Black in Serbia use UNSCR 1325 to make visible and try to implement their radical feminist (re-)conceptualization of security, away from militarism toward a more human-focused conceptualization of security involving reconciliation and deep structural changes. Such interpretations are not mirrored in the governmental Serbian National Action Plan nor in the agenda of the UNDP's South-Eastern European Arms Clearinghouse. Nevertheless, McLeod argues that the tensions between these different conceptualizations of gender security can pave the way for discussion and deliberation over the meaning of gender security. However, different contexts may be more or less amenable to such deliberations.

In Palestine, as Farr shows, although some women's organizations find 1325 useful in their work on women's security and empowerment and to get a hearing in international circles, the asymmetry between Israel and the Palestinians is so pronounced that 1325 has not yielded any tangible results. Moreover, many ordinary Palestinians are understandably distrustful of the UN and, consequently of 1325, as a path to justice (see also Richter-Devroe 2009, 2011; Farr this volume). Iraqi women's rights activist Sundus Abbas believes that 1325 does provide a framework for women's peace and security activism, and has helped women in framing their demands (successfully) for a 25 per cent quota in parliament. Yet, she argues that the UN has failed to systematically implement the Resolution in the context of its mission in Iraq, particularly with regards to the protection of women refugees and women who are kidnapped and trafficked, which has become a huge problem in the context of violent conflict, weakened state institutions and the limited rule of law following the fall of the Ba'th regime (Abbas this volume).

On the other hand, 1325 may actually become an obstacle to achieving gender justice and security in some contexts. Aroussi's study compares 112 peace agreements signed between the adoption of UNSCR 1325 and the end of 2008, finding that only five of these include provisions linked to accountability for gender-based violence. In other words, even the UN's narrow conceptualization of (gender) justice for victims of sexual violence (mainly through sanctions and prosecutions) has not been included in peace agreements. However, even those five agreements that do include

> significant gender sensitive provisions on transitional justice [...] have been characterised by very high levels of international involvement and pressure

and the presence of the ICC in the country. This international involvement, while it may have facilitated the inclusion of model provisions on justice for gender based violence, both in the cases of Uganda and Sudan has created significant threats to the peace process and resulted in peace agreements that carry very little hope of implementation.

(Aroussi this volume)

In these contexts, it is not only necessary to question the utility of 1325 as a framework for gender justice for victims of sexual violence, but also to understand the ways in which foreign intervention in the name of 'gender justice' may actually undermine peace and reconciliation.

Gibbings' ethnographic study at the UN sheds light upon the discrepancies between international and local agendas concerning women, peace and security. Her article not only tells the story of the two Iraqi activists labeled 'angry' by the UN gender advocates, but also the contrasting story of Basma Fakri's address to the UN Arria Formula meeting in 2005, which followed the speech norms of the UN. Gibbings demonstrates how 1325 risks constraining some women's agency, but also how the UN's agenda on 'women, peace and security' and its associated speech norms risks exacerbating divisions among local women's movements and between women's movements in different contexts. Resolution 1325, as Gibbings (this volume) argues,

> is supplemented by a scalar logic where representatives of women who come to speak to the Security Council are situated as local and connected to grassroots organizations, while also being allied to the transcendental goals of the UN, which is imagined as 'above'.

When 1325 calls for empowering women and supporting so-called indigenous women's peace strategies, we thus need to ask critically *which* women and *which* indigenous strategies? By selecting certain local actors and portraying their forms of agency as legitimate and as 'not tied to local politics, ethnic or class divisions' (Gibbings this volume), 1325 and the 'women, peace and security' agenda render other actors and their forms of agency as deviant. Yet, at the local level, the NGO-ized women's groups that attempt to formulate their demands using 1325 often fail to mobilize women at the grassroots. The liberal peacebuilding agenda that is privileged by the UN and gender advocates working at/through the UN represents a limited strategy for those women's movements engaged in a more radical agenda of social and political transformation. Women's 'resistance' to global capitalism and forms of colonialism (rather than 'peacebuilding' *per se*), for example, is not supported by the 1325 agenda, although women might in fact find their involvement in such initiatives 'empowering', perhaps even more so than their participation in the 1325 gendered peace agenda (see also Richter-Devroe 2009, 2011).

Interventions by the international community to 'empower' and 'protect' women (through providing technocratic, legalistic gender mainstreaming and humanitarian relief) are legitimized by 1325 and may replace the mobilization of genuine political will and commitment, treating symptoms rather than structural root causes of war. The case studies in this volume call into question the purported universality of UNSCR 1325, but also the attempts to make hegemonic the liberal 'women, peace and security' agenda.

CONCLUSION – BEYOND UNSCR 1325: TOWARD FEMINIST PEACEBUILDING?

Returning to the questions regarding the implementation of UNSCR 1325 and its implications for women's activism and for peace and security that we originally posed for this volume, we find that the contributors provide different, often contradictory, answers. Resolution 1325 is being translated into programs and measures on the ground in some places but with different consequences for women in Serbia (McLeod) versus women in Sudan and Uganda (Aroussi). In Palestine (Farr), Iraq (Abbas) and Nepal (Owen) women activists are using 1325 to frame the demands specific to the contexts in which they work, yet only in Nepal have activists yielded tangible results. The gender focus of 1325 and the subsequent resolutions provide a strategic tool for feminist engagement for some contributors (McLeod, Shepherd), while other contributors illustrate how the 'women, peace and security' agenda delegitimizes some women's agency (Farr, Gibbings). Several contributors suggest that the Resolution's focus on armed conflict, as opposed to other forms of structural violence, is problematic in that it marginalizes discussion of those structural factors that are an obstacle to women's agency (Shepherd) and may even exclude consideration of violence against women that is not strictly a 'weapon of war', such as random rapes, trafficking and kidnap (Abass, Aroussi). Nevertheless, other contributors to this volume do not regard the focus on armed conflict *per se* as the problem but rather the essentialized representation of women within the Resolution (Gibbings), the selective implementation of the Resolution (Farr, Owen) and the way in which the Resolution may be instrumentalized to bolster US global hegemony (Harrington). Contributors are divided over whether 1325 and the 'women, peace and security' agenda represents a shift toward a more inclusive, gender-sensitive global governance, whether it undermines women's grassroots struggles for justice and security or whether it is mere rhetoric that changes little in practice.

To some degree, differences between contributors may be accounted for by different epistemological and ontological approaches. Some privilege women's agency while others privilege structures in evaluating the significance of 1325. To a certain extent, these different approaches are, themselves, embedded within different understandings of feminism(s) as a political project. The power of 1325 and its associated discourse is, arguably, that it appropriates some key concepts in feminist theorizings (namely, the gendered dimensions of war and peace). However, the focus on gender as an analytical category (typical of liberal, radical and cultural feminisms) marginalizes discussion of 'the intersectionality of structural inequalities at the national, regional and transnational levels' (Al-Ali and Pratt 2009: 18) that are integral to other strands of feminist thinking – namely, post-colonial and Marxist feminisms. Different feminisms may underpin different visions of peace and, consequently, different projects of peacebuilding. Ultimately, this volume, while answering the questions that we originally posed, throws up new questions about feminist praxis:

- How can we mobilize, support and demand women's active involvement in conflict resolution and peacemaking without romanticizing, homogenizing and/or essentializing their diverse experiences and forms of activism, or providing a justification for foreign (military) intervention?
- How can we understand and support non-liberal forms of women's political agency?
- How can the political force of the international feminist peace/anti-war/ justice movement be maintained if difference is accounted for?

These questions are not necessarily new for transnational/international feminists and women activists. However, Resolution 1325 and the 'women, peace and security' agenda make it essential that we revisit these questions. The final evaluation of 1325 may depend on how we answer them.

Notes

1   While pointing out possible potentials of UNSCR 1325 authors, of course, also highlight contradictions and/or shortcomings inherent in the resolution. See, for example Hill (2002), Hill et al. (2003), Cohn (2004, 2008), Cohn et al. (2004), Whitworth (2004), Cockburn (2007), Anderlini (2007).
2   See Enloe (1993, 2001), Cockburn (1998), Lorentzen and Turpin (1998), Sorensen (1998), Jacobson (1999), Jacobs et al. (2000), Meintjes et al. (2001); among others.
3   These 25 countries are Austria, Belgium, Bosnia-Herzegovina, Canada, Chile, Cote d'Ivoire, Denmark, DRC, Holland, Estonia, Finland, France, Iceland, Liberia, Nepal, Norway, Philippines, Portugal, Rwanda, Sierra Leone, Spain, Sweden, Switzerland, Uganda and the United Kingdom. See http://www.peacewomen.org for updates.

4   For such critical enquiries see, among others, Orford (2002), Otto (2009, 2010), Chinkin and Charlesworth (2006), Shepherd (2008) and Cohn (2008).
5   This edited volume emerged from a series of panels organized at the international joint meeting of the Brazilian Association of International Relations and the International Studies Association, July 2009, in Rio de Janeiro. We would like to thank all the participants in those panels for the stimulating discussions that led to this special issue.
6   See Anderlini (2007), Whitworth (2004), Hill et al. (2003) and Cockburn (2007: 132–43) for a more detailed account on the build-up to the passing of UNSCR 1325.
7   See http://www.peacewomen.org for an up-to-date account of activities and strategies developed to support and enforce the implementation of 1325 in different country contexts.
8   For full details, see UNSC (2008, 2009a, 2009b).
9   For such critical evaluation see, for example, NGOWG (2004, 2005) as well as Abbas, Aroussi, Farr and Owen in this volume.

References

Ahmed, L. 1992. *Women and Gender in Islam: Historical Roots of a Modern Debate.* New Haven: Yale University Press.
Al-Ali, N. and Pratt, N. (eds). 2009. 'Introduction', *Women and War in the Middle East*, pp. 1–31. London: Zed Books.
Anderlini, S. N. 2007. *Women Building Peace: What They Do, Why it Matters.* Boulder, CO: Lynne Rienner.
Booth, K. (ed.). 2005. *Critical Security Studies and World Politics.* Boulder, CO: Lynne Rienner.
Caprioli, M. 2000. 'Gendered Conflict', *Journal of Peace Research* 31 (1): 51–68.
Caprioli, M. 2005. 'Primed for Violence: The Role of Gender Inequality in Predicting Internal Conflict', *International Studies Quarterly* 49 (2): 161–78.
Chinkin, C. 1994. 'Rape and Sexual Abuse of Women in International Law', *European Journal of International Law* 5 (3): 326–41.
Chinkin, C. and Charlesworth, H. 2006. 'Building Women into Peace: the International Legal Framework', *Third World Quarterly* 27 (5): 937–57.
Cockburn, C. 1998. *The Space Between Us: Negotiating Gender and National Identities in Conflict.* London: Zed Books.
Cockburn, C. 2007. *From Where We Stand: War, Women's Activism and Feminist Analysis.* London: Zed Books.
Cohn, C. 2004. 'Feminist Peacemaking', *The Women's Review of Books* 21 (5): 8–9.
Cohn, C. 2008. 'Mainstreaming Gender in UN Security Policy: A Path to Political Transformation?,' in Rai, S. and Waylen, G. (eds) *Global Governance: Feminist Perspectives*, pp. 185–206. Basingstoke: Palgrave Macmillan.
Cohn, C., Kinsella, H. and Gibbings, S. 2004. 'Women, Peace and Security, Resolution 1325', *International Feminist Journal of Politics* 6 (1): 130–40.

Ekiyor, T. 2006. 'Engendering Peace: How the Peacebuilding Commission Can Live Up to the UN Security Council Resolution 1325', *FES Briefing Papers Dialogue on Globalisation*, New York: FES New York Office. Available at http://library.fes.de/pdf-files/iez/global/50420.pdf (accessed 29 June 2011).

Enloe, C. 1993. *The Morning After: Sexual Politics at the End of the Cold War.* Berkeley: University of California Press.

Enloe, C. 2001. *Bananas, Beaches and Bases: Making Feminist Sense of International Politics.* Berkeley: University of California Press.

Hill, F. 2002. 'NGO Perspectives: NGOs and the Security Council', *Disarmament Forum* 1: 27–30. Available at: http://www.unidir.ch/pdf/articles/pdf-art9.pdf (accessed 29 June 2011).

Hill, F., Aboitiz, M. and Poehlman-Doumbouya, S. 2003. 'Nongovernmental Organizations' Role in the Buildup and Implementation of Security Council Resolution 1325', *Signs: Journal of Women in Culture and Society* 28 (4): 1255–69.

Jacobs, S., Jacobson, R. and Marchbank, J. (eds). 2000. *States of Conflict: Gender, Violence and Resistance.* London and New York: Zed Books.

Jacobson, R. 1999. 'Complicating "Complexity": Integrating Gender into the Analysis of the Mozambican Conflict', *Third World Quarterly* 20 (1): 175–87.

Lorentzen, L. and Turpin, J. (eds). 1998. *The Women and War Reader.* New York: New York University Press.

Meintjes, S., Turshen, M. and Pillay, A. (eds). 2001. *The Aftermath: Women in Post-Conflict Transformation.* London: Zed Books.

NGOWG. 2004. *Four Years On: An Alternative Report and Progress Check on the Implementation of Security Council Resolution 1325.* New York: NGOWG. Available at http://www.un-ngls.org/orf/cso/cso5/FourYearsOnOct04.pdf (accessed 29 June 2011).

NGOWG. 2005. *From Local to Global: Making Peace Work for Women.* New York: NGOWG. Available at http://womenpeacesecurity.org/media/pdf-NGOWG_5_Years_On_Report_EN.pdf (accessed 29 June 2011).

NGOWG/UNIFEM. 2005. *The UN Peacebuilding Commission: A Blueprint for Amplifying Women 's Voices and Participation, Issue Brief.* New York: UNIFEM and NGOWG. Available at http://www.womenpeacesecurity.org/media/pdf-pbc_amplifying_women_2006.pdf (accessed 29 June 2011).

Orford, A. 2002. 'Feminism, Imperialism and the Mission of International Law', *Nordic Journal of International Law* 71 (2): 275–296.

Otto, D. 2009. 'The Security Council's Alliance of "Gender Legitimacy": The Symbolic Capital of Resolution 1325', in Charlesworth, H. and Coicaud, J.-M. (eds) *Fault Lines of International Legitimacy*, pp. 239–275. Cambridge: University Press Cambridge.

Otto, D. 2010. 'Power and Danger: Feminist Engagement with International Law through the UN Security Council', *Australian Feminist Law Journal* 32: 97–121.

Peterson, V. S. (ed.). 1992. *Gendered States: Feminist (Re)Visions of International Relations Theory.* Boulder, CO: Lynne Rienner.

Rehn, E. and Sirleaf, E. J. 2002. *Women, War, Peace: The Independent Expert's Assessment on the Impact of Armed Conflict.* New York: UNIFEM. Available at http://www.unifem.org/resources/item_detail.php?ProductID=17 (accessed 29 June 2011).

Richter-Devroe, S. 2009. '"Here, It's Not about Conflict Resolution – We Can Only Resist": Palestinian Women's Activism in Conflict Resolution and Non-Violent Resistance', in Al-Ali, N. and Pratt, N. (eds) *Women and War in the Middle East*, pp. 158–90. London: Zed Books.

Richter-Devroe, S. 2011. *Gender and Conflict Transformation in Palestine: Women's Political Activism between Local and International Agendas*, PhD Thesis, Exeter University.

Seifert, R. 1994. 'War and Rape: A Preliminary Analysis', in Stiglmayer, A. (ed.) *Mass Rape: The War against Women in Bosnia-Herzegovina*, pp. 54–73. Lincoln: University of Nebraska Press.

Shepherd, L. J. 2008. *Gender, Violence and Security*. London: Zed Books.

Sorensen, B. 1998. *Women and Post-Conflict Reconstruction: Issues and Sources. War-torn Societies Project*. Geneva: UNRISD.

Tickner, J. A. 1992. *Gender in International Relations: Feminist Perspectives on Achieving Global Security*. New York: Columbia University Press.

United Nations (UN). 1995. *The United Nations Fourth World Conference on Women: Platform for Action*. Beijing: UN. Available at, Beijing September www.un.org/womenwatch/daw/beijing/platform/plat1.htm#concern (accessed 29 June 2011).

United Nations (UN). 2002. *Women, Peace and Security: Study submitted by the Secretary-General pursuant to Security Council resolution 1325 (2000)*. New York: UN. Available at http://www.un.org/womenwatch/daw/public/eWPS.pdf (accessed 29 June 2011).

United Nations Security Council (UNSC). 2008. 'Resolution 1820', S/RES/1820. Available at http://www.un.org/Docs/sc/unsc_resolutions08.htm (accessed 29 June 2011).

United Nations Security Council (UNSC). 2009a. 'Resolution 1888', S/RES/1888. Available at http://www.un.org/Docs/sc/unsc_resolutions09.htm (accessed 29 June 2011).

United Nations Security Council (UNSC). 2009b. 'Resolution 1889', S/RES/1889. Available at http://www.un.org/Docs/sc/unsc_resolutions09.htm (accessed 29 June 2011).

United Nation Secretary General. (UNSG). 2008. *Women and Peace and Security: Report of the Secretary-General*. New York: UN. Available at http://www.peacewomen.org/assets/file/PWandUN/UNImplementation/Secretariat/DepartmentAndOffices/OSG/osg_secgenreportwps_2008.pdf (accessed 29 June 2011).

Vaughan-Williams, N. 2006. 'Towards a Problematisation of the Problematisations that Reduce Northern Ireland to a "Problem"', *Critical Review of International Social and Political Philosophy* 9 (4): 513–26.

Väyrynen, T. 2004. 'Gender and UN Peace Operations: The Confines of Modernity', *International Peacekeeping* 11 (1): 125–42.

Waller, M. R. and Rycenga, J. 2001. *Frontline Feminisms: Women, War, and Resistance*. New York: Routledge.

Whitworth, S. 2004. *Men, Militarism and UN. Peacekeeping*. London: Lynne Rienner.

Yuval-Davis, N. and Anthias, F. 1989. *Gender, Nation, State*. London: Sage.

Zalewski, M. 2006. 'Intervening in Northern Ireland: Critically Re-thinking Representations of the Conflict', *Critical Review of International Social and Political Philosophy* 9 (4): 479–97.

Sex, Security and Superhero(in)es: From 1325 to 1820 and Beyond

LAURA J. SHEPHERD
University of New South Wales, Australia

Abstract

United Nations Security Council Resolution 1325 was adopted in October 2000 with a view to ensuring that all aspects of conflict management, post-conflict reconstruction and peacebuilding be undertaken with a sensitivity towards gender as an axis of exclusion. In this paper, I do not dwell on the successes and shortcomings of UNSCR 1325 for long, instead using a discussion of the Resolution as a platform for analysis of subsequent Resolutions, including UNSCRs 1820 (2008), 1882 (2009), 1888 (2009) and 1889 (2009). This last relates specifically to the participation of women in peacebuilding and post-conflict reconstruction and is the most recent pronouncement of the Security Council on the issue of 'women and peace and security'. Through this analysis, I draw attention to the expectations of and pressures on (some) women in the arena of peace and security, which can only be alleviated through discursive and material change in attitudes towards equality and empowerment. I argue that the Council is beginning to recognize – and simultaneously to constitute – (some/most) women as agential subjects and suggest that the fragmented and mutable representations of women in Council resolutions offer a unique opportunity for critical engagement with what 'women' might be, do or want in the field of gender and security.

INTRODUCTION

> Cuz I have had something to prove as long
> as I know there's something that needs improvement,
> and you know that every time I move
> I make a woman's movement.
> Ani DiFranco, 'Hour Follows Hour' (1995).

Are we expecting more from women (super heroines) than we expect of men?
Cohn et al. (2004: 136)

The engagement of the United Nations with issues of gender and security acquired significant impetus in 2000 with the adoption of United Nations Security Council Resolution 1325. This Resolution, often described in relevant literature as 'groundbreaking' or similar (Cohn 2008: 185, see also Charlesworth 2008; Otto 2006/7)[1] was drafted with the aim of ensuring that all efforts towards peacebuilding and post-conflict reconstruction, as well as the conduct of armed conflict itself, would entail sensitivity towards gendered violence and gendered inequalities.

> Resolution 1325 is a watershed political framework that makes women – and a gender perspective – relevant to negotiating peace agreements, planning refugee camps and peacekeeping operations and reconstructing war-torn societies. It makes the pursuit of gender equality relevant to every single Council action, ranging from mine clearance to elections to security sector reform. (Rehn and Sirleaf 2002: 3)

As a Security Council Resolution, UNSCR 1325 is legally binding upon states that are signatories of the UN Charter, and must therefore be taken seriously as a political document worthy of analysis, not least because it is argued that, despite the Resolution's many successes, significant obstacles remain in the translation of the Resolution from policy document to effective advocacy tool and action plan (in addition to the works cited below, see Rehn and Sirleaf 2002; Cohn et al. 2004). At the time of writing (June 2011), there were 102 translations of UNSCR 1325 available, in languages from Albanian to Zulu, and 16 national actions plans that commit the respective governments to the full implementation of UNSCR 1325 in their international and domestic activities.[2] These data indicate that national governments are taking seriously the challenge of UNSCR 1325 and thus pursuing policies geared towards full and equal participation of women in all peace and security initiatives, as well as mainstreaming of gender issues in the context of armed conflict, peacebuilding and reconstruction processes. In itself, UNSCR 1325 represents not only successful claims on gender equality and empowerment but also significant moves towards the same.

In this article, I begin to unpack some of these claims and hope to contribute to ongoing debates about the successes and shortcomings of UNSCR 1325, looking both briefly back at the circumstances of its production and forward to trace shifts in policy discourse that are both produced by and productive of the ways in which we think about gender and security. Specifically, in the first section of this paper I sketch a short account of UNSCR 1325 and highlight some of the arguments I have made about the Resolution elsewhere (Shepherd 2008a, 2008b) as a way to frame subsequent discussions about resistance and agency. I go on in the second section to analyse UNSCRs 1820 (2008), 1882 (2009), 1888 (2009) and 1889 (2009). This last relates specifically to the participation of women in peacebuilding and post-conflict reconstruction and is the most recent pronouncement of the Security Council on the issue of 'Women and peace and security'. In this analysis, I pick out the concept of participation for closer engagement and draw attention to the expectations of and pressures on (some) women in the arena of peace and security. Specifically, I investigate the ways in which the UNSC currently writes (about) women and argue that activity, in the form of political participation, has become conflated with agency. This elision has profound implications for future debates about empowerment and equality; as I discuss below, the definitive conceptual component of agency is the achievement of change, whereas action presumes no such transformation. I conclude that this is an important historical moment for feminist engagement with peace and security policy, as the Council moves towards writing women as agents, and suggest that productive ways to confront and address power and powerlessness in UN visions of the sexed subject of security could still be found through critical engagement with UNSCR 1325 more than 10 years on.

UNDERSTANDING UNSCR 1325

When I began working on UNSCR 1325, my hunch was that the ideas and ideals about gender, violence and security that were represented in the Resolution could be tracked back to ideas and ideals held in the institutions involved in the crafting of the document – what I term the 'discursive terrain' of the institutions, constituted through time- and location-specific legal systems, cultural and socio-political traditions, geopolitical positioning and histories and so on. If this was shown to be the case (and ultimately I believe I demonstrated that it was), then the implications for policy-making would be profound: the frequently unreflective and unconscious ideas that people have are being written into policy documents and are functioning to order and organize those documents – and those of whom the documents speak – in very specific ways. In UNSCR 1325, I identify constructions of gender that assume it largely synonymous with biological sex and, further, reproduce logics of identity that characterized women as fragile, passive and in need of protection and constructions of security that locate the responsibility for providing that protection firmly in the hands of elite political actors in the international system, despite the Resolution

> *Reaffirming* the important role of women in the prevention and resolution of conflicts and in peace-building, and *stressing* the importance of their equal participation and full involvement in all efforts for the maintenance and promotion of peace and security, and the need to increase their role in decision-making with regard to conflict prevention and resolution. (UNSC 2000: Preamble, emphasis in original)

UNSCR 1325 offers a coherent and convincing account of actions that both can and should be undertaken by the Member States of the United Nations in order to ameliorate 'the impact of armed conflict on women and girls' (UNSC 2000: Art. 16). The emphasis placed on 'representation of women at all decision-making levels' (UNSC 2000: Art 1) and on the participation of women in formal political processes (differentiated from representation by the emphasis on 'role and contribution' rather than presence, see UNSC 2000: Art. 4) is particularly interesting. Here, I undertake an exploration of how the Security Council has continued, since the adoption of UNSCR 1325, to delimit an inclusive vision of women as crucial actors in processes of peacebuilding and post-conflict reconstruction. In the following section, I trace the shifts in Security Council discourse on the sexed subject of security and examine how women (and, importantly, women's bodies) have become sites of such significant regulatory practices.

MIND THE GAP: FROM UNSCR 1325 TO UNSCR 1889

In June 2008, the United Nations Security Council voted unanimously to accept Resolution 1820, in which the Council '*Notes* that rape and other forms of sexual violence can constitute a war crime, a crime against humanity, or a constitutive act with respect to genocide' and, further, '*Demands* the immediate and complete cessation by all parties to armed conflict of all acts of sexual violence against civilians with immediate effect' (UNSC 2008: Art. 2–4, emphasis in original). The violation of the human body is central to UNSCR 1820; indeed, the Resolution is premised on a vision of the human body as inherently violable. On closer inspection, 'women and girls' are particularly vulnerable to violation (UNSC 2008: Art 3), particularly embodied in a way that their constitutive others ('civilians') are not. This is a construction that echoes the essentialist logics of gender in UNSCR 1325, logics which draw a clear link between sex and security in suggesting that women are 'metaphor[s] for vulnerable/victim in war' (Charlesworth 2008: 358). The discursive constitution of women as subjects of security does not, at first glance, seem to have changed very much in the eight years elapsed between UNSCR 1325 and UNSCR 1820.

Through the nodal point of participation, however, I suggest that we can begin to identify small discursive shifts. In the Preamble of UNSCR 1325, women are represented as having an 'important role [...] in the prevention and resolution of conflicts and in peacebuilding' (UNSC 2000: Preamble), which Otto argues 'provided important new leverage for local women's groups to claim a role in peace negotiations and post-conflict decision-making' (Otto 2004: 1). UNSCR 1820 emphasizes the need to 'tak[e] into account, inter alia, the view expressed by women of affected local communities' (UNSC 2008: Art. 3), to consult 'with women and women-led organizations as appropriate' (UNSC 2008: Art. 10) and to 'ensur[e] effective representation of women's civil society' (UNSC 2008: Art. 11). The Secretary-General and his Special Envoys are *urged* 'to invite women to participate in discussions pertinent to the prevention and resolution of conflict, the maintenance of peace and security and post-conflict peacebuilding' (UNSC 2008: Art. 12). In UNSCR 1820, representation is abstracted from the body in a way that differs from UNSCR 1325: in the latter, the 'representation of women' is to be increased (UNSC 2000: Art. 1), while the former speaks of the representation of and consultation with 'women's civil society' (UNSC 2008: Art. 11). Both assume that women are unproblematically identifiable as women, but I propose that participation supplants representation in UNSCR 1820 as the crucial mechanism for empowerment, and that this has important implications for how the Security Council writes (about) women. The activities of women, whether in the sphere of 'civil society', in 'women-led organizations' (UNSC 2008: Art. 10) or as 'peacekeepers or police' (UNSC 2008: Art. 8), are constituted in UNSCR 1820 as expressions of agency and as resistance to both structural and direct violences. I identify this as agency given the emphasis on change. Implicit in UNSCR 1820 is the assumption that participation of women will lead to transformation of political environment. The female subject of security, according to UNSCR 1820, is perhaps in the process of becoming an agent of security.

UNSCR 1888 also reaffirms the Security Council's commitment to increasing the representation and participation of women in formal politics (UNSC 2009a: Art. 16) and its recognition of 'the important role of women in rebuilding society' (UNSC 2009a: Art. 18). Similarly, UNSCR 1888 notes *with concern* the underrepresentation of women in formal peace processes [...] and the lack of women as Chief or Lead peace mediators' (UNSC 2009a: Preamble, emphasis in original). The rationale for this concern is spelled out quite clearly:

> women and children affected by armed conflict may feel more secure working with and reporting abuse to women in peacekeeping missions, and ... the presence of women peacekeepers may encourage local women to participate in the national armed and security forces, thereby helping to build a security sector that is accessible and responsive to all (UNSC 2009a: Preamble)

It is clear, therefore, that the participation of women is expected to transform the 'security sector': the women in UNSCR 1888 are recognizable as positive actors and putative agents.

Resolution 1889 continues in this vein, with the Preamble almost wholly devoted to accounts of women's activities in conflict, conflict resolution and post-conflict reconstruction. The Security Council expresses 'deep concern about the under-representation of women at all stages of peace processes' and '*reiterat[es]* the need for the full, equal and effective participation of women at all stages of peace processes given their vital role in the prevention and resolution of conflict and peacebuilding' (UNSC 2009b: Preamble). The first recommendation contained in the Resolution is that 'Member States, international and regional organizations ... take further measures to improve women's participation' (UNSC 2009b: Art. 1). A crucial enabler of participation, according to UNSCR 1889, is active engagement by Member States with civil society, 'including women's organizations', in order to address the 'needs and priorities' of women and girls (UNSCR 2009b: Art. 10). These needs include:

> inter alia support for greater physical security and better socio-economic conditions, through education, income-generating activities, access to basic services, in particular health services, including sexual and reproductive health and reproductive rights and mental health, gender-responsive law enforcement and access to justice as well as enhancing capacity to engage in public decision-making at all levels. (UNSC 2009b: Art. 10)

According to this list, a lack of 'access' and diminished 'capacity' only account for some of a range of impediments to women's participation. In order to ensure 'full, equal and effective participation', the international community would need to find solutions to the plethora of socio-political problems that result in the 'needs and priorities' of 'women and girls' remaining unmet.

There are two aspects of this short passage worthy of further exploration. First, as Naila Kabeer (1999: 443) has noted, 'access' to resources as an indicator of empowerment is both complex and problematic: 'How changes in women's resources will translate into changes in the choices they are able to make will depend, in part, on other aspects of the conditions in which they are making their choices.' The existence of capacity-building programmes and the impact of those programmes on participation in decision-making must be analysed with reference to specific socio-cultural context as 'not all [decisions] have the same consequential significance' (Kabeer 1999: 446) or status. There is also a danger that participation is equated with voice; the presence of women in a decision-making forum can sometimes legitimate the policies put forward by that forum when the women present have been explicitly or implicitly marginalized during discussion and been able to contribute little or nothing to its eventual conclusion.

The second aspect that strikes me as interesting is the minimal reflexive relationship of the factors listed above to gender identity, with the possible exception of reproductive health, although this itself is contentious; women have frequently and for too long been defined by their assumed capacity to bear children, as if masculine subjects have no reproductive capacity or health needs. I would venture that there are very few people in a post-conflict society who *don't* require 'greater physical security', 'better socio-economic conditions', 'health services [...] and access to justice'. These 'needs and priorities' are not specific to women and girls, although the distribution of material resources available to ameliorate scarcity in these realms is of course gendered. The latter is hinted at in the final article of UNSCR 1889, which requests that the UN Secretary-General reports to the Security Council by October 2010 with:

> Recommendations for improving international and national responses to the needs of women and girls in post-conflict situations, including *the development of effective financial and institutional arrangements* to guarantee women's full and equal participation. (UNSC 2009b: Art. 19d, emphasis added)

In giving this account of Security Council resolutions since 1325, I do not wish to suggest that 'women's full and equal participation' is not a worthy goal. I am not suggesting that women should not be invited 'to participate in discussions pertinent to the prevention and resolution of conflict' (UNSC 2008: Art. 12), nor that the Council should not be concerned about 'the under-representation of women in formal peace processes [...] and the lack of women as Chief or Lead peace mediators' (UNSC 2009a: Preamble). Rather, I propose that we look closely at the 'women' in question and ask how the Council writes (about) women in recent UNSC resolutions.[3] Minimally, as I discuss in the fol-lowing sections, I suggest that the resolutions analysed here write *some* women as victims, in keeping with my analysis of UNSCR 1325, but also – and perhaps more interestingly – that the Resolutions assume that *most* women speak for *all* women and, further, equate action with agency. Agency – the capacity to engage in formal and informal political discussion and decision-making, capacity to represent the interests of a post-conflict community and capacity to insist upon 'the development of effective financial and institutional arrangements' needed to ensure equality of participation – is circumscribed by the lack of infrastructural support for and recognition of the amount of pro-ductive and reproductive labour undertaken by the most marginalized, disen-franchized and under-resourced members of post-conflict society. In sum, while the UN Security Council has written (about) women as putative agents since 2000, this agency is both a rupture in the familiar representation of women-as-victim and an additional burden for (some) women to bear.

'WOMEN HOLD UP HALF THE SKY' (MAO ZEDONG)

They say that 'behind every great man there's a woman';[4] my mother used to have a postcard on her fridge bearing her favoured alternative: 'Behind every famous woman, there's often a rather talented cat.'[5] Based on information cur-rently available, that cat must be not only talented but also rather tired. To put it another way, in contemporary global politics – and there is no reason to suppose that post-conflict society should be a marked exception from these trends – 'women hold up half the sky', support a significant proportion of earthly labours and fulfil the majority of the world's duties of care and repro-duction as well (see *inter alia* Bergeron 2003; Bedford 2007, 2008; Peterson 2010). In feminist literature, this has long been a key policy concern when addressing international development institutions: 'childcare, housework, sub-sistence agriculture, cooking, voluntary work to sustain community organis-ations, and so on [...] dominant models of growth overlook the economic value of these activities' (Bedford 2008: 86). I would argue that feminist scho-lars of security and post-conflict need to engage closely with these debates, in order to explore fully the ways in which the assumptions made about capacity during conflict, in conflict resolution and in post-conflict reconstruction not only rely on writing women as victims in need of protection but also (and somewhat schizophrenically, as I discuss further in the concluding section of this article) as superheroines, agents of their own salvation, capable of representing the needs and priorities of others and with the capacity to effect positive transformation in their given environments.

Fifteen years after Beijing, women occupied an average of 18.9 per cent of positions in upper and lower houses of parliament globally (Inter-Parliamentary Union 2010). The United Nations Secretary-General 'boasted' in 2009 'about the increasing number of women he has appointed to senior positions in the world body since he took office in 2007' (Deen 2009) but 'posts that are committed to gender equality work are at lower levels than comparable posts on other issues' (Yasmeen Hassan, Dir. of Programs at *Equality Now* cited in Deen 2009). According to the UN Economic and Social Council, of the 850 million people in the world who remained 'chronically hungry' in 2007, 60 per cent were women and children (UN ECOSOC 2007: 8). Women and children are 14 times more likely to die during natural disasters than men (UNFPA 2009). The global gender disparity in earned income sees women earning 'on average slightly more than 50 per cent of what men earn' (UNDAW 2000); this 'gender pay gap' increased in 2008/9 in both the UK and the USA (ILO 2009: 8). In short, not much has changed since the formulation of the 'informal slogan' of the UN Decade for Women (1976–85): 'Women do two-thirds of the world's work, receive 10 per cent of the world's income and own 1 per cent of the means of production' (Robbins cited in Shah 2010). There have, of course, been some changes. Anup Shah (2010) points to the implementation of microcredit schemes enabling 'greater access to savings and credit mechanisms' and the 'dwindling number of countries that do not allow women to vote' (Shah 2010).

In a typically elegant turn of phrase, Kabeer describes statistics as 'simple windows on complex realities' (1999: 447). The point of recounting these dismal statistics (and the temporary suspension of suspicion about not only the validity of statistical evidence but also the assumptions that inform many of these statements; for example, to be outraged at the lack of women in positions of formal political leadership requires the implicit acceptance of the conflation of descriptive and substantive representation and, relatedly, the concept of critical mass. See, for example, Childs and Krook (2006, 2008)) is neither to simplify the 'complex realities' they attempt to capture, nor to depress any reader so thoroughly that it effectively precludes any kind of critical political action, although this would be an understandable reaction. The point is to demonstrate the existence of serious, (infra-) structural inhibitors that may well impede the (superheroic) activities of the women in post-conflict societies on whom the UN Security Council relies in its efforts to achieve empowerment and gender equality in those same societies. If a woman – even a superwoman – has to spend upwards of six hours per day sourcing and gathering water and wood (UNDP 2004: 28) her capacity for engaging in formal political activity or even informal community-based organization is likely to be severely limited. In short, just because the UN Security Council recognizes, albeit belatedly, that women are actors, this does not automatically ensure that those same women necessarily have agency – the capacity to act.

'Actors [...] are much more than, and much less than, agents' (Alexander cited in Campbell 2009: 408). As Andrea Cornwall explains, whereas actors are engaged in a consultative mode of participation, agents are better conceived of as transformative (2003: 1327) of both direct (immediate) and structural (removed) concerns. If it is indeed the case that UN Security Council discourse on gender and security is beginning to constitute gendered subjects as actors rather than agents, this nonetheless represents a potentially enabling move away from its representation of those same subjects as objects or instruments of security policy (these categories are explained in Cornwall 2003). It still behoves us, however, to explore the regulatory mechanisms (both tangible and discursive) that prevent the transition from actor to agent. Sam Cook, for example, investigates 'in very practical terms' some inhibitors to the expression of agency, arguing that '[t]his is where [...] flashlights, raincoats and rooms with doors come into play' (2009: 131):

> One [...] anecdote concerns a UN peacekeeping mission in a country with a high prevalence of sexual violence. A visiting researcher questioned the police about a pattern of attacks at night and in inclement weather. The police admitted that patrols in such conditions were limited, and thus the risk of violence was indeed higher. The reason for the limited patrols? The police were unwilling to patrol at night and in bad weather because they did not have flashlights and raincoats; there was no money provided for those in their budget. (Cook 2009: 132)

Furthermore, Kabeer (1999) identifies a range of 'pre-conditions', the presence of which facilitates the exercise of agency, including physical proximity to resources, control over life choices, mobility, decision-making opportunity and status. Agency, the ability to exercise choice and to achieve change, is multi-dimensionally constituted, and Kabeer illustrates persuasively how difficult it is to operationalize measures of the pre-conditions she investigates.

Women may 'hold up half the sky', but they do so in the face of 'inadequate budgeting for the gender components of projects, insufficient development of analytical skills, poor supervision of the implementation of gender components, and a general lack of political commitment both within the [UN] and at the country level' (Charlesworth 2005: 11). As a former Senior Gender Advisor for the UN surmised succinctly in an end of mission report, there is 'a *lack of political will* to take gender seriously' (Puechguirbal 2010: 183, emphasis in original). At the outset of this article, however, I suggested a cautious feminist optimism at the current historical moment. This optimism is not unrelated to the above explorations of what it means to be an actor or an agent in UN discourse on sex and security, explorations that are underpinned by an understanding of agency not simply as 'power to' or 'power over' but as 'the fourth face of power' (Digeser 1992: 980), where subject, agency and structure are inextricably intertwined. In the section below, I move to a brief discussion of how poststructural theories of identity constitution can facilitate a different kind of understanding of the UNSC policy on peace and security, with potentially transformative effects.

'TO INFINITY AND BEYOND!' (BUZZ LIGHTYEAR)

There is a complex relationship between academic International Relations (IR), the discipline from which I write, and the formulation of international policy. While in the areas of social policy, planning studies and public administration, academic engagement with policy analysis is frequently nuanced and theoretically informed, IR appears to have a somewhat ambivalent relationship with theories of policy and theory in policy.[6] Christopher Hill (1994) refers to the 'siren song of policy relevance', in a particularly interesting metaphor: readers will recall that, according to Greek mythology, sailors were lured to their deaths by the enchanting voices of the sirens. From Hill's representation, we might infer that scholars are the hapless mariners and the ultimately unattainable goal of policy relevance entrances us to the extent that we risk (career?) death to achieve it.

Recent years have certainly seen a proliferation of essays on the subject of policy relevance in the social sciences more broadly (see, for example, Duvall and Varadarajan 2003; Walt 2005; Youngs 2008). This literature, in general, seeks to suggest ways in which we as academics might find ways to facilitate productive dialogue between ourselves and practitioners. Eriksson and Sundelius, for example, suggest three distinct modes of engagement between scholars and practitioners, concluding that both communities can benefit from combining 'two sets of knowledge for the purpose of better practice and improved theory' (2005: 67). They emphasize, however, that 'public officials and civil society practitioners should make room for [...] the unorthodox, the imaginative and the politically incorrect' (Eriksson and Sundelius 2005: 67) and this is in tension with much other writing on the subject. The conventional wisdom, within IR literature at least, tends to be that policy relevant work should be 'theory-lite'. Indeed, Alexander George cautions against using the word 'theory' when talking with policy-makers lest their eyes 'glaze over' (1994: 171–2). If academics do wish to produce work that is explicitly informed by theoretical musings, Stephen Walt (2005: 26–7) provides a handy overview of the characteristics of 'good theory', which include logical consistency, empirical validity, clarity about causal mechanisms and explanatory power.

This article, then, somewhat goes against the grain, as I propose that the above reflections on international policy in the area of gender, peacebuilding and security are usefully understood through the lens of poststructural theory. Poststructuralism and postcolonialism 'alert . . . us to the epistemic violence of Eurocentric discourses of the non-West' (Mohan 2006) that are particularly relevant to discussions of postconflict reconstruction and peace(state)building (see Darby 2009) and encourage us to investigate the discursive practices and regulatory mechanisms through which the reality we take for granted, which includes disparities of power and multiple forms of (sometimes violent) oppression, comes to be accepted as such. Even those with only a rudimentary knowledge of poststructural theory will recognize that it tends not to speak of explanations or causal mechanisms. However, this does not mean that its policy relevance is null. Power is understood by Michel Foucault as 'a productive network which runs through the whole social body, much more than [...] a negative instance whose function is repression' (1977: 119), productive of practices of knowledge (including UNSC Resolutions), conditions of meaning (of those same Resolutions), and identity (as marked and made in the Resolutions, and elsewhere). Ideas about agency (the efficacy of the subject), structural inhibitors of that agency and the construction of the subject itself all emerge in a particular discursive context and are both produced by and productive of practices of power.

Whereas other approaches can analyse capability of the agent and/or determinism of the structure, a discourse-theoretical approach can conceive of power as productive and therefore implicated in the production of meaning. That is to say, the ways in which discursive practices construct an intelligible reality that then itself acts as a referent for the construction of meaning are intrinsically related to power. Crucially, a distinctively poststructural form of policy analysis highlights the ambiguities and tensions inherent in any policy document; 'alternative visions provide a promise of empowerment, through ambiguity rather than certainty; through struggles to create new spaces where they[/we] can think "other-wise"; where there is a proliferation of many voices rather than a few and where we continue to create knowledge as we resist by avoiding "paradigmatic conceit"' (Ashley and Walker cited in Rai 2008: 180). There is, of course, no guarantee that the transformation of knowledge will be regarded as positive – but that there will be transformation is itself cause for optimism.

I use the quotation from Buzz Lightyear, a character in Disney's popular animated film *Toy Story*, to head this section for two reasons: first, to admit to the intertextual reference in my own choice of title for this article; and second, to emphasize that feminist engagement with international policy must continue 'to infinity and beyond'.[7] My wariness of gender mainstreaming discourse is rooted in its teleological formation; the transformation of the concept into a verb implies to me that gender can be (successfully or otherwise) *mainstreamed* and the project thus concluded. Feminist scholars, practitioners and policy-makers know, of course, that this is not the case (see True 2003, 2010), but it can be hard to resist such attempts at closure when key figures (such as the UN Secretary-General, for example) are publicly trumpeting the increase (in this case, of 40 per cent) of women in positions of institutional power (cited in Deen 2009). I conclude this discussion by suggesting that resistance, far from being futile, is crucial, and especially at this juncture. As discussed above, the discursive constitution of female subjectivity in the UNSC policy discourse is currently somewhat fragmented. This represents, to me, a unique historical moment, and a significantly enhanced possibility of change.

In the course of this article, I have traced shifts in the UNSC policy discourse, drawing attention to the ways in which the various Resolutions that speak to 'women and peace and security' write the subject of women and constitute the concepts of peace and security. UNSCR 1325, as I have argued elsewhere, assumes 'that gender is synonymous with women and, moreover, that gender signifies need/want/lack' (Shepherd 2008b: 171–2). In UNSCR 1820 and beyond, I have identified ruptures and shifts in the organizational logics of these discourses. While in UNSCR 1325 'women-as-informal-organisers and women-as-formal-actors are still, primarily, essentially women-in-need-of-protection' (Shepherd 2008b: 120), UNSCR 1820 represents the policy beginnings of contestation over this discursive construction.[8] UNSCR 1888 continues this dual trajectory, on the one hand still inscribing 'sexual violence in situations of armed conflict' on the bodies of 'women and children, notably [...] girls' (UNSC 2009a: Preamble) but on the other insisting upon recognizing that:

> sexual violence, when used or commissioned as a tactic of war in order to deliberately target *civilians* or as part of a widespread or systematic attack against *civilian populations*, can significantly exacerbate situations of armed conflict and may impede the restoration of international peace and security. (UNSC 2009a: Art. 1, emphasis added)

The articulation of this recognition, in the first substantive article of the Resolution, and in terms of the impact of sexual violence on *civilians* rather than 'women and children' (Enloe 1990) perhaps signifies a move towards the ascription of agency to female subjects that is further consolidated in UNSCR 1889.[9] This latter explicitly challenges the fact that 'women in situations of armed conflict and post-conflict situations continue to be often considered as victims and not as actors' (UNSC 2009b: Preamble), suggesting that the Council is beginning to recognize – and simultaneously to constitute – (some/most) women at least as actors, if not fully agential subjects.

So here we are, more than 10 years after the unanimous adoption of UNSCR 1325, perhaps wondering how and why it took so long for the UN Security Council to write women as actors, but also curious about where we go from here. Some scholars have written 'essays in despair' (Rai 2008) regarding the transformative potential of UNSCR 1325 given that 'it has been used as a means of coopting gender dynamics in order to preserve the existing gender status quo' (Puechguirbal 2010: 184) and that 'the war system [has been left] essentially undisturbed' (Cohn 2008: 203). I fully understand the frustration evidenced in these arguments, but suggest that perhaps the fragmented and mutable representations of women in Council resolutions at the current time offer a unique opportunity for critical engagement. Alan Swingewood suggests that partiality and fluidity are characteristic of discursive fields: a discourse 'does not constitute a totality since it lacks a unifying centre but consists of fragments, perspectives, discontinuity' (2000: 198). However, in order to be intelligible, discourses, which are always multiple and competing, must temporary 'fix' meaning. 'Any discourse is [...] an attempt to dominate the field of discursivity, to arrest the flow of differences, to construct a centre' (Laclau and Mouffe 2001: 112).

I have identified here three possible emergent 'centres' in discourses of gender, peace and security issuing from the United Nations Security Council: women as victims; women as superheroines; women as representative of (some/most/all) other women. Of course, all of these – and none of them – are 'true';

> identities are always contingent and depend on specific forms of identification. Rather than presupposing some kind of homogenous identity, then, looking at the ways in which people identify themselves with others or with particular issues can provide a more effective basis for advocacy and for action. (Cornwall 2003: 1338)

As W.B. Yeats suggested (an early unrecognized discourse theorist?), 'Things fall apart; the centre cannot hold' (Yeats [1921] 2003: 19). This recognition is cause for great feminist optimism at the present moment. The practices of the UN Security Council regarding 'women, peace and security' (as the agenda is termed in the UNSC) have already had profound effects: NGO activists and practitioners use UNSCR 1325 'in multiple strategic ways' to enhance equality, empowerment and accountability in conflict and post-conflict zones (Cohn 2008: 189–91). 'Whether by reconfiguring the rules of interactions in public spaces, enabling once silenced participants to exercise voice, or reaching out beyond the "usual suspects"' in decision-making' (Cornwall 2003: 1338), it is likely that this grassroots engagement will continue in productive ways. What is interesting is how feminist engagement with these policy discourses might enable the construction of a 'centre' that pays attention to diversity, supports capacity-building without conforming to the imperial logic of 'a "trickle-down" theory of expertise' (Shepherd 2008b: 97), embraces a translocal, multiperspectival politics and refuses to effect arbitrary and ultimately regressive closure on what 'women' might be, do or want in the field of gender and security.

Notes

1 I am grateful to the reviewer who noted that there is a distinctive difference between *claiming* the Resolution as groundbreaking and the Resolution *being* groundbreaking. As this introductory section is meant only to provide a descriptive account of the analysis that follows, I engage more fully with this debate in the second substantive section of the article.

2 At the time of writing, 24 states have implemented national action plans (Peace-Women n.d.).

3 It is of course also interesting to ask *why* the Council writes (about) women in the ways that it does. '[I]s it because women are good at peace; or because women have equal rights to participate in peace operations?' (Charlesworth 2008: 351). This discussion is, however, beyond the scope of this paper, as I seek to explore the possibilities that are created or foreclosed by *how* the Council writes.

4 The origins of this phrase are unclear. The first printed citation of it was apparently in 1946 in a Texan newspaper, when the athlete commented, upon receiving an award, 'said "They say behind every great man there's a woman. While I'm not a great man, there's a great woman behind me"' (The Phrase Finder, n.d.).

5 I have been unable to trace its author or production company.

6 Richardson (1996: 289) makes this distinction in his discussion of policy-making and planning theory, drawing on the Foucauldian concept of a power/knowledge nexus to suggest that while the dualism is 'convenient', it perpetuates the obfuscation of practices of power in the policy-making process, thus 'enhanc[ing] the possibility of imposition of normative values, confusion and manipulation'. While I do not entirely agree with Richardson's attribution of intentionality, it is nonetheless refreshing to see discourse-theoretical analysis being taken seriously in debates about policy and planning.

7 This is a prosaic echo of Ani DiFranco's (1995) lyric cited at the outset: 'I have had something to prove as long as I know there's something that needs improvement.'

8 Of course, in a wider academic and practitioner literature, these contestations have been actively explored and expanded upon for many decades (see, for example, Moser and Clark 2001; El Jack 2003; Afshar and Eade 2004; Giles and Hyndman 2004; Mazurana et al. 2005; Sweetman 2005).

9 Another reading of this discursive move is in keeping with feminist literature on the constitution of the subject of 'civilian', which elucidates the frequency with which gendered assumptions 'stow away' (Carpenter 2006: 31) within the norm of civilian immunity (see also Sjoberg 2006), rendering civilians effectively feminised.

Acknowledgements

I am grateful for the comments of the two anonymous reviewers and the editors of this Special Issue. Their input and constructive engagement with my analysis and argument were both valuable and encouraging.

References

Afshar, H. and Eade, D. (eds). 2004. *Development, Women and War: Feminist Perspectives*. Oxford: Oxfam GB.

Bedford, K. 2007. 'The Imperative of Male Inclusion: How Institutional Context Influences World Bank Gender Policy', *International Feminist Journal of Politics* 9 (3): 289–311.

Bedford, K. 2008. 'Governing Intimacy in the World Bank', in Rai, S. and Waylen, G. (eds) *Global Governance: Feminist Perspectives*, pp. 84–106. Basingstoke: Palgrave Macmillan.

Bergeron, S. 2003. 'The Post-Washington Consensus and Economic Representations of Women in Development at the World Bank', *International Feminist Journal of Politics* 5 (3): 397–419.

Campbell, C. 2009. 'Distinguishing the Power of Agency from Agentic Power: A Note on Weber and the "Black Box" of Personal Agency', *Sociological Theory* 27 (4): 407–18.

Carpenter, R. C. 2006. *'Innocent Women and Children': Gender, Norms and the Protection of Civilians*. Aldershot: Ashgate Press.

Charlesworth, H. 2005. 'Not Waving but Drowning: Gender Mainstreaming and Human Rights in the United Nations', *Harvard Human Rights Journal* 18 (n.i): 1–18.

Charlesworth, H. 2008. 'Are Women Peaceful? Reflections on the Role of Women in Peacebuilding', *Feminist Legal Studies* 16 (n.i): 347–61.

Childs, S. and Krook, M. L. 2006. 'Gender and Politics: The State of the Art', *Politics* 26 (1): 18–28.

Childs, S. and Krook, M. L. 2008. 'Critical Mass Theory and Women's Political Representation', *Political Studies* 56 (3): 725–36.

Cook, S. 2009. 'Security Council Resolution 1820: On Militarism, Flashlights, Raincoats and Rooms Without Doors – A Political Perspective on Where it Came From and What it Adds', *Emory International Law Review* 23 (n.i): 125–39.

Cohn, C. 2008. 'Mainstreaming Gender in UN Security Policy: A Path to Political Transformation?', in Rai, S. and Waylen, G. (eds) *Global Governance: Feminist Perspectives*, pp. 185–206. Basingstoke: Palgrave Macmillan.

Cohn, C., Kinsella, H. and Gibbings, S. 2004. 'Women, Peace and Security: Resolution 1325', *International Feminist Journal of Politics* 6 (1): 130–40.

Cornwall, A. 2003. 'Whose Voices? Whose Choices? Reflections on Gender and Participatory Development', *World Development* 31 (8): 1325–42.

Darby, P. 2009. 'Rolling Back the Frontiers of Empire: Practising the Postcolonial', *International Peacekeeping* 16 (5): 699–716.

Deen, T. 2009. 'Gender Empowerment at UN Still Cloudy', Terraviva Europe via Global Policy Forum. Available at http://www.globalpolicy.org/home/218-injustice-and-inequality/48570-gender-empowerment-at-un-still-cloudy.html (accessed 25 May 2010).

DiFranco, A. 1995. *'Hour Follows Hour, Not A Pretty Girl'*. Buffalo, NY: Righteous Babe Records.

Digeser, P. 1992. 'The Fourth Face of Power', *The Journal of Politics* 54 (4): 977–1007.

Duvall, R. and Varadarajan, L. 2003. 'On the Practical Significance of Critical International Relations Theory', *Asian Journal of Political Science* 11 (2): 75–88.

El Jack, A. 2003. 'Gender and Armed Conflict: Overview Report', *BRIDGE Cutting Edge Pack Series*. Brighton: Institute of Development Studies

Enloe, C. 1990. 'Women and children: Making Feminist Sense of the Persian Gulf Crisis', *Village Voice*, 25 September 1990.

Eriksson, J. and Sundelius, B. 2005. 'Molding Minds That Form Policy: How to Make Research Useful', *International Studies Perspectives* 6 (1): 51–71.

Foucault, M. 1977. 'Truth and Power', in Gorden, C. (ed.) *1980. Power/ Knowledge: Selected Interviews and Other Writings 1972–1977 by Michel Foucault*, pp. 109–33. London: Harvester [trans. Fontana and Pasquino].

George, A. L. 1994. 'Some Guides to Bridging the Gap', *Mershon International Studies Review* 39 (2): 171–72.

Giles, W. and Hyndman, J. (eds). 2004. *Sites of Violence: Gender and Conflict Zones*. London and Berkeley, CA: University of California Press.

Hill, C. 1994. 'Academic International Relations: The Siren Song of Policy Relevance', in Hill, C. and Beshoff, P. (eds) *Two Worlds of International Relations*, pp. 3–28. London: Routledge.

International Labor Office (ILO). 2009. 'Global Wage Report: Update 2009'. Available at http://www.ilo.org/wcmsp5/groups/public/-dgreports/-dcomm/documents/publication/-wcms_116500.pdf (accessed 25 May 2010).

Inter-Parliamentary Union. 2010. 'Women in National Parliaments: Situation as of 31 March 2010'. Available at http://www.ipu.org/wmn-e/world.htm (accessed 25 May 2010).

Kabeer, N. 1999. 'Resources, Agency, Achievements: Reflections on the Measurement of Women's Empowerment', *Development and Change* 30 (n.i): 435–64.

Laclau, E. and Mouffe, C. 2001. *Hegemony and Socialist Strategy: Towards a Radical Democratic Politics* 2nd edn. London: Verso.

Mazurana, D., Raven-Roberts, A. and Parpart, J. (eds) 2005. *Gender, Conflict and Peace-keeping*. Oxford and Lanham, MD: Rowman and Littlefield.

Mohan, G. 2006. 'Beyond Participation: Strategies for Deeper Empowerment', in Cooke, B. and Kothari, U. (eds) *The New Tyranny*, pp. 153–67. London: Zed. Available at http://oro.open.ac.uk/4157/1/TYRANNY3.pdf (accessed 23 August 2010).

Moser, C. and Clark, F. (eds). 2001. *Victims, Perpetrators or Actors? Gender, Armed Conflict Armed Conflict and Political Violence*. London: Zed Books.

Otto, D. 2004. 'Securing the 'Gender Legitimacy' of the UN Security Council: Prising Gender From its Historical Moorings', *Legal Studies Research Paper No. 92*. Available at http://www.er.uqam.ca/nobel/juris/Lamarche/Droitsdesfemmes/Documents/ssrn-id585923%5B1%5D-otto.pdf (accessed 23 August 2010).

Otto, D. 2006/7. 'A Sign of "Weakness"? Disrupting Gender Certainties in the Implementation of Security Council Resolution 1325', *Michigan Journal of Gender and Law* 13 (n.i): 113–75.

PeaceWomen. n.d. 'National Action Plans'. Available at http://www.peacewomen.org/pages/about-1325/national-action-plans-naps (accessed 16 June 2011).

Peterson, V. S. 2010. 'International/Global Political Economy', in Shepherd L. J. (ed.) *Gender Matters in Global Politics: A Feminist Introduction to International Relations*, pp. 204–17. London: Routledge.

Puechguirbal, N. 2010. 'Discourses on Gender, Patriarchy and Resolution 1325: A Textual Analysis of UN Documents', *International Peacekeeping* 17 (2): 172–87.

Rai, S. 2008. *The Gender Politics of Development: Essays in Hope and Despair.* London: Zed.

Rehn, E. and Sirleaf, E. 2002. *Women, War and Peace: The Independent Experts' Assessment on the Impact of Armed Conflict on Women and Women's Role in Peace-building.* New York, NY: UNIFEM. Available at http://www.reliefweb.int/rw/lib.nsf/db900SID/LGEL-5FMCM2/$FILE/unicef-WomenWarPeace.pdf?OpenElement (accessed 25 May 2010).

Richardson, T. 1996. 'Foucauldian Discourse: Power and Truth in Urban and Regional Policy Making', *European Planning Studies* 4 (3): 279–292.

Shah, A. 2010. 'Women's Rights', *Global Issues*, 14 March. Available at http://www.globalissues.org/print/article/166 (accessed 25 May 2010).

Shepherd, L. J. 2008a. 'Power and Authority in the Production of United Nations Security Council Resolution 1325', *International Studies Quarterly* 52 (2): 383–404.

Shepherd, L. J. 2008b. *Gender, Violence and Security: Discourse as Practice.* London: Zed Books.

Sjoberg, L. 2006. *Gender, Justice and the Wars in Iraq: A Feminist Reformulation of Just War Theory.* Oxford: Lexington Books.

Sweetman, C. (ed.). 2005. *Gender, Peacebuilding and Reconstruction.* Oxford: Oxfam GB.

Swingewood, A. 2000. *A Short History of Sociological Thought* (3rd ed.). Basingstoke: Palgrave.

The Phrase Finder. No date. 'Behind Every Great Man, There's a Great Woman'. Available at http://www.phrases.org.uk/meanings/60500.html (accessed 25 May 2010).

True, J. 2003. 'Mainstreaming Gender in Global Public Policy', *International Feminist Journal of Politics* 5 (3): 368–96.

True, J. 2010. 'Gender Mainstreaming in International Institutions', in Shepherd L. J. (ed.) *Gender Matters in Global Politics: A Feminist Introduction to International Relations*, pp. 189–203. London: Routledge.

United Nations Development Programme (UNDP). 2004. 'Water Governance for Poverty Reduction: Key Issues and the UNDP Response to Millennium Development Goals'. Available at http://www.undp.org/water/pdfs/241456_UNDP_Guide_Pages.pdf (accessed 25 May 2010).

United Nations Division for the Advancement of Women (UNDAW). 2000. 'The Feminization of Poverty'. Available at http://www.un.org/womenwatch/daw/followup/session/presskit/fs1.htm (accessed 25 May 2010).

United Nations Economic and Social Council (UN ECOSOC). 2007. 'Strengthening Efforts to Eradicate Poverty and Hunger, Including Through the Global Partnership for Development'. E/2007/71. Permanent available URL http://www.un.org/docs/ecosoc/ecosoctest/docs/jump2ods.asp?symbol=E/2007/71 (accessed 16 June 2011).

United Nations Population Fund (UNFPA). 2009. 'Climate Change Connections'. Available at http://www.unfpa.org/webdav/site/global/shared/documents/publications/2009/climateconnections_1_overview.pdf (accessed 25 May 2010).

United Nations Security Council (UNSC). 2000. 'Resolution 1325', S/RES/1325. Permanent available URL http://www.un.org/Docs/scres/2000/sc2000.htm (accessed 25 May 2010).

United Nations Security Council (UNSC). 2008. 'Resolution 1820', S/RES/1820. Permanent available URL http://www.un.org/Docs/sc/unsc_resolutions08.htm (accessed 25 May 2010).

United Nations Security Council (UNSC). 2009a. 'Resolution 1888', S/RES/1888. Permanent available URL http://www.un.org/Docs/sc/unsc_resolutions09.htm (accessed 25 May 2010).

United Nations Security Council (UNSC). 2009b. 'Resolution 1889', S/RES/1889. Permanent available URL http://www.un.org/Docs/sc/unsc_resolutions09.htm (accessed 25 May 2010).

Walt, S. M. 2005. 'The Relationship Between Theory and Policy in International Relations', *Annual Review of Political Science* 8: 23–48.

Yeats, W. B. [1921] 2003. *Michael Robartes and the Dancer.* Whitefish, MT: Kessinger.

Youngs, G. 2008. 'From Practice to Theory: Feminist International Relations and "Gender Mainstreaming"', *International Politics* 45 (4): 688–702.

No Angry Women at the United Nations: Political Dreams and the Cultural Politics of United Nations Security Council Resolution 1325

SHERI LYNN GIBBINGS
Institute of Asian Research, University of British Columbia, Canada

Abstract

From the start, United Nations (UN) Security Council Resolution 1325 was celebrated as an achievement for Member States and activists around the world with the promise that gender would be considered in all peace and security-related decisions and planning. This paper describes how two Iraqi women who spoke at an informal meeting at the UN generated embarrassment for some UN-based gender advocates when their performance did not follow the norms expected by the attending NGOs, Member States and UN officials. The reaction to their performance can be explained by two main factors. First, the cultural norms of the UN require issues to be framed in a positive manner. Second, Resolution 1325 is supplemented by discourses that place value on the knowledge produced by women and situate women as peacemakers. When the two Iraqi women denounced the US- and UK-led invasion of Iraq and used terms like 'imperialism', they spoke outside of UN-based norms. The subsequent reaction illustrated how agency among gender advocates at the UN is socially and historically contingent.

INTRODUCTION

Since its passage, United Nations (UN) Security Council Resolution 1325 has generated a noteworthy amount of discussion within academia, political circles and the press. Scholars have begun to document the use of the

resolution by grassroots organizations, NGOs (non-governmental organizations) and UN agencies (e.g. Neuwirth 2002; Bahdi 2003; Shah 2006). Resolution 1325 has also served as a reference point for UN Member States in
shaping the policies and programmes of a wide range of organizations that
are working to integrate gender-sensitive approaches to peace building and
human security efforts. As of 2010, twenty-two countries have developed
National Action Plans on Women, Peace and Security (Bachelet 2010).

My interest in studying the gender advocates at the UN arose from my
experience working as an intern and then Program Associate for the WILPF-
UN (Women's International League for Peace and Freedom UN Office, an
NGO with consultative status at the UN) between 2001 and 2002.[1] Resolution
1325 was 1 year old at the time I started working at WILPF-UN, and I became
quickly immersed in the efforts to spread the word about the resolution and
ensure its implementation at the UN headquarters in New York. My experience
working for WILPF-UN and the NGO Working Group on Women, Peace and
Security made me interested in reflecting further on the work that gender
advocates were doing at the UN. In June 2003 I returned to the UN headquarters in New York to conduct 4 months of anthropological fieldwork for my
Master's thesis.[2]

In particular, during my research I investigated the shifting practices and
ideologies of WILPF-UN. I also examined United Nations Development Fund
for Women (UNIFEM) and the NGO Working Group on Women, Peace and
Security (of which WILPF-UN was a member), a coalition formed in June
2000 to advocate for a discussion on women, peace and security in the Security
Council. In focusing on these particular groups, I aimed to gain a deeper understanding of how NGOs and UN agencies working on the 'Women, Peace and
Security' agenda were engaging and seeking to transform the UN system to
be more gender sensitive.

The majority of my fieldwork involved participant observation. I took part
in the daily activities of my research consultants, which included writing
reports, attending meetings and strategizing for future interventions. From
these observations and encounters, I wrote daily field notes. Informal discussions were complemented by semi-structured interviews with twelve individuals from these NGOs and UN agencies.[3] I also obtained archival materials
from the offices of Amnesty International (for the period of 2000–2003) and
WILPF-UN (for the period of 1990–2004). Through meeting minutes, email
archives, drafts of documents and advertisements, I was able to understand
the conversations taking place during the build-up, passage and implementation of Resolution 1325. The data I use in this paper are also drawn from
the large repository of information at PeaceWomen.org (a website dedicated
to collecting information about the implementation of UNSCR 1325).

Resolution 1325 is a product of major changes to the Security Council.
Throughout the 1990s, Member States pressured the Security Council to
become more democratic (Malone 2004). Interacting with NGOs was considered a move towards this objective. Arria Formula meetings were developed

to facilitate informal, off-the-record encounters between Security Council members and non-members such as NGOs. Even though the first Arria Formula meeting took place in 1993, it was only in 2000 that an agreement was reached among Members States that NGOs should be consulted in this manner (Paul 2004: 379). Much of the material used in this paper is drawn from Arria Formula meetings where women from conflict zones were invited to speak with Security Council members.

ANGER AT THE UN

In the spring of 2003, the NGO Working Group on Women, Peace and Security was confronted with a precarious dilemma. On the one hand, they wanted to advocate for Iraqi women's participation in their country's 'post-conflict' reconstruction efforts. On the other hand, they did not want to grant legitimacy to the invasion by the USA and UK. In May 2003 the NGOs formulated recommendations for the Security Council calling for women's participation in the reconstruction of Iraq by employing Resolution 1325. In October 2003, two Iraqi women, Amal Al-Khedairy and Nermin Al-Mufti, toured various parts of the USA, including Washington, DC, area universities and civic organizations.[4] One research consultant, a member of the NGO Working Group on Women, Peace and Security, described the unexpected response they received from Al-Khedairy and Al-Mufti when they visited the UN and met with NGO, Member State and UN representatives at the UNIFEM office:

> We assumed that there would be interest in Resolution 1325, but we did not consider how the sanctions had affected [the Iraqi women]. We did not [expect] that they would not even want to consider this Resolution because [they] did not want to associate with the Security Council that has caused them so much pain.[5]

Several NGOs with consultative status at the UN facilitated the expedition of the Iraqi women to the UN. Even though they were denied permission to speak in front of the Security Council in a formal way (it was considered too controversial at the time), the NGOs arranged for Al-Khedairy and Al-Muftito participate in an informal meeting attended by gender officers of the UN agencies, NGOs and several representatives from Member States. At the meeting the two Iraqi women voiced their opposition to the occupation. They spoke in nationalist terms, condemned the invasion by the USA and UK as imperialist and critiqued the UN for its lack of support. There were approximately thirty people at the event and many of the participants were disappointed and embarrassed by Al-Khedairy and Al-Mufti's performance and labelled their comments as 'angry'.

After the meeting, I spoke with several of its organizers. They were concerned about the impact on their own credibility within the UN, since the Iraqi women they had invited to speak had presented themselves in a way that did not meet the expectations of attendees.[6] Although the UN-based NGOs had known ahead of time that Al-Khedairy and Al-Mufti were not familiar with Resolution 1325, they had been told by the tour organizers that the women were 'leading women's rights advocates in Iraq'. They had expected their guests to speak positively about women's efforts in the reconstruction of Iraq and the role the UN could play. The meeting's organizers discussed the possible damage done (in particular, there was concern that the US ambassador's wife might have been offended) and how they might rectify the situation. It was concluded that next time more briefing and background research were needed before organizing a meeting with officials. These gender advocates knew that if they did not speak in accordance with UN discourses (which presented women as peacemakers and emphasized that there was an important role for the UN to play in the reconstruction), they risked being dismissed entirely. It was not that they intended to silence the two Iraqi women, but speaking in terms of imperialism was avoided at UN meetings. It was a known fact in meetings with Security Council members that NGOs were not allowed to make reference to specific Security Council members in ways that questioned their tactics or approaches to peace.[7] Al-Khedairy and Al-Mufti's performance illustrated that powerful norms exist around the Women, Peace and Security agenda, and that certain performances could be anticipated and expected, while others were discouraged. Those who did not meet these expectations caused embarrassment and discomfort.

Because of my relatively low status as an intern at UNIFEM, I did not feel at the time it was appropriate for me to approach Al-Khedairy or Al-Mufti after the meeting to inquire further. I therefore do not know why they spoke the way they did. However, I do know that they had just toured the USA speaking to audiences of activists. At a meeting at University of California, Los Angeles (UCLA) in November 2003 one of them said, 'I see your beautiful universities here, and I ask why did your government have to destroy our universities?' (Basarudin and Shaikh 2003). At the UN they spoke likewise in bold ways about how it was an 'unjust war' and 'illegal occupation' that was destroying their country and people. They also critiqued the Security Council's years of severe sanctions against them. They did not use language, symbols and acronyms that were normal at the UN but rather drew on the idea that the national heritage (monuments, museums and artefacts) of Iraq was being destroyed during the American-led occupation. Perhaps the Iraqi women did not consider peace to be made in the halls of the Security Council. As one of the UN gender advocates explained to me, Al-Khedairy and Al-Mufti were not particularly convinced that they wanted to draw upon Resolution 1325 to achieve their rights. Instead, they could have purposely hoped to have their message of criticism heard by the American diplomats who sat in the audience. In any case, their message was not necessarily against Resolution 1325, which defends their right to speak, but it was at odds with the UN's powerful speech norms.

The necessity of following certain speech norms at the UN was illustrated 2 years later when another Iraqi woman presented herself very differently to

Security Council members. In 2005 Basma Fakri spoke on behalf of Hanaa Edwar, Secretary General of the Iraqi Al-Amal Association (Hanaa Edwar would have spoken at the Arria Formula meeting herself had she received a visa). In the speech Fakrisaid:

> Iraqi women show a rare courage, challenging all aspects of terrorism and vio-
> lence. They continue to work to ensure a lasting and just peace and security in
> Iraq. We are proud to say that Iraqi women won 31 percent of the seats in the
> National Assembly. This achievement speaks to the aspiration of Iraqi women
> to participate in political leadership, to the importance of international law
> and international pressure, as well as to the adherence to the rule of law – par-
> ticularly CEDAW and Resolution 1325.
>
> [...]
> After the fall of the dictatorial regime, Iraqi women were on the front lines
> working for peace, often at great personal sacrifice, and many are paying with
> their lives. Iraqi women proved their capability in different ministries and in pro-
> posing and implementing government policies.
>
> [...]
> The women of Iraq are determined to see peace and justice in our country. Res-
> olution 1325 has been instrumental in giving women a voice in the process, and
> we thank you and hope we can count on your continued support. (Edwar and
> Fakri 2005)

This speech, made only a couple of years after the informal meeting with Al-Khedairy and Al-Mufti, was very similar to others presented to the Security Council by 'representatives of women' from various countries in Arria Formula meetings. From my experience working for WILPF-UN and later during my research, guests speakers were typically briefed and their speeches written in collaboration with the NGO Working Group on Women, Peace and Security and UNIFEM. The specifics of the particular country and its women's activities were framed into a motivational and inspiring story.

In the meeting with the Iraqi women in 2003, the agency of women was inter-preted differently from what might be expected. Rather than celebrating the women's performance as an act of resistance, which might assume a 'subversion and re-inscription of norms' (see Mahmood 2005: 9), the gender advocates actu-ally upheld the discursive tradition of the UN, which does not situate blame on particular Member States but rather places the possibility of hope and change onto women. In the corridors of the UN discourses that are uplifting, positive and present women as peacemakers are the most valued. Those who work at the UN deploy this master narrative, and citizens' success at being intelligible in this space depends on their capacity to reproduce the master narrative.[8] In other words, a particular way of speaking at the UN shapes the possibility of action and limits a supposed freedom of political participation. I am not arguing that women, through using this discourse, are resisting or subordinate to the UN system; I believe the social relations of power are shifting and cannot be removed from the social and political conditions from which they emerged (see Mahmood 2005). I am arguing that one of the key ways that power is negotiated at the UN is through language (see Bourdieu 1991).

In some ways the gender advocates of WILPF-UN and the NGO Working Group were operating on their own norms and their own assumptions of agency, which were working self-consciously against what they considered the patriarchies of the UN system. Their attempt to speak to the Security Council using the normative speech style of the UN can be understood as a form of agency, established by understanding the structures and discourses of the UN system and using them to their own advantage. These gender advocates imagined themselves as agents, and assumed the two Iraqi women shared similar goals. Al-Khedairy and Al-Mufti, however, had little knowledge or experience with UN practices and norms. That being said, whether the gender advocates were constrained by the UN or the Iraqi women were acting freely must be examined rather than assumed. In the next section, I will situate the incident with Al-Khedairy and Al-Mufti within a description of the discourses that were produced around Resolution 1325, drawing attention to the supplementary discourses that lie beyond the rights-based arguments present in Resolution 1325.

Utopian Visions

The discourse on Women, Peace and Security must be seen as part of a practice at the UN where narratives are expected to be positive, hopeful and future oriented (see Apthorpe 1997; Barnett 1997: 556) with a use of 'mobilizing metaphors' (Shore and Wright 1997: 15).[9] The following statements on Resolution 1325 illustrate this [author's emphasis]:

> Our greatest indicator of success must, however, remain the extent to which *our collective energies* contribute to building a sustainable, nationally-owned platform from which local women, working with men, can themselves define, shape and influence the course of peace in their countries. (Department of Public Information 2010, statement by Alain Le Roy, Under-Secretary-General for Peacekeeping Operations)

> The ultimate goal of the international community, and therefore of the United Nations, is to *build a world free of conflict*. By adopting this resolution three years ago, the Security Council showed its *wisdom* by fully recognizing the important roles played by women and girls in the process of building and maintaining peace and security. (Permanent Mission of Japan to the United Nations 2003)

Therefore, the production of this powerful discourse on Women, Peace and Security must be understood in relation to the discursive practices of the UN, which inspire and empower the listener toward action. Phrases such as 'active participation', 'indispensable agents' and 'collective energies' are vague. Consequently, they mobilize a vision that enrols a number of different interests and masks any ideological differences (Shore and Wright 1997). This is a vision wherein women are no longer abused and their contributions are recognized. It is a 'world free from conflict'. These statements situate Resolution 1325 in relation to the UN's historical goal to make the world a better place and are part of the UN's master narrative, presented in a style of language that often goes unnoticed (see Apthorpe 1997).

Moving Beyond a Rights-Based Discourse

At a very basic level, Resolution 1325 makes three central arguments. The first is for the increased participation of women in various bodies, institutions and processes related broadly to peace and security (such as peacekeeping missions and peace and security decision-making). The second is for the incorporation of a gender perspective into all these processes and institutions (through developing gender-sensitive training materials). 'Gender perspective' has a specific meaning: to 'recognize the special needs of women and girls' and to protect their human rights during and after a conflict. Central to taking this gender perspective is to also 'take special measures to protect women and girls from gender-based violence, particularly rape and other forms of sexual abuse, and all other forms of violence in situations of armed conflict' and to consider their 'special needs' as women (in designing refugee camps, for instance). Integrating gender throughout these policies and programmes is referred to as 'gender mainstreaming'. The third central argument of Resolution 1325 is that there should be a mechanism through which the Security Council can take into account gender and the rights of women. This is accomplished through 'consultation with local and international women's groups' (United Nations Security Council [UNSC] 2000).

These arguments are rights based. The arguments for the increased participation of women and for the incorporation of a gender perspective are based on the premise that women as half of the population have the right to equal participation in all programmes related to peace and security. If the special needs of women and girls are not recognized, it is suggested that the needs of half of the population are being ignored. Yet I observed in my fieldwork that although the gender advocates used the rights argument in reports, speeches and meetings at the UN, it was often supplemented by other arguments, including contributor rights.

Contributor rights are similar to what Muehlebach (2001: 217) noticed with regard to indigenous organizing. The Women, Peace and Security agenda has been influenced by this shift to 'knowledge as industrial capital'. By this I mean that rights are derived or given worth because of their contribution and value in relation to achieving peace. I am arguing that although not stated explicitly in Resolution 1325 itself, supplementary discourses exist around the resolution, in speeches, reports and talk. These supplementary discourses used by the NGO Working Group and Member States suggest that the rights of women are based on the specific claims that women are local (connected to grassroots movements) and that their stakes are derived from universal principles (peace and justice) rather than loyalty to other interests (i.e. tribal, political or national). In other words, these NGOs present a hybrid discourse of 'special-treatment rights' (which argue that women and girls need to be paid attention because conflict affects them differently) and also 'contributor rights' (which argue that women can make a difference when it comes to peace) (see Holston 2008: 253–62).

In the lead-up to the passage of Resolution 1325, gender advocates purposely sought to shift perceptions of women away from just 'victims' of war to also 'agents' of peace building.[10] Consequently, in addition to the rights-based discourse, another discourse was produced and deployed at the UN that closely linked women to practices of peace and argued for their value. A statement by the director of UNIFEM provides an example of this discourse: 'Women can more readily embrace the collaborative perspective needed to cut through ethnic, religious, tribal and political barriers. They also embrace a more sustainable concept of security' (Heyzer 2003). In the second Arria Formula meeting on Women, Peace and Security on 30 October 2001, a member from the NGO Working Group said [author's emphasis],

> Your mission visits to East Timor, DRC and Sierra Leone really made a difference to women's organisations. The deliberate emphasis placed on meeting with women's organisations and valuing their input through your reports has encouraged the UN missions in the field *to tap this under utilised resource.* We urge you to routinely meet with women's organisations on your mission visits. (NGO Working Group on Women, Peace and Security 2001)

One of the discourses that is not specifically located in Resolution 1325 but appears in many of the documents written on the topic is the idea of women as a resource. References are continually made to women as 'untapped resources' (e.g. Anderlini 2003). The Norway Mission to the UN stated in a speech that, 'women are a resource that should be included at all levels of peace planning and peace-making' (Permanent Mission of Norway to the UN 2002). In *Ms. Magazine*, an article title asserts that, 'In UN Peacekeeping, Women are an Untapped Resource' (Kirshenbaum 1997). The competition between agendas at the Security Council leads to women being 'marketed', and women's abilities are framed to convince the current decision-makers of the utility of their abilities and knowledge. This idea of women as a resource needs to be situated in the larger transformation of arguments at the UN, linked to the 'shifting concepts of "value" in the global marketplace, as well as new trends in developmental discourse...' (Muehlebach 2001: 432). As in the case of the value placed on the local knowledge of indigenous organizations to prevent environmental destruction, the concern over conflict has situated women as repositories of community knowledge.

It was through the reports and documents leading up to and after the passage of the resolution that women were presented as having valuable knowledge. The *Women at the Peace Table* report produced by Sanam Naraghi Anderlini for UNIFEM in 2001 states, 'While women clearly need access to the peace table in order to advance toward the goal of gender equality, the peace table also requires women's participation to truly uphold the principle of democracy and to lay the foundations for sustainable peace' (Anderlini 2000: 56). The report noted, however, that not all women would necessarily work in the interest of women, but that 'the question therefore is how to develop effective mechanisms during conflicts to ensure that women leaders are committed to presenting and defending grassroots priorities' (Anderlini 2000: 57). Although the gender advocates writing these reports were aware that women, as women, had the right to participate, this right was not necessarily enough. It was instead their connection to the grassroots movement and peace movements that made them valuable. For example, during an Arria-style meeting between members of the Security Council and NGOs on the Fifth Anniversary of Resolution 1325 in 2005, Swanee Hunt from Women Waging Peace argued:

> Why should we include women in peace processes? Of course, women constitute over half the population, so sidelining them is discriminatory and fundamentally undemocratic. But the rights argument is persuasive only to those who cherish fairness. For those who prioritize efficacy, ignoring them is patently unwise. Worldwide, women make profound contributions to peace building. If we hope to transform instability and violence into prosperity, we must incorporate the expertise of women. (Hunt 2005)

Scholars have noted how the logic of the market has been extended to the operation of state functions (e.g. Rose and Miller 1992). This shift to an enterprise model is also occurring at the UN with the appearance of discourses that focus on the value of women's knowledge and their contribution to great efficiency (see Muehlebach 2001).

Civil Society: Perspectives from 'On the Ground'

Anthropologists have increasingly looked at states not just as bureaucratic apparatuses but as the sites of symbolic and cultural production, and as a 'fiction' or a unified body and centre of power that conceals the disjointed nature of its practices and discourses (e.g. Abrams 1988; Aretxaga 2003). In this framework, civil society is often imagined as coming 'from below' and acting separately from the state (Ferguson and Gupta 2002; Van Klinken and Barker 2009). This imagined separation also exists at the UN, where women from conflict zones are invited to speak to the Security Council because they are viewed as bringing a 'grounded' voice that is more authentic or real and thus more valuable. The NGOs that I worked with were also imagined as mediators working to connect the 'up there' with the 'on the ground women', and they gained their legitimacy by reproducing this image.

An important part of providing legitimacy to Resolution 1325 and convincing leaders of its value has been the statements made by women activists from the field who have spoken in Arria Formula meetings before the Security Council. In 2001 Jamila Akbarzi from Afghan Women's Welfare Department and a founding member of the Afghan Women's Network said:

> I have often heard that Afghan women are not political. That peace and security is man's work. I am here to challenge that illusion. For the last 20 years of my life, the leadership of men has only brought war and suffering.
>
> [...] We see larger grants channeled through Afghan men's organizations and wonder why? Women's organizations work in the refugee camps and reach out to the refugee communities in Peshawar, Islamabad, Rawalpindi and Quetta, where Afghan refugees do not receive UN assistance. We are the role models for our youth; we are working for security and peace. (Akbarzi 2001: 1)

Central to Resolution 1325 is the imagination that there is a distinction between state and society and that the NGOs working on the subject are able to bring the voices of women to the 'up there' (i.e. the UN). At the same time, however, the way that women from these conflict zones, such as Afghanistan, were able to speak to the 'higher up' Security Council was by claiming to embody the universal principles of peace and security as opposed to the local (tribal or ethnic) interests of particular communities. Jamila Akbarzi says in her speech, 'Most women's organizations do not have political affiliations and are providing humanitarian assistance to all of our people, regardless of ethnic background. We are Pushtun, Tajik, Hazara, and Uzbek' (Akbarzi 2001: 1–2). Resolution 1325 is supplemented by the idea that women work across political and ethnic divisions, and the gender advocates utilize these images to qualify them as rightful participants.

In these speeches the loyalty of women transgressed geographical areas, class and other divisions. As a result, their principles came to mirror the discourse of the 'higher ups' at the UN. Men in conflict zones, in contrast, were often silently situated as unable to move across class, ethnic or political divisions of the nation. In practice, however, the connections and boundaries between the 'up there' and the 'grounded' were more blurred. One way this was demonstrated was by the fact that most of the speeches given by representatives for women at the Arria Formula meetings were drafted and written with the NGOs and UNIFEM working from the UN. It was through their guidance that the speeches were framed in the appropriate language. Al-Khedairy and Al-Mufti in 2003 who did not receive this guidance spoke in nationalist and anti-imperialist terms that directly contradicted the UN vision of women (as inhabiting the universal, civil and humanitarian domain), and as a result they were labelled as 'angry' and their message dismissed.

The Women, Peace and Security agenda thus assigns supplementary legitimacy for women through two moves. They assign authority to women first as local agents (who understand and are connected to the local) and second as upholders of universal interests that represent the greater good. Through these 'scaled' assignments, the NGOs were able to give the gender perspective and women's participation greater authority. Arguably this is another example of where the UN encourages activists and grassroots organizations to take up a greater role and responsibility in an emerging system of transnational governmentality (see Dean 1999; Li 2007). In the process, the UN promotes a particular idea of what it means be a woman or what is considered appropriate feminine behaviour, which can be used as a rationale to privilege certain voices and exclude others.

Compromising Anti-militarism

My attempt in this article has been to de-naturalize the Women, Peace and Security agenda and discourse. I do not doubt that female peace activists have something to contribute to peace and my intention is not to undermine their important work. I am suggesting, however, that there is movement to supplement the rights-based approach with one based on possible contributions. I also want to highlight that this discourse could have been different in another institutional setting. Indeed, the powerful discourse that emerged with the Women, Peace and Security agenda was not without its critics. Prior to the passage of Resolution 1325, the WILPF-UN office was including recommendations such as the 'reduction of military expenditures' and the alteration of 'military priorities' in their documents.[11] After reviewing WILPF-UN's documents for 10 years prior to the passage of Resolution 1325, I noticed that they continuously proposed a reduction in military spending, the cessation of nuclear testing and the prevention of the arms trade. Yet, the arguments presented to the Security Council immediately prior to and after Resolution 1325 included little, if any, reference to these points.

These critiques of militarism, military budgets and military priorities were curtailed and reformulated into positive calls for women's participation and a gender perspective in peace and security. This illustrates how the Women, Peace and Security agenda was shaped by the practices and expectations within the Security Council and the UN, where positive and uplifting speech is valued. If language is power, then to use the same speech forms as the Security Council members allowed the NGO Working Group and UNIFEM to situate themselves on a similar playing field as Member States. Adopting the UN language norms situated these groups as worth listening to, which allowed them to push their agenda forward. The UN thus imposes certain practices onto speakers, and power operates in this symbolic domain.

After reviewing the WILPF-UN office and Amnesty International archives, I asked one of my research consultants, who worked for WILPF during the passage of Resolution 1325, whether she believed that the aims of WILPF-UN had been altered. She had worked for the WILPF-UN Office for several years prior to, and for 1 year after, the passage of Resolution 1325. She responded,

> WILPF's work on 1325 has not maintained this political message [anti-militarism], which has saddened and enraged me. The strategy was to provide a platform for multiple views and information in order to locate the facts and analysis WILPF brings to the table, not to let that fade while working to facilitate NGO information.[12]

Prior to the passage of Resolution 1325, WILPF-UN often portrayed women as agents of peace but also provided an explicit critique of militarism and masculinity. This WILPF member's response reinforced my observation that WILPF-UN was encouraged to formulate its arguments using the positive and uplifting language of the UN, with a focus towards gender equality and gender mainstreaming and away from militarism, in their collaborative work with the NGO Working Group on Women, Peace and Security. The route to peace and ending war in this approach was no longer a reduction in military spending but the integration of women and a gender perspective; women were viewed and constructed as peacemakers, fitting with the more utopian visions circulating at the UN.

CONCLUSION

In this article I have illustrated how the UN and its speech norms around gender are a space of inclusion but also exclusion. Certain narratives are sanctioned while others are discouraged, as seen in the example of the Arria Formula responses to Al-Khedairy and Al-Mufti in 2003. The story of the Iraqi women is particularly powerful in helping to make visible the norms of acceptable speech at the UN. It illustrates that operating at the UN is akin to acquiring a second language. Women's participation within the Security Council is thus structured by, and upholds, certain UN performance and speech practices that I have described. In particular, I have illustrated that the NGO Working Group on Women, Peace and Security and UNIFEM acted as mediators, instructing most of the activists who visited the UN on how to speak and perform at Security Council and other informal meetings, in ways that accord with the UN's speech styles and master narratives.

These gender advocates are thus at the forefront of producing a discursive space for 'women' and 'gender' in the peace and security agenda of the UN. Exploring the discourses of the Women, Peace and Security agenda, I have argued that Resolution 1325 is supplemented by a scalar logic where representatives of women who come to speak to the Security Council are situated as local and connected to grassroots organizations, while also being allied to the transcendental goals of the UN, which is imagined as 'above'. This connection made between the local and the global is through the idea that women share a sense of good, and uphold global goals rather than being tied to local political, ethnic or class divisions. Therefore, in this supplementary discourse women are positioned as overcoming conflict as agents of the local, but simultaneously as having interests in universal good. Their claim to know the local, to be part of the 'grassroots', is also what provides them with greater authority, because they are imagined as separate and distinct from the 'higher ups' at the UN headquarters.

The possible identities women embody are influenced by multiple sources. There are many different forms of desire and discipline at work beyond Resolution 1325 and the UN. However, at the space of the UN a certain kind of performance is demanded of women; one that asks women to be loyal to the global while also showing their connection to the local, and one that encourages them to speak in positive ways. Women who represent this agenda are expected to embody and reproduce this image as upholders of peace in their communities. Whether these women enact similar performances outside the corridors of the UN remains to be seen, but in the rituals and representations of the Women, Peace and Security agenda at the UN headquarters, women are expected to justify their right to participate by drawing on these supplementary discourses. I have also argued that these supplementary discourses are part of a larger trend at the UN that privileges 'value-based knowledge' within a larger context of neoliberal logics.

Consequently, claims that women may make in support of particular groups like a local Islamic movement, or groups that critique the UN as imperialist, are not well received. The UN speech styles encourage positive visions and utopian dreams; little space exists for more critical interventions in public forums beyond these essentialized visions of gender. The efforts of the gender advocates I studied to transform the UN were also structured by, and upheld, some of the discursive traditions of the UN system. More attention needs to be paid to the possibilities and closures that exist with these linguistic practices; how certain speech styles become more valued and carry more authority than others at the UN. The case of the Iraqi women is important because it illustrates the contradictions inherent in Resolution 1325 between the idea of the 'free acting subject' and the constraints of the UN system, which sets frameworks for action and intervention. If the ability to effect change is historically and culturally contingent, then the meaning and sense of agency that gender advocates assume with relation to Resolution 1325 must be studied. We must examine how agency is embedded in the realities, desires and norms of the UN system that shape and produce assumptions about the capacity for action.

'It is time for action, not words', said Ms. Awori from the Civil Society Advisory Group to the United Nations on Women, Peace and Security at the Security Council Meeting in October 2010. Later in the same speech, she stated, 'We cannot wait another ten years for action' (Department of Public Information 2010). In the press release from the meeting, the word 'action' was used over eighty-three times. Even scholars such as Binder et al. (2008) ask, '[...] have the commitments of Resolution 1325 remained empty words without further impact?' During my fieldwork, almost everyone I met working within the UN claimed that the UN was all talk and that there was not enough action. The main problem was converting these speeches into willpower and action by Member States and UN bodies. At the same time as the NGO network and gender advocates complained that the UN was just words, however, they afforded importance to its speeches and language. The UN expects sincerity, but there is also recognition that what is said there might not become a reality; that it is a mere vision for a future that might not come. This followed the general concerns that gender advocates expressed to me, that Member States might be making public statements that express their commitment to gender equality, but in reality they would act differently. There thus remains opacity behind the claims made by Member States and UN bodies, and questions of sincerity arise. The gender advocates I spoke with knew that the decisions to pass a resolution and to hold talks on the Women, Peace and Security agenda were part of larger political exchanges where favours were granted and debts were repaid. Although the commitment to discuss gender in the Security Council was seen as important, the NGO network and gender advocates also treated it with suspicion, and hence academics and advocates call continuously to put this language into action. As I have suggested, many of the gender advocates make metalinguistic claims about the limits of speech at the UN, pointing out that there is something inherently unbelievable about it. The language is based on utopian visions, generating a hope for radical change that is always deferred to a future date, and thus it is always haunted by an impossibility.

Notes

1   WILPF was founded in 1915 by a group of women who met at The Hague to speak out against World War I (Birchem 1998: 44).
2   I am grateful to the Martin Cohnstaedt Graduate Research Award for Studies in Non Violence, York Centre for International and Security Studies at York University, for financial support during my research.
3   I have omitted details about the positions and personal histories of my research consultants in order to protect their anonymity.
4   The New York-based Fellowship of Reconciliation organized the 'Women of Iraq Tour of the United States.'

5   Member of NGO Working Group on Women, Peace and Security, email message to author, August 2004.

6   I documented this discussion in my field notes in October 2003.

7   This statement was made in a summary report written on the Arria Formula meeting by a member of the NGO Working Group on Women, Peace and Security (Member of WILPF-UN, email message to NGO Working Group, October 2001).

8   See Borneman's (1992: 77) concept of 'master narrative' and his discussion of how states produce narratives that provide models 'that give form to everyday experiences of the citizens'. I thank Andrea Muehlebach for drawing my attention to this work.

9   They describe how 'their mobilizing effect lies in their capacity to connect with, and appropriate, the positive meanings and legitimacy derived from other key symbols of government such as "nation", "country", "democracy", "public interest" and "rule of law"' (Shore and Wright 1997: 15).

10 Member of the NGO Working Group on Women, Peace and Security, email message to NGO Working Group, October 2000.

11 In a document produced for the Commission on the Status of Women in 1999 on the follow-up to the Beijing Conference, WILPF wrote, 'When only one quarter of current military spending is necessary to eradicate all health, social, political, economic and environmental challenges faced by humanity, the complex issues of peace are urgently relevant. Militarism, arms trade and the permanent war economy that in the late 1990s drains 780 billion per year from the global economy, contributes to normalization of violence, the cultural production of gender roles, poverty, environmental degradation – clearly affecting every one of the 12 Critical Areas of Concern of the Platform For Action' (found by author in WILPF-UN Archives, WILFP-UN office, New York).

12 WILPF-UN Member, interview with the author, August 2003.

References

Abrams, P. 1988. 'Notes on the Difficulty of Studying the State', *Journal of Historical Sociology* 1 (1): 58–89.

Akbarzi, J. 2001. 'United Nations Security Council Meeting on the Implementation of Resolution 1325 on Women, Peace and Security 30 October 2001, Afghanistan'. Available at http://www.peacewomen.org/assets/file/SecurityCouncilMonitor/ArriaFormula/Oct2001/jamila_afgh_oct2001.pdf (accessed 16 December 2010).

Anderlini, S. N. 2000. 'Women at the Peace Table: Making a Difference'. United Nations Development Fund for Women. Available at http://www.reliefweb.int/library/documents/peacebk.pdf (accessed 10 December 2010).

Anderlini, S. N. 2003. 'The Untapped Resource: Women in Peace Negotiations', *Conflict Trends, Special Issues on Women, Peace and Security* 3: 18–22.

Apthorpe, R. 1997. 'Writing Development Policy and Policy Analysis or Clear: On Language, Genre and Power', in Shore, C. and Wright, S. (eds) *Anthropology of Policy: Critical Perspectives on Governance and Power*, pp. 34–46. London: Routledge.

Aretxaga, B. 2003. 'Maddening States', *Annual Review of Anthropology* 32: 393–410.

Bachelet, M. 2010. 'Security Council Open Debate on Women, Peace and Security, Tuesday, 26 October 2010, Security Council Chamber (GA-TSC-01). Statement by Under-Secretary-General Michelle Bachelet, Executive Director for UN Women'. Available at http://www.peacewomen.org/assets/file/SecurityCouncilMonitor/ Debates/WPS/WPS2010/unwomen_wps_2010.pdf (accessed 28 November 2010).

Bahdi, R. 2003. 'Security Council Resolution 1325: Practice and Prospects', *Refuge* 21 (2): 41–51.

Barnett, M. 1997. 'The UN Security Council, Indifference, and Genocide in Rwanda', *Cultural Anthropology* 12 (4): 551–78.

Basarudin, A. and Shaikh, K. 2003. 'Voices of Resistance: Two Iraqi Women Speak Out: Azza Basarudin and Khanum Shaikh Interview Amal Al-Khedairy and Nermin Al-Mufti', *The Middle East Women's Studies Review* 18 (3–4): 1–4.

Binder, C., Lukas, K. and Schweigher, R. 2008. 'Empty Words or Real Achievement? The Impact of Security Council Resolution 1325 on Women and Armed Conflicts', *Radical History Review* 101 (1): 22–41.

Birchem, R. 1998. 'The Women's International League for Peace and Freedom', in Auth, J. (ed.) *To Beijing and Beyond: Pittsburg and the United Nations Fourth World Conference on Women*, pp. 43–45. Pittsburgh, PA: University of Pittsburg Press.

Borneman, J. 1992. *Belonging in the Two Berlins: Kin, State, Nation.* Cambridge: Cambridge University Press.

Bourdieu, P. 1991. *Language and Symbolic Power.* J. Thompson (ed.). Trans. G. Raymond and M. Adamson. Cambridge, MA: Harvard University Press.

Dean, M. 1999. *Governmentality: Power and Rule in Modern Society.* Los Angeles, CA: Sage Publications.

Department of Public Information. 2010. 'Security Council Supports "Taking Forward" Indicators of Progress in Implementing Landmark Text on Women, Peace and Security as Organization Marks Tenth Anniversary'. Available at http://www.un. org/News/Press/docs//2010/sc10071.doc.htm (accessed 2 December 2010).

Edwar, H. and Fakri, B. 2005. 'United Nations Security Council "Arria Formula" Meeting 5th Anniversary of Security Council Resolution 1325 Women, Peace and Security October 25, 2005'. Available at http://www.peacewomen.org/assets/file/ SecurityCouncilMonitor/ArriaFormula/October2005/hanaaedwar_statement_oct_ 25_2005.pdf (accessed 10 December 2010).

Ferguson, J. and Gupta, A. 2002. 'Spatializing States: Toward an Ethnography of Neoliberal Governmentality', *American Ethnologist* 29 (4): 981–1002.

Heyzer, N. 2003. 'Foreword', in *Conflict Trends, on Women, Peace and Security.* International Knowledge Network of Women in Politics. Available at http://www. iknowpolitics.org/en/node/1120 (accessed 10 December 2010).

Holston, J. 2008. *Insurgent Citizenship: Disjunctions of Democracy and Modernity in Brazil.* Princeton and Oxford: Princeton University Press.

Hunt, S. 2005. 'Arria-Style Meeting Between Members of the Security Council and NGOs Security Council Resolution 1325, 5th Anniversary, Hosted by Denmark October 25, 2005'. Available at http://www.peacewomen.org/assets/file/SecurityCouncilMonitor/ ArriaFormula/Nov2008/swaneehunt_oct_25_2005.pdf (accessed 15 December 2010).

Kirshenbaum, G. 1997. 'In the U.N. Peacekeeping, Women are an Untapped Resource', *Ms. Magazine* January/February: 20-1.

Li, T. 2007. *The Will to Improve: Governmentality, Development, and the Practice of Politics*. Durham and London: Duke University Press.

Mahmood, S. 2005. *The Politics of Piety: The Islamic Revival and the Feminist Subject*. Princeton, NJ: Princeton University Press.

Malone, D. 2004. *The UN Security Council: From the Cold War to the 21st Century*. Boulder, CO: Lynne Rienner.

Muehlebach, A. 2001. 'Making Place at the United Nations. An Anthropological Inquiry into the United Nations Working Group on Indigenous Populations', *Cultural Anthropology* 16 (3): 415-35.

Neuwirth, J. 2002. 'Women and Peace and Security: The Implementation of U.N. Security Council Resolution 1325', *Duke Journal of Gender Law and Policy* 9: 253-60.

NGO Working Group on Women, Peace and Security. 2001. 'United Nations Security Council "Arria Formula" Meeting on the implementation of Resolution 1325 30 October 2001'. Available at http://www.peacewomen.org/assets/file/SecurityCouncilMonitor/ArriaFormula/Oct2001/maha_ngowg_oct2001.pdf (accessed 9 September 2011).

Paul, J. 2004. 'Working with Nongovernmental Organizations', in Malone, D. (ed.) *The UN Security Council: From the Cold War to the 21st Century*, pp. 373-90. Boulder, CO: Lynne Rienner.

Permanent Mission of Japan to the United Nations. 2003. 'Statement by H.E. Mr. Toshiro Ozawa Ambassador, Permanent Mission of Japan to the United Nations at the Open Meeting of the Security Council on "Women, Peace and Security" United Nations, New York, 29 October 2003'. Available at http://www.un.emb-japan.go.jp/statements/ozawa031029.html (accessed 7 February 2011).

Permanent Mission of Norway to the United Nations. 2002. 'Statement by H.E. Mr. Ole Peter Kolby Ambassador Permanent Representative to the United Nations, in his National Capacity, on the Implementation of Security Council Resolution 1325 on Women, Peace and Security, in the Security Council, New York, 28 October 2002', Press Release SC/7550. Available at http://www.un.org/News/Press/docs/2002/sc7550.doc.htm (accessed 7 February 2011).

Rose, N. and Miller, P. 1992. 'Political Power Beyond the State: Problematics of Government', *British Journal of Sociology* 43 (2): 173-205.

Shah, P. 2006. 'Assisting and Empowering Women Facing Natural Disasters: Drawing from Security Council Resolution 1325', *Columbia Journal of Gender and Law* 15 (3): 711-37.

Shore, C. and Wright, S. 1997. 'Policy: A New Field for Anthropology', in *Anthropology of Policy: Critical Perspectives on Governance and Power*, pp. 3-34. London: Routledge.

United Nations Security Council (UNSC). 2000. 'Resolution 1325 Adopted by the Security Council at Its 4213th Meeting', 31 October. Available at http://www.un.org/events/res_1325e.pdf (accessed 17 December 2010).

Van Klinken, G. and Barker, J 2009. 'Introduction: State in Society in Indonesia', in *State of Authority: The State in Society in Indonesia*, pp. 1-16. Ithaca, NY: Cornell University Press.

UNSCR 1325 and Women's Peace Activism in the Occupied Palestinian Territory

VANESSA FARR

UNDP Programme of Assistance to the Palestinian People, East Jerusalem

Abstract

Palestinian women's organized resistance to the Israeli occupation is decades old and has been well-documented and analysed by feminists in the occupied Palestinian territory (oPt) and outside. Some of the most recent attempts to formulate and shape this resistance make reference to UNSCR 1325. The application of the Resolution in the work of three women's organizations in the Gaza Strip, the West Bank and Palestinian–Israeli peace-making attempts are analysed in this paper. However, the paper concludes that the disconnects between women's activism on the ground and in academia, the intentions stated in UNSCR 1325, and the Israel–Palestine peace process are so vast that there is little evidence that the Resolution offers an effective mechanism for women to make their voices heard.

INTRODUCTION

In her brilliant new book on the impacts on women of the war in Iraq, Cynthia Enloe observes that '[a]ny war takes place at a particular moment in the history of gender – that is, in the history of women's organizing, in the history of women's relationships to the state, in the history of contested masculinities, in the history of patriarchy's rationalization and reach' (Enloe 2010: 4). In this article, I reflect on how UNSCR 1325 relates to the long history of Palestinian women's contribution to resisting the ongoing Israeli occupation of the Palestinian territory. I also analyse their recent record of trying to cope with and oppose the internal fragmentation of Palestinian politics since Hamas took over the Gaza Strip in June 2007, effectively extending the geographical division of the territory into a political split that was only overcome in May 2011 with the signing of a unity accord in Cairo.

Following what Enloe describes as 'a feminist curiosity' and her 'feminist discovery that paying serious attention to any woman's life can make us smarter about war and about militarism' (Enloe 2010: xii; see also Enloe 2004), I speculate on the relevance and visibility of women's activities and their possible efficacy in an endeavour to make peace that seems to be both stuck and utterly inaccessible to women. My observations derive from field-work conducted in the occupied Palestinian territory (oPt) since mid-2008, which includes ongoing semi-structured interviews with women's networks that are trying to advance peace in the different parts of the oPt.

UNSCR 1325 seems by now to be quite widely known in the oPt – at least theoretically – and, as a result, it crops up in the discourse of many organizations. This paper will show, however, that a large gap still exists between women's abilities to use UNSCR 1325 to make visible their activities and ideas on peace and security (see also Cockburn 2007: 154), and the normative patriarchal peace-building discourses and praxis that fixedly define notions of 'peace-making' and more recently 'state-building' in this always asymmetrical, old and seemingly intractable conflict.[1] I shall confine my reflections to three organizations which use UNSCR 1325 in defining their strategies: the well-established and internationally known MIFTAH (The Palestinian Initiative for the Promotion of Global Dialogue and Democracy) in Jerusalem/West Bank, founded by the politician Hanan Ashrawi in 1998; the Wisal Coalition in the Gaza Strip, formed with the aid of The United Nations Population Fund (UNFPA) to focus on women's well-being and crisis impacts on their access to healthcare; and the recently disbanded International Women's Commission (IWC), which included Palestinian, Israeli and international members and was founded with assistance by The United Nations Development Fund for Women (UNIFEM) in 2005 as a deliberate attempt to advance UNSCR 1325 by creating a group 'which would be capable of an intervention in any future Israeli/Palestinian peace negotiations' (Cockburn 2007: 154).[2]

As an international civil servant who can move relatively freely around the oPt, I have been privileged to talk to members of these organizations both formally and informally in the course of my daily work, drawing comparisons between their responses. Such comparative research would be much more difficult, if not impossible, for Palestinian feminists to do given the extreme movement restrictions imposed on them by the Israeli military authorities. The findings of my field research are supplemented by secondary literature, especially that produced by academics at Birzeit University's Institute of Women's Studies, with whom I am also privileged to have regular contact.

PALESTINIAN WOMEN AND STATE-BUILDING

As state-building and improving weak governance systems have become central foci of international engagement in so-called fragile states, women peace activists have more vocally challenged the limited strategic priorities set by both the international community and national governments, which bypass the interests of ordinary people, especially women. UNSCR 1325 and subsequent Resolutions on women in conflict zones came about to try to broaden both the conceptual and the operational aspects of peace- and state-building (particularly as these relate to governance and security). Yet despite the formal recognition that it led to – that gender analysis matters for international peace and security – efforts made so far to integrate gendered concerns into peace- and state-building programmes have been paltry. A few women may have been allowed some access, but there is still no intention to use gender analysis to shift power relations.

This silence in the face of power inequities is particularly salient in the oPt, since the hoped-for independent Palestinian state has not yet come into being. Its birth relies on successful final status negotiations with Israel taking place, adding another layer of complexity to the process of state-building to which the thirteenth government of the Palestinian Authority, under Prime Minister Fayyad, committed itself in 2009.[3]

Because so many actors external to the oPt have a stake in it, there is quite a large gap between stated commitments to building the state and its governing structures in such a way that the polity feels engaged in the process, and the gestures towards state-building, including all forms of negotiation, that are actually taking place. These happen in an abstract and high-level manner in which elites speak to elites; and decisions are made with neither democratic participation from those who will have to live with them nor accountability to report the results of such high-level encounters to ordinary people (Johnson and Kuttab 2001; Shalhoub-Kevorkian 2008).

In this, the oPt is like most other conflict-stricken places. As the international women's movement has observed, current state-building practices rarely consider, or derive from, what a population needs or wants.[4] All too often the creation of post-conflict institutions is driven by a perceived lack of time and by financial constraints, especially when it comes to supporting machineries for women's political inclusion. As a result, priorities are set, and processes and institutions put in motion, that are divorced from the reality in the conflict or post-conflict zone. Nor are they fundamentally about examining and re-negotiating power to make state institutions more accessible and accountable to citizens, and therefore able to understand or respond to the needs of women and other marginalized stakeholders (Farr 2004).[5]

Not surprisingly, evidence from state-building efforts shows that stated commitments to ensure gender-responsive engagement with fragile states are not made operational. Certain areas are still stereotyped as gender-relevant while others, especially security, are overlooked. Worse, gender considerations are too often sidelined to subordinate parallel tracks or de-prioritized altogether (Castillejo 2010; Schoofs and Smits 2010). Most problematically, far from advancing a feminist aim for social transformation, gender inclusion language is often misused to maintain the *status quo.*

In the Palestinian peace process, elites maintain their privileged positions using language and processes that grassroots activists cannot control or understand. This is also somewhat true of UNSCR 1325, which is not, in itself, something that ordinary women can wield effectively as a means to describe their peace and security-building work. Nor does it enhance their existing capacities to apprehend and use the sophisticated language and political procedures that form the currency of high-level negotiations, as fieldwork in Jerusalem has shown (UNDP/PAPP 2010b). This has important consequences for Palestinian civil society's ability to act in the present, let alone to influence the kind of state and institutions that may eventually result from a successful peace process.

Finally, the weakest element of UNSCR 1325 is that it does not focus on '*ending war itself,*' which after all, was the main reason the United Nations was established and is precisely the Security Council's brief' (Cockburn 2007: 147; her italics). As such, the Resolution risks being yet another tool to underpin the neo-liberal peace-making approach characteristic of the Israel–Palestine conflict, which makes no effort to tackle the huge power differential between the two parties.

Although it is now seen as a failure, the international community initially described the 2-year period following President Obama's declaration of a new negotiation process (which saw six rounds of proximity talks and official leaders' visits to Washington, DC) as a 'critical juncture' (Malley and Agha 2010) in ongoing efforts to resolve the Israeli–Palestinian conflict.[6] The talks, like all those before them, were never designed to be inclusive of all walks of Palestinian life. The unexpected Fatah–Hamas unity agreement of May 2011 was similarly elitist. In all aspects of this extraordinarily visible high-level discourse around ending one of the world's most intractable conflicts, gender issues and women themselves are nowhere to be seen.[7] The rest of this article will ask why this is so.

CONTEXT: POLITICAL ACTIVISM IN THE OPT

Before looking in depth at how three organizations have used UNSCR 1325 in their work, I shall offer a brief review of the history of Palestinian women's resistance to military occupation and disenfranchisement by the State of Israel. Generations of Palestinians, old, young, female and male, urban and rural, have struggled, both violently and non-violently, to achieve an independent state.[8] As in other protracted conflicts that have drawn in an entire population, leading and sustaining the movement for freedom has become a shared responsibility amongst Palestinians, although there have been a few particularly outspoken leaders who have made a strong mark on the public imagination (Johnson and Kuttab 2001). Because it is a popular resistance struggle, an understanding of contemporary activism should be grounded in an analysis of local gender issues as well as an understanding of how political and social differences have played out in the oppositional strategies of generations of Palestinians.[9] This is definitely not just the story of a few 'big men'.

A hard look at the history also shows that there is slim chance that a new 'peace' process with Israel will not be just another excuse for the subjugation of Palestinians. In the past, such processes have only ever resulted in more suffering on the ground. As a result, official leaders are often not the ones most trusted by Palestinians.

In addition to political pressure from the State of Israel and the international community, local leaders have also been vulnerable to internal party-political violence and repression, or to arrest or assassination by Israel, so they do not always conduct their work in the open or as part of an official political process.[10] The risk associated with political leadership is one among many reasons why few women have emerged as local leaders, but independent-minded men are also marginalized from public roles. Sadly, while the Palestinian–Israeli peace process is possibly the most visible one on earth, and while Palestinians everywhere have articulate and passionate political opinions, it is important not to overstate the level of political involvement of ordinary people. Because of the duration and complexity of the struggle for independence, and the overwhelming impact of the Israeli occupation on their daily lives, no Palestinian can remain politically unaware or, to some extent, politically uninvolved. Yet there is, today, a desperate paucity of independent-minded and outspoken leaders at both local and national levels and a sense of directionless in how people see and use political processes and structures. Their wariness of the international community also means that few Palestinians know and use international instruments such as Security Council Resolutions to help them articulate and organize their struggles against both occupation and violent internal fragmentation.[11]

Israeli-imposed movement restrictions in the West Bank and the military blockade of the Gaza Strip, the increasing impoverishment and isolation of Palestinians, restrictions on oppositional activism within Israel, the legacy of the Hamas–Fatah political split and a strongly patriarchal culture all mean that, as in many conflict zones, there are very few women who have either the courage or the economic, educational and social means to become and remain politically active. Hanan Ashrawi is a notable example of a woman leader, but it remains to be seen whether her long years of service to the Palestinian people will be recognized with a high-level official post in the government of national unity. Today, when asked their opinions on politics and resistance, the majority of Palestinian women respond that they have other, more pressing concerns to deal with.[12] They focus on daily survival and express a generalized mistrust of their leaders and the international community including the United Nations. Instruments such as UNSCR 1325 are not widely known or seen as relevant to their daily lives. That ordinary women have become very distant from the grassroots liberation struggle is obvious in an examination of the new non-violent resistance movements that are being used by communities near the Separation Wall. With a few exceptions, these are male-organized and run and have scarcely any female members and no women leaders.[13] At the same time, elite women are mistrusted and invisible at home and wield no local influence, although some have retained an international support base (UNDP 2010b).

Yet on the ground, UNSCR 1325 can and does help a small number of feminist analysts and activists think differently about their political engagement. A tiny percentage of Palestinian women use it in their work and have interesting things to say about what it helps them achieve, but there is scant evidence that their work is being usefully promulgated so that it can be taken seriously by activists, policy-makers and politicians. Gendered divisions of labour and different spheres of interest are obvious: what women do in their daily work (predominantly in private) to survive and resist this decades-old complex humanitarian and political crisis, is not reflected in what politicians (local and international) say in public they are doing to overcome the crisis.[14] To use Enloe's words, the Palestinian struggle is shrouded in 'militarized gendered silences' (Enloe 2010: 217). Palestinians are disempowered in the final status process; women doubly, or even triply so if they are also refugees. Yet little 'feminist sense' is being made of this multiply asymmetrical conflict (Enloe 2010: 221). Instead, women's analyses, concerns, calculations and voices are invisible and of little influence even as the occupation daily worsens their lives.

Women's Actions in the oPt

While they are nowhere to be seen in formal processes, women's actions in Palestine predate UNSCR 1325 by several decades (Torres 1989; Johnson and Kuttab 2001; Shalhoub-Kevorkian 2008). Throughout the decades of the occupation, Palestinian women have been important players in non-violent resistance, in state-building processes and in peace-making with their Israeli counterparts when this was considered strategic. Women's movements in Palestine, as elsewhere, have varied interests. Starting from a base that did not prioritize women's liberation, women found themselves increasingly involved in various forms of resistance and in service provision as political conditions worsened from the 1970s onwards, until, in December 1988, the impacts of the first intifada led to the establishment of a Higher Women's Committee which articulated, as an explicit goal, the need to address gender equality alongside national liberation (Torres 1989). Women were also instrumental in creating manifestos that captured their democratic ambitions; for example, the rights 'to freedom of movement and the right to full nationality' claimed in the Women's Charter of 1994 issued by the General Union of Palestinian

Women. These rights remain, until today, 'denied to all the population' (Johnson and Kuttab 2001: 23).

Palestinian women's movements face a central dilemma: the reality and necessity of their political engagement in resistance to the occupation contrasts strongly with the continued, and growing, impacts of conservative gender ideologies that aim to constrain their movements and choices (Kuttab 2008). So, even while the family is a source of strength in resisting the occupation, the emphasis placed on men's control over women (husbands over wives, fathers and sons over daughters and sisters) and its resultant attempts to confine women to the private sphere, remains powerful. It deprives women of full access to their rights, including their right to organize for an independent Palestine (Shalhoub-Kevorkian 2008; Jad 2010).

Palestinian women's organizing is also profoundly shaped by what Islah Jad describes as an 'NGOization' process, through which women's energy and attention is directed into 'dealing with aspects of women's lives such as health, education, legal literacy, income generation, advocacy of rights and research' that cannot be properly addressed in the absence of a state (Jad 2004: 43; see also Johnson and Kuttab 2001 and UNDP/PAPP 2010b). Trying to provide services that women need but do not get means that the most capable and dynamic women are fully occupied and have little time left for political work.

Yet, as in other countries engaged in complex processes of political and social change, there are still ways in which engagement in the struggle has increased women's participation in public life and, to some extent, challenged patriarchal control. Male and female Palestinians alike acknowledge that the depredations of the occupation have been in some measure kept in check by civil society, especially women's organizations, which have been directly involved in a spectrum of activities including the provision of basic services, humanitarian care and early childhood education. The women's movement has also played an important role in civic education, especially in such taboo issues as violence in the family, and it has become quite skilful at helping Palestinians understand the interconnections between public, militarized violence and violence in the home. Women were crucial to helping their families survive during the 2008–9 Israeli military incursion into the Gaza Strip, otherwise known as 'Operation Cast Lead'. They are challenging age-old gendered divisions of labour in the reconstruction of the Gaza Strip, even as they remain largely excluded from its political sphere (Al Saqqa 2009; Muhanna and Qleibo 2009).

Some Impacts of Women's Exclusion

At the time of writing, despite high-level rhetoric and the recent unity process, things are getting worse on the ground in both the blockaded Gaza Strip and a West Bank threatened by ongoing illegal settlement and severe movement restrictions. Talks between Israeli and Palestinian leaders, when they take place at all, are remote from people's lives and bring little in terms of tangible resolutions to the multiple crises Palestinians face. Today, Palestinians are more sceptical than ever about the efficacy of the United Nations or the international community, in particular the USA, as partners in solving the crisis, and they question why the administration of President Obama is increasing pressure on Israeli and Palestinian leaders to resume face-to-face talks when there are no efforts to stop Israeli territorial expansion.[15]

In such circumstances, women's ground-level activism and political organizing has proven all too easy to ignore. Both Palestinian and Israeli women activists are completely excluded from such formal processes as exist. Palestinian women have also been left out of the recent unity process. They are clear about the impacts of these exclusions, contending that it is because activist women have never been seriously consulted or played a central role in how peace and security is imagined, in either the oPt or Israel, that no progress is being made. They propose that the inclusion of women with a feminist and social equality mandate would fundamentally change how peace and state-building are envisaged, negotiated and implemented.[16] Most practically, they argue that the gap between where ordinary people find themselves and where politicians focus is so significant that nothing decided at the top will have meaning when attempts are made to apply it on the ground. Their arguments make sense because the Israel–Palestine peace process is, indeed, making no progress. Nor can it until a real commitment is made to address the fundamental inequalities in power between the State of Israel and the people it militarily occupies. I neither wish to oversimplify a terribly complicated issue, or to fall into the hoary old trap of equating women with peacefulness when I agree with what Palestinian women peace activists say. In my view, recognizing women not as 'peaceful', but as multiply subordinated rights claimants who have valid opinions on peace-making, would profoundly shift the nature of final status negotiations. It would, at the very least, force a proper engagement with the core problem: power difference and the violence and dispossession it inevitably causes.

If women are to be included, significant shifts are needed in local and international understanding of how they could and should contribute to a peaceful solution. Their question is exactly the one posed by UNSCR 1325: do women represent a constituency that could look at the multiple challenges of this crisis with a new mind, and if so, what would and could they do to make a difference? To address these questions, the next section of this article looks at three women's initiatives that use UNSCR 1325 in their work.

WOMEN'S GROUPS AND UNSCR 1325

The International Women's Commission

In 2005, tired of waiting for their activism to be noticed and recognized formally, a group of highly educated and well-connected Palestinian and

Israeli women, with the support of international women and UNIFEM, formed the *IWC for a just and lasting peace*.[17] Based on UNSCR 1325, it positioned itself as a women-focused policy-making entity with 'fresh, incisive analysis and innovative proposals from women leaders for actions and strategies that can serve to advance the peace process'.[18] One of the first initiatives by the IWC was to ensure the formal recognition of UNSCR 1325 by both parties; in Israel the resolution has been passed into law, if not acted on.[19] On the Palestinian side, a Presidential Decree (a *de facto* law) from 26 September 2005 endorses both UNSCR 1325 and Palestinian participation in the IWC.[20] This formal recognition has had no visible policy impacts in either location.

In 2011, having survived many challenges to its commitment to present a unified Palestinian and Israeli women's perspective on peace, the IWC disbanded. Some of its members argue that it had succeeded in opening windows in the European Union through which women's issues could be addressed. However, from an observers' perspective, while they were impressive to listen to and spoke with an authority borne of political experience, diplomatic skills and academic accuracy, the IWC's political analysis was not always timely, alternative or particularly visible.[21]

Palestinian members of the IWC always struggled with the forum because it was set up for both Palestinian and Israeli women. In a tussle that mirrors the one facing men in the official negotiations, it was difficult for them to find common ground in the face of Israeli military aggression, especially Operation Cast Lead. More than anything else, then, the IWC ended up challenging the liberal feminist assumption that their shared gender oppression is enough to effectively bring together women from bitterly opposing sides and significantly different power bases, as a unified influence on larger peace processes.

There were other problems too. The IWC remained an obscure and even mistrusted initiative at home. Three reasons I can discern for this are: (1) while its members were, by necessity, from the elite (and thus had the support base to enable them to join this initiative) they were unsuccessful in communicating their work to ordinary Palestinians and Israelis; (2) while it failed to learn from or sharpen grassroots activism, there is a perception that it diverted scarce financial resources from more effective, inclusive and challenging work[22]; and (3) it became increasingly difficult for Palestinian women to work with Israelis in the face of Palestinian calls to end joint projects, a matter that became gravely more problematic after the last Israeli incursion into Gaza. When this was not condemned by all Israeli IWC members, it led to considerable internal challenges from which the local members of the Commission never fully recovered, despite ongoing international efforts to keep going.[23]

Most cruel, however, is the fact that the regard with which the IWC was seen in some quarters of the international community did not translate into substantial changes in peace-making practice at home. Its members still could not make effective public contributions to the high-level political processes it was designed to influence – either the intra-Palestinian dialogue or efforts to end the military occupation and build a viable Palestinian state.

The IWC, with its outward-looking focus, operated very differently from two other women's networks that also make use of UNSCR 1325 in their peace activism. These organizations approach their peace work very much as Palestinians, with little or no profile abroad and no interest in working with Israelis. They represent and reach very different constituencies from those for whom and to whom the IWC spoke.

The West Bank: MIFTAH

MIFTAH, founded in 2003 to focus on politics in the oPt, is not exclusively a women's initiative but, not surprisingly as it was founded by Hanan Ashrawi, it has a programme for the Empowerment of Palestinian Women's Leadership in which women's role in negotiations and elections has been a primary focus, along with advocacy and capacity-building endeavours for women, especially youth (MIFTAH 2007). As part of its efforts, MIFTAH has produced a booklet entitled *Palestinian Women and UNSCR 1325* and it is working on a training manual to give women practical ideas about how to utilize the Resolution in their work.

The primary obstacles faced by MIFTAH in using UNSCR 1325 are that it is little known and used among donors and international observers and participants in the peace process, and that its credibility among Palestinian women is tarnished by their mistrust of the United Nations. MIFTAH has also found that its partners' lack of technical capacity in navigating UN documentation, reporting and hearing structures means that they are not always able to collect the right information, analyse it in ways that can contribute to broader advocacy efforts, or use it effectively in lobbying. They are working to develop training materials to help address these problems.

MIFTAH is also concerned that dealing with increasing gender-based violence (GBV) within the oPt itself is distracting women's attention from more strategic concerns: because there is no state to serve the people, women do significant amounts of service delivery work and have fewer resources, including time, to focus on their rights, their political participation, and their contributions to resisting the violence of the occupation (Sanders 2010). This is a problem throughout the oPt, given the scarce resources available for women to work on violence prevention and the cultural taboos surrounding discussions of this problem. While sexual violence is not, thankfully, used in a widespread or systematic manner in the Israeli–Palestinian conflict, sexual harassment and sexual humiliation at checkpoints and in prisons by Israeli Security Forces (against Palestinian women and men) is common. However, it is extremely difficult to react to it in effective ways given the power asymmetries between Palestinians and the Israeli Security Forces.[24]

At the same time, domestic violence is a severe and under-reported problem that is being fuelled by the constant, low-level aggression experienced daily as a result of the occupation and the lack of an effective Palestinian national response. MIFTAH argues that dealing with domestic problems of violence against women drains a lot of activist and advocacy energy, and financial resources, from women's groups. Palestinian women also face a great deal of difficulty in addressing this 'private' problem in such a way that their assessment of levels of domestic GBV and their suggestions for appropriate responses do not become part of the propaganda wars being waged by men in the political sphere, either internally in Palestine or in the Israeli–Palestinian conflict.

MIFTAH reports that the different intensities of conflict in the different parts of the territory challenge women's ability to use UNSCR 1325 coherently: while the Gaza Strip, Area C of the West Bank and East Jerusalem are clearly facing an escalating humanitarian crisis, the rest of the West Bank is comparatively stable and may even be thought of as a 'post-conflict' zone. This reality, in combination with the difficulties of moving around within and across the territory, suggests that strategies such as the development of a National Action Plan that have been successfully employed in other parts of the world are not a straightforward answer for the oPt.

Nonetheless, MIFTAH's future plans include scaling up their work with UNSCRs 1325, 1820, 1888 and 1889. They see these Resolutions as a way to continue to keep a focus on the oPt as an ongoing conflict zone and one means to unite liberation efforts within historic Palestine, in the refugee camps and in the wider Diaspora. It also helps them reach out to a global audience working on women, peace and security.[25]

Gaza Strip: The Wisal Coalition

Perhaps the greatest among the many challenges to achieving a functioning unity between Palestinians is the fact that the Gaza Strip and the West Bank are so decisively cut off from each other, both by the geographical fragmentation of the territory and by the occupation with its draconian movement and access regime, including the full military blockade of the Strip. It is not surprising, then, that the Gaza Strip has its own UNSCR 1325-focused network, known as the Wisal Coalition, which does not, at present, work with any other oPt women's groups on UNSCR 1325.

Founded with support from UNFPA, this network of about twenty women's organizations across the Gaza Strip has been using UNSCR 1325 to advance its work since 2008, in concert with the Convention on the Elimination of All Forms of Discrimination against Women (CEDAW) and other conventions on human rights and equality. With a significant focus on women's health, Wisal considers the prevention of GBV to be a cornerstone of its work. In discussions with its members, it was clear that the same difficulties facing MIFTAH in its work on GBV are a concern in Gaza, possibly even more so since Hamas is imposing an increasingly restrictive gender regime in the Strip and making it ever more difficult for women to speak out, conduct research or maintain contact with outside organizations which share their political and advocacy goals.[26]

The Wisal Coalition does, however, report some successes in its advocacy work which it attributes to UNSCR 1325. In 2009, Wisal members led a demonstration to the Office of the United Nations Special Coordinator for the Middle East Peace Process (UNSCO) building in Gaza City demanding that the Secretary General's Special Envoy to the Middle East, Robert Serry, state his position on UNSCR 1325 and its applicability to the oPt. In discussions, the leader of the Coalition, Mariam Zaqout, described how 'a most powerful moment was meeting Kofi Annan and being able to argue with him on women and security based on my 1325 experience'. The Coalition reports that it has been successful in discussing human rights from a UNSCR 1325 perspective and thinks its inputs, including the annual Secretary-General's report on women in Palestine, have become weightier because they are grounded in references to the Resolution.

The Coalition has focused on its networking within the Gaza Strip and is trying to find ways to get moderate Hamas and Fatah women members to work together to sustain national unity. It is building women's capacity for political participation and offering training on UNSCR 1325 and CEDAW. These efforts are not, however, either easy to maintain or presently bearing any fruit. Wisal members consider the current situation to be a 'depressing one, in which we see no real avenues for women's participation and limited space for us to work'.[27]

CONCLUSION

Palestinian women have the capacity and the will to organize themselves, using international instruments such as UNSCR 1325 to magnify their efforts on the ground and to reach out to others who understand the complexities of organized resistance in a long-drawn-out conflict. Yet their efforts do not yield tangible results. Their struggles to be heard are one more reason to view the strident rhetoric around the Palestine–Israel peace process sceptically and, despite the hope that regional events may open up more spaces for critical thinking on political evolution, none of the feminists I talk to in my daily work, and whose opinions I have drawn from in preparing this article, feel positive about the outcome of contemporary efforts to negotiate for peace.

Indeed, the degree of asymmetry between what Palestinians can negotiate for and how Israelis can choose to react is so severe that a meaningful and durable solution does not seem imaginable. Within this imbalanced arena, the powerlessness and marginality of women are extreme. Put starkly, no matter what instruments they use to help them position their peace-building arguments, Palestinian women are trying to organize a response to a process that clearly does not prioritize or value women's voices for peace.

They are also hampered by acute forms of separation that are even bleaker, I would suggest, than what Enloe describes as a general condition of 'women in warring states *not* discovering their connections with each other' (Enloe 2010: 3). While they are inside the oPt, women are not able to do much as political activists because of deep political, geographical and social divisions; they lack a platform or any sense of a national strategy around which to organize; and they have no effective counterparts. Their marginal position does not always seem to result from women's lack of capacity to debate important peace and security issues. As this paper has shown, women are quite well organized within the extremely limited space granted them by the occupation and Palestinian political patriarchy. Their capacity is also very obvious once they are able to present themselves outside the oPt, when they speak strongly and courageously, receiving recognition as 'women peace activists' with interesting political insights and vision.

The significant discrepancy between how they are perceived outside and what they can actually do at home means that women who could be serious counterparts in the peace process remain invisible and ineffectual where they are needed most. Like women in so many conflict zones, they cannot break through the patriarchal attitudes of either international or local leaders and political parties (Castillejo 2010) to forge a new space in which women's diverse and non-mainstream opinions are taken seriously. Yet they continue to express creativity, fortitude, pragmatism and sheer hopefulness when they discuss their work. Their courage attests to the importance of continuing to support their diverse efforts to influence political processes.

Women activists and academics in the Gaza Strip and the West Bank still seem to see better organization as one means to move forward. They always articulate a strong desire to find more effective common platforms and strat-egies for action to advance both their understanding of peace and security from a gendered perspective, and their participation in formal and informal processes towards a solution for Palestinians. In reality, however, more efforts to create networks would be futile because of the endless constraints on the ground that overwhelm activism. The only way to do this networking at present is by the cumbersome and not very effective means of video-conferencing or expensive, difficult and unsustainable attempts to help women meet each other outside historic Palestine – an approach which is par-ticularly challenging for Gazan women, given how hard it is to get exit permits. Nothing but the full removal of the blockade on the Gaza Strip and the lifting of movement restrictions in the West Bank is going to solve this problem.

At the time of writing, a shrill rhetorical battle dominated by Israeli and US voices is once more raging about the question of Palestinian statehood. Palestinians, yet again, have few possible responses. Yet regional changes suggest that something new can – and urgently must – be done. If a new approach were possible, my strongest recommendation would be that women leaders globally agree (with like-minded men) to bring a halt to the current, futile attempts to 'make peace' without addressing the asymmetry between the parties. No more costly efforts should be made by male politicians in closed rooms. What is needed is a radical departure from the well-worn paths that are currently being trod. There should be no further actions, proximal or face-to-face, until well-prepared women – Palestinians, Israelis, global leaders and experts on women, peace and security – are invited to share their insights, to discuss possible solutions to the conflict and offer alternative views on building a sovereign Palestinian state. If such women came into a process that has exhausted and baffled generations of male leaders, the results might surprise us all.

Notes

1   The literature on the Israel–Palestine conflict is legion. For some of the earliest reflections, see Edward Said's groundbreaking *Orientalism* (Said 2003 [1978]). A feminist analysis of women's peace activism in Israel and oPt is found in Cynthia Cockburn's *From Where We Stand: War, Women's Activism and Feminist Analysis* (Cockburn 2007). The best contemporary academic resource on Palestinian women's organizing is the annual *Review of Women's Studies*, published by the Institute of Women's Studies at Birzeit University.

2   See http://www.miftah.org/ and http://www.iwc-peace.org/ (accessed 2 June 2011). The Wisal Coalition is a very humble, grassroots-based network that does not run an English-language website.

3   Entitled 'Homestretch to Freedom', the plan calls for the recognition of an independent Palestinian State by 2011 (Palestinian National Authority 2010). At the time of writing, the PNA intends to call for this state at the United Nations General Assembly in September 2011, even if a final status agreement with the State of Israel has not been reached.

4   See West 1997; Cockburn 2007; Castillejo 2010; Enloe 2010.

5   For an excellent account of this problem, see Enloe's 'Conclusion: the Long War' for a detailed analysis of how Nawal al-Samaraie, Iraq's minister for women's affairs, fared trying to run a poorly resourced, isolated Ministry, from which she resigned in protest in 2009 (Enloe 2010: 211–25).

6   President Obama appointed Senator George Mitchell as his Middle East Peace Envoy as he entered his Presidency in 2009. Mitchell's role was to facilitate 'proximity talks' between Prime Minister Netanyahu and President Abbas. Indirect negotiations were intended to be launched in March 2010, but were derailed by the announcement of increased illegal settlement activity, including building 1,600 new housing units, in East Jerusalem. By 14 December 2010, Robert Malley and Hussein Agha, in an article published in the *International Herald Tribune*,

acknowledged that there was 'nothing left to talk about' between Israel and Palestine, and declared the last two years' efforts 'for all practical purposes and for the foreseeable future, over' (Clemons 2011). Mitchell himself resigned as Envoy on the 13 May 2011. Obama has, since then, made renewed attempts to revitalize the talks: the impacts of this effort remain to be seen.

7   No women representatives have taken part in the six rounds of proximity talks. One woman delegate from the Palestinian Legislative Council did participate in the 2009 Egyptian-led process to reconcile Fatah and Hamas, but she was not characterized by women peace activists as representing their aims. There were two women at the unity talks in Cairo in May 2011 but not in leadership roles. It is important to note that the rights of Bedouins as an occupied minority people, of youth, of the disabled and other marginalized individuals, also do not receive attention.

8   For a highly detailed account of Palestinian history, see Farsoun and Aruri (2006). While they offer a fairly detailed discussion of women as victims of violence and as workers, no mention is made in their study of how women have organized politically over the years.

9   For an in-depth discussion of Palestinian human security, see UNDP 2010a.

10   See Johnson and Kuttab 2001; Jad 2004, 2010; Farsoun and Aruri 2006; Johnson 2010.

11   See Johnson and Kuttab (2001) for an excellent account of the marginalization of Palestinian civil society from the political process from the Oslo period (1993 to present), especially as it manifested in the Second Intifada (2000). See also UNDP (2010b).

12   Despite public rhetoric about the improving economy of the West Bank, recent research shows that those living in Area C, the Seam Zone (areas between the 1949 Armistice Line and the Separation Wall) and East Jerusalem are experiencing growing poverty (see Save the Children 2009).

13   The documentary film *Budrus* records a popular struggle in which women were centrally engaged, but this example remains an exception (see http://www.justvision.org/budrus).

14   The Special Coordinator for the Middle East Peace Process, Robert Serry, as part of the UN-organised Global Open Days on Women and Peace, has recently held a series of meetings with women representatives and has given his assurances that UNSCR 1325 will be reflected on in his reports to the Security Council, but this process is in its infancy and no impacts can be reported yet.

15   For some of the many accounts following Benjamin Netanyahu's May 2011 speech in the US Congress, see Richard Falk (2011a, 2011b).

16   The goal of the IWC was to change this, so that women who represent women's interests would be included in every aspect of the peace process. The example of successful popular organizing including women, in Budrus for one, shows that the inclusion of women really does make a substantial difference on the ground – including in changing how young male activists behave.

17   See http://www.iwc-peace.org

18   Statement 15 September 2006 (http://www.iwc-peace.org); see also the more recent statements issued in 2010 (http://unispal.un.org/UNISPAL.NSF/0/BDB7

6830578DFB0C8525773700685943, accessed 30 May 2011). I am also grateful to Amal Khreishe, General Director of Palestine Working Women Society for Development and a member of the IWC, for her analysis of the IWC's work and impacts in informal discussions in Ramallah throughout 2010.

19 In July 2005, the Israeli 'Equal Representation of Women Act' was updated by the Knesset, demanding the inclusion of women in teams appointed for peace negotiations as well as in committees setting guidelines for domestic and foreign security policy.

20 See http://www.wilpfinternational.org/middleeast/palestine1325.html (accessed 15 December 2010).

21 Their website, for example, was rarely updated. I have been unable to find an official statement announcing the disbanding of the IWC in any online source.

22 Arguments over resource allocation are difficult to assess, but it is certainly true that organisations older than the IWC struggle to find funding, for reasons I do not have space to discuss here. One grouping that has been severely marginalised is the Israeli Coalition of Women for Peace, founded in November 2000 after the Second Intifada broke out. It brings together ten feminist organizations as well as independent activists and conducts a variety of activities inside Israel and in solidarity with Palestinian women in the oPt. See http://www.coalitionofwomen. org/?lang=en (accessed 2 June 2011).

23 Supported by UNIFEM, the IWC held what turned out to be their last large international meeting, a colloquium on *Advancing Women's Leadership for Sustainable Peace in the Palestinian-Israeli Conflict and Worldwide*, as late as 1–2 June 2010 in Madrid.

24 The Israeli Security Forces comprise several inter-related organizations (government, military and civilian) that focus on Israel's security.

25 Interview with Bisan Mousa, Gender Desk Coordinator, MIFTAH, 10 June 2010. The MIFTAH website is also very informative.

26 Hamas has been intent on defining itself as a movement which imposes a strict gender regime based on its interpretation of Islamic religious codes. Recent evidence of this was a ban on women smoking *argila* (water pipes) in public. See Palestine News Network 2010 and Guardian Newspaper Online 2010.

27 The account of the Wisal Coalition is based on discussions with Mariam Zaquot and Maha Aria of the Wisal Coalition held in Gaza City throughout 2010, including at a public discussion on the occasion of UNSCR 1325's tenth anniversary which was hosted by Mary Robinson, Ela Bhatt and Lakhdar Brahimi of the Elders on 17 October 2010. Quotes are from these discussions.

Acknowledgements

I would like to thank Maha Aria of the Wisal Coalition, Bisan Mousa of MIFTAH, Rela Mazali of New Profile, Dr Islah Jad of Birzeit University and women who worked with the IWC, especially Amal Khreishe of the Palestinian Working Women Society for Development and Dareen Khattab, for their generosity in discussing their organizations and their opinions on UNSCR 1325 in oPt. The interpretation of the data as presented in this paper is my own and is not to be ascribed to any other organization or individual.

References

Al Saqqa, M. 2009. 'War Diary from Khan Younis: "My Life Is Not my Life"', *Review of Women's Studies* 5: 8–22.

Castillejo, C. 2010. *Building a State that Works for Women: Integrating Gender into Post-conflict State Building*. Madrid, Spain: FRIDE.

Clemons, S. 2011. 'Thoughts on George Mitchell Resignation'. Available at http://www.huffingtonpost.com/steve-clemons/thoughts-on-george-mitche_b_861953.html (accessed 15 May 2011).

Cockburn, C. 2007. *From Where We Stand: War, Women's Activism and Feminist Analysis*. London, New York: Zed Books.

Enloe, C. 2004. *The Curious Feminist: Searching for Women in the New Age of Empire*. Berkeley, Los Angeles, London: University of California Press.

Enloe, C. 2010. *Nimo's War, Emma's War: Making Feminist Sense of the Iraq War*. Berkeley, Los Angeles, London: University of California Press.

Falk, R. 2011a. 'Who Cares in the Middle East What Obama says?' *The Independent* Online, 30 May. Available at http://www.independent.co.uk/opinion/commentators/fisk/who-cares-in-the-middle-east-what-obama-says-2290761.html (accessed 30 May 2011).

Falk, R. 2011b. 'A UN Secretary General vs Freedom Flotilla 2', *Al-Jazeera*, 2 June. Available at http://english.aljazeera.net/indepth/opinion/2011/06/201161820392 43894.html (accessed 2 June 2011).

Farr, V. 2004. 'Voices from the Margins: A Response to "Security Sector Reform in Developing and Transitional Countries"', Berghof Research Centre for Constructive Conflict Management. Available at http://www.berghof-handbook.net/documents/publications/dialogue2_farr.pdf (accessed 2 June 2011)

Farsoun, S. K. and Aruri, N. H. 2006. *Palestine and the Palestinians: A Social and Political History* (2nd ed.). Boulder, CO: Westview Press.

Guardian Newspaper Online. 2010. 'Hamas Bans Women from Smoking Water Pipes'. Available at http://www.guardian.co.uk/world/2010/jul/18/hamas-women-smo king-pipes (accessed 30 May 2011).

Jad, I. 2004. 'The NGOization of the Arab Women's Movements', *Review of Women's Studies* 2: 42–56.

Jad, I. 2010. 'Feminism Between Secularism and Islamism: The Case of Palestine (West Bank and Gaza)', Beirut and London: Conflicts Forum. Available at http://conflictsforum.org/briefings/CaseOfPalestine.pdf (accessed 2 June 2011).

Johnson, P. 2010. 'Displacing Palestine: Palestinian Householding in an Era of Asymmetrical War', *Politics and Gender* 6 (2): 295–304.

Johnson, P. and Kuttab, E. 2001. 'Where Have All the Women (and Men) Gone? Reflections on Gender and the Second Palestinian Intifada', *Feminist Review* 69: 21–43.

Kuttab, E. 2008. 'Palestinian Women's Organisations', *Cultural Dynamics* 20 (2): 99–117.

Malley, R. and Agha, H. 2010. 'Israel/Palestine: Nothing Left to Talk About', *International Herald Tribune*, 14 December. Available at http://www.crisisgroup.org/en/regions/middle-east-north-africa/israel-palestine/malley-israel-nothing-left-to-talk-about.aspx (accessed 19 December 2010).

MIFTAH. 2007. '9th Annual Report', Jerusalem: MIFTAH. Available at http://www.miftah.org/Mact/MiftahActivityReport2007.pdf#page=17 (accessed 20 July 2010).

Muhanna, A. and Qleibo, E. 2009. 'Negotiating Survival: The Impact of Israeli Mobility Restrictions on Women in Gaza', *Review of Women's Studies* 5: 23–40.

Palestine News Network. 2010. 'Hamas Bans Water Pipes For Women'. Available at http://middleeastconflict.org/palestine-news-network/hamas-bans-water-pipes-for-women.php (accessed 2 June 2011).

Palestinian National Authority. 2010. 'Homestretch to Freedom: The Second Year of the 13th Government Program. Palestine: Ending the Occupation, Establishing the State'. Available at http://www.miftah.org/Doc/Reports/2010/Second_year_of_the_government_program_English.pdf (accessed 2 June 2011).

Said, Edward 2003 1978. *Orientalism*. London: Penguin Books.

Sanders, E. 2010. 'Palestinian Says Women's Rights Forgotten in Gaza', *The Los Angeles Times*, 27 June. Available at http://www.latimes.com/news/nationworld/world/la-fg-gaza-feminist-qa-20100627,0,6959559.story?page=1 (accessed 26 July 2010).

Save the Children. 2009. *Life on the Edge: The Struggle to Survive and the Impact of Forced Displacement in High Risk Areas of the occupied Palestinian territory*. Available at http://www.crin.org/docs/Save_Research_Report_with_Cover_low_res.pdf (accessed 20 July 2010).

Schoofs, S. and Smits, R. 2010. *Aiming High, Reaching Low: Four Fundamentals for Gender-Responsive State-building*. Clingendael Conflict Research Unit, 13 March. Available at http://www.clingendael.nl/publications/2010/20100300_cru_policy_brief_13_rosan_smits.pdf (accessed 2 June 2011).

Shalhoub-Kevorkian, N. 2008. *Militarization and Violence Against Women in Conflict Zones in the Middle East: A Palestinian Case-Study*. Cambridge: Cambridge University Press.

Torres, M. 1989. *Women in the Intifada*. Published online as part of the Palestine Papers. Available at http://www.sonomacountyfreepress.com/palestine/women2.html (accessed 8 October 2009).

UNDP/PAPP. 2010a. *Palestinian Human Development Report 2009/10, Investing in Human Security for a Future State*. Jerusalem: UNDP/PAPP. Available at http://204.200.211.31/contents/file/PHDR2010/PHDR_Book_Eng.pdf (accessed 30 October 2010).

UNDP/PAPP. 2010b. *Palestinian Women Organizing in Jerusalem*. Jerusalem: UNDP/PAPP. Available at http://www.undp.ps/en/newsroom/publications/pdf/other/womenorg.pdf (accessed 27 November 2010).

West, L. (ed.). 1997. *Feminist Nationalism*. New York and London: Routledge.

Resolution 1325 and Post-Cold War Feminist Politics

CAROL HARRINGTON
Victoria University of Wellington, New Zealand

Abstract

Social movement scholars credit feminist transnational advocacy networks with putting violence against women on the United Nations (UN) security agenda, as evidenced by Resolution 1325 and numerous other UN Security Council statements on gender, peace and security. Such accounts neglect the significance of superpower politics for shaping the aims of women's bureaucracies and non-governmental organizations in the UN system. This article highlights how the fall of the Soviet Union transformed the delineation of 'women's issues' at the UN and calls attention to the extent that the new focus upon 'violence against women' has been shaped by post-Cold War US global policing practices. Resolution 1325's call for gender mainstreaming of peacekeeping operations reflects the tension between feminist advocates' increased influence in security discourse and continuing reports of peacekeeper perpetrated sexual violence, abuse and exploitation.

INTRODUCTION

In October 2000, the unanimous passage of United Nations Security Council Resolution 1325 linked gender, peace and security and recognized the need to 'mainstream a gender perspective in peacekeeping operations' (UNSC 2000). The Resolution authorizes monitoring of peacekeeping operations by gender experts and condemns military sexual violence. As a policy artifact this Resolution gives evidence of startling tensions in the gender politics of mainstream international security discourse in the final years of the twentieth century. How did 'gender' and 'violence against women' become mainstream security issues at this particular point in history? What does Resolution 1325 signify about feminist capacity to intervene in questions of international security?

Social movement theorists have answered such questions with celebratory accounts of how feminist activists inside and outside United Nations (UN) institutions managed to get the problem of violence against women onto the international security agenda. They argue that activists' success in influencing international security discourse depended upon the leadership of 'moral entrepreneurs' and their formation of a 'transnational advocacy network' of insiders and outsiders that framed violence against women as a human rights issue. Moreover, a number of feminist scholars have argued that the intrinsic nature of the problem of violence against women as a violation of female bodily integrity forged unity in the previously divided field of women's organizations active around the UN.

This article argues that such accounts fail to analyze how the collapse of the Soviet Union transformed discourse on both 'women' and 'human rights' as problems for international government. In the post-Cold War order the USA poses as leader of the democratic world and defender of women and children against brutal men who instigate 'new wars' characterized by mass rape. Since its foundation, women's politics in the UN system formed a terrain of superpower struggle: the Soviet argument that the problem of 'women's oppression' should be located within a broader analysis of international political economy attracted many women's organizations active in the UN. Consequently, representatives from mainstream US women's organizations often felt isolated from other women's groups while US officials tended to view women's politics with suspicion. Thus, the sudden unity forged in the post-Cold War UN field of women's politics owes less to the intrinsic properties of the violence against women issue than to a sudden absence of superpower conflict. Furthermore, the significance of the human rights frame for the success of the international feminist campaign on violence against women only makes sense when considered in the context of broader transformations in security discourse which followed the collapse of the Soviet Union. According to security experts, the 'new wars' of the post-Cold War era require new forms of peacekeeping that include attention to women's rights, particularly violence against women. Ironically, these new forms of peacekeeping create environments in which sexual violence, abuse and exploitation flourish. Resolution 1325 speaks to these tensions within contemporary peacekeeping operations, proposing the technical solution of gender mainstreaming.

TRANSNATIONAL FEMINIST NETWORKS

Scholarly accounts of how and why violence against women made it onto the mainstream security agenda build upon social movement theory to highlight transnational activists' agency in bringing about change globally and locally. Social movement analysts use the concepts of 'political opportunities', 'mobilizing structures' and 'framing' to explain both the achievements and failures of social reform efforts (Joachim 2003: 247). Keck and Sikkink combine social network analysis with the social movement approach to show how 'transnational advocacy networks' have achieved reform by working simultaneously at the international, national and local levels. They define 'transnational advocacy networks' as 'those relevant actors working internationally on an issue, who are bound together by shared values, a common discourse and dense exchanges of information and services' (Keck and Sikkink 1998: 2).

One of Keck and Sikkink's case studies analyzes how 'violence against women' came onto the international security agenda through the efforts of women active in the UN and women's NGOs who held organizing meetings and events at the Center for Women's Global Leadership at Rutgers University. In 1989, when she became founding director of the Center, Charlotte Bunch decided that, given the increasing importance of 'the human rights concept' to international politics, women needed to 'claim it and be in on it' (Bunch quoted in Friedman 1995: 25). She held a meeting of activists who agreed that violence against women would be the best point of intersection between feminism and human rights discourse as it was:

> [t]he issue which most parallels a human rights paradigm and yet is excluded. You can see in violence all the things the human rights community already says it's against: it involves slavery, it involves situations of torture, it involves terrorism, it involves a whole series of things that the human rights community is already committed to [fighting, but which] have never been defined in terms of women's lives. (Bunch quoted in Friedman 1995: 20)

The Center for Women's Global Leadership's location at Rutgers made it possible to gather women from all over the world located in the New York area and active in the UN or in non-governmental organizations (NGOs) that worked with the UN. As Jacqui True emphasizes, transnational advocacy networks' capacity to achieve change within major global governing institutions depends upon their fostering of 'alliances of [institutional] insiders and outsiders', such alliances 'work within the system with institutional actors and as a part of larger policy communities to bring about incremental change' (True 2008: 7). Thus, transnational advocacy networks constitute a form of elite women's politics closely integrated into the UN system.

Valentine Moghadam argues that changes in the global economy since the 1980s favored the formation of transnational *feminist* networks in particular, which she calls 'structures organized above the national level that unite women from three or more countries around a common agenda, such as women's human rights, reproductive health and rights, violence against women, peace and antimilitarism, or feminist economics' (Moghadam 2005: 4). Moghadam's concept of transnational feminist network covers a wider range of political actors than Keck and Sikkink's concept of transnational advocacy networks, which work for change in the mainstream institutions of international government. However, like Keck and Sikkink, she argues that the increased salience of gender in international politics reflects increased global unity among women activists. In her account, the impetus for women's global unity increased from the mid-1980s because of three related factors: the decline of the welfare state in rich countries, a new international division of labor that relied on cheap female workers and the emergence of patriarchal fundamentalist movements (Moghadam 2005: 19). She also points to new information technologies that allow transnational networks to 'retain flexibility, adaptability and nonhierarchical features' (Moghadam 2005: 17). Although Moghadam pays attention to global structural changes and their significance for driving international unity among women's organizations, she does not mention the collapse of the Soviet Union.

Women active on 'women's issues' in UN conferences, organizations and debates had typically divided over the political questions of the day along North/South or along Cold War lines, over nationalist questions and over the question of Israel/Palestine. At the UN women's conferences in Mexico (1975) and Copenhagen (1980) women delegates from poor countries accused those from wealthy countries of focusing too much on sexuality and legal equality rather than economic and political questions (Keck and Sikkink 1998: 170; Moghadam 2005: 5). Keck and Sikkink emphasize the role of political leadership in forging unity in a divided movement (Keck and Sikkink 1998: 184–8; also, Joachim 2003; Carpenter 2007). They discuss feminist leader Charlotte Bunch as an example of a 'global moral entrepreneur', who cleverly framed various grievances women had about bodily violation as 'violence against women' and a human rights problem (Keck and Sikkink 1998: 184–5). They contend that Bunch's astute linkage of human rights with violence against women highlighted common experiences and interests of women from rich and poor countries and bridged the North–South divide (Keck and Sikkink 1998: 195–8). They also argue that the reason women in the UN more readily united on violence, rather than other issues 'is intrinsic to the issue itself' since it concerns 'the preservation of human dignity' and 'bodily integrity' (Keck and Sikkink 1998: 195).

The activities of the Global Center for Women's Leadership certainly made a difference to production of information on violence against women. In 1989, Bunch gave a speech to Amnesty International about gender and human rights which provided a catalyst for Amnesty to begin investigating women's rights and sexual violence as specific human rights concerns. Similarly, the Center worked with Human Rights Watch on a women's rights project which began documenting sexual violence in the sex industry, against refugees and during conflict (Harrington 2010: 122–3). The feminist entry into mainstream human rights organizations transformed the discourse and activities of those organizations, turning their machineries to documenting women's experience of violence.[1] Interventions planned by the Center for Women's Global

Leadership at the UN Human Rights conference in Vienna in 1993 and the Women's Conference in Beijing in 1995 helped consolidate the slogan 'women's rights are human rights', echoed in the name of an Amnesty International publication which came out that same year (Amnesty International 1995b).

Keck and Sikkink's (1998) account assumes a UN context in which human rights discourse provides a master frame which feminists could appropriate (see also Joachim 2003: 259; Carpenter 2007: 101). Yet violence against women became a mainstream international issue at the very same time as human rights increased in salience at the UN. Joachim (2003) argued that the fall of the Soviet Union allowed the USA to assume global leadership in the cause of violence against women, but fails to address why the USA had never championed this issue in the international arena before. Nor does she question why the Soviets, who had previously advocated gender equality and opposed sexual violence and harassment, had not brought this issue to the international table. The following section considers how bipolar Cold War politics shaped feminist discourse at the UN and kept the problem of violence against women off the international agenda.

WOMEN'S POLITICS AT THE UN DURING THE COLD WAR

I argue that Cold War politics and the end of the Cold War profoundly affected which issues women could speak with authority on *as* women at the UN. Cold War politics exacerbated the North/South divisions that other authors have considered a barrier to unified action among women's organizations active in the UN. These divisions isolated mainstream US women's organizations and government officials from more radical and socialist feminist groups internationally and in their own country. While vibrant feminist anti-sexual violence politics developed outside the Soviet sphere during the 1970s, Cold War politics kept such questions off the international women's agenda at the UN.

The UN incorporated a separate women's bureaucracy providing official sanction of the notion that some international issues counted as 'women's issues' and fuelling superpower intervention in international women's politics. As the Cold War intensified following the founding of the UN, the UN Status of Women Commission provided 'a testing group of the respective programs and achievements of eastern and western attitudes', according to one US observer (Frieda Miller to the US Office of International Labor Affairs quoted in Laville 2002: 114). The UN made provision for NGOs to seek 'consultative status', which gave them access to UN debates and resources. Thus women's NGOs emerged with the specific goal of intervening at the UN. Such NGOs became sites of active intervention by agents of the USA and the Soviets. After the Second World War, communist women of the French Resistance had called a women's conference which founded the Women's International Democratic

Federation (WIDF). The Soviet Union supported this new international women's organization, supporting its access to UN consultative status and using it as an opportunity to propagate the socialist program for women's liberation (Weigand 2001: 46–64).

Socialist commitment to gender equality and analysis of the connections between sexism and capitalism intrigued many feminists, although few outside the socialist bloc accepted the Soviet Union's claim to have ended women's oppression. Nevertheless, such intellectual interest in communism meant that even anti-communist feminists in the USA came under investigation and suspicion during the McCarthy era (Weigand 2001; Laville 2002: 102–11). Walt Disney testified to the House Committee on UN-American Activities that the League of Women Voters was a communist front, although a few days later when he checked his documents he apologized and said he actually meant the League of Women Shoppers. In similar confusion, League of Women Voters activist Anna Lord Strauss often found herself confused with communist activist Anna Louise Strong. The American WIDF affiliate, which included leading international activists such as Susan B. Anthony (Jr), had to close in 1950 after being forced to register as 'subversive' (Laville 2002: 105). Meanwhile, the US branch of the International Alliance of Women disassociated from the international organization in 1950, having expressed dissatisfaction with its 'feminist angle' since the end of the war: in the US 'feminism' was too akin to socialism (Laville 2002: 56–9, 200).

Both the State Department and Central Intelligence Agency (CIA) found allies in American women's organizations, anti-communist leaders of which eagerly impressed upon US officials the dangers of Soviet influence in the international women's organizations (Laville 2002: 114). In the early 1950s, concerned about Soviet hegemony over 'the women question', the CIA secretly sponsored the 'Committee of Correspondence', an organization of patriotic American women which held international conferences to 'emphasize the favorable position of women in the free world' as compared to that under communism (Committee memorandum quoted in Laville 2002: 175). However, the Committee's efforts did not meet with much success. A member admitted that on a trip to Europe she 'felt at once a certain distrust and resentment of our communications. The criticisms were too much US propaganda, too obvious a campaign against the USSR' while on a trip to Japan she found women there 'agreed with our European friends that US propaganda was just as abhorrent to them as Communist propaganda' (quoted in Laville 2002: 178, 188). In 1967, media revelations broke about covert CIA activity in NGOs including women's NGOs, discrediting American women's organizations (Agee 1975; Willetts 1996: 33–43, 41–2; Laville 2002: 171–92).

Championing women's rights was one of the ways the Soviets intervened in developing countries. Their linkage of 'the woman question' with problems of capitalism, imperialism and racism attracted large national women's organizations in poor countries (Ghodsee 2010: 5–6). In the early 1960s, the Soviets successfully argued at the Status of Women's Commission that women's full integration into economic development would eliminate discrimination and inequality. In 1970, the Assistant Director responsible for the Commission on the Status of Women noted it had 'recast its programme of work giving less emphasis to "rights" and more to the "roles" of women' (Margaret Bruce in Connors 1996: 158). This approach embedded questions of women's status in an analysis of economic relationships and broader political economy. The 'women and development' issue area formed the main focus of the Women's Commission and expanding international women's bureaucracy in the 1970s and 1980s. UNIFEM launched in 1976 and funded burgeoning numbers of women's NGOs to implement women and development projects. The question of 'women' became so firmly linked with economic development in the UN that the Convention on the Elimination of All forms of Discrimination against Women (CEDAW), although technically a human rights instrument, found its home with the Center for Social Development and Humanitarian Affairs in Vienna rather than the UN's human rights offices in Geneva (Berkovitch 1999: 142).

Thus until the end of the twentieth century, UN debates about women's status revolved around a critique of capitalism. According to Leticia Ramos Shahini, who served on the UN Women's Commission during the decade on women from 1975 to 1985: 'A constant topic of debate in the commission between those who came from the East and their Western counterparts was the superiority of women's status in the Socialist bloc as against the advantages of women in market oriented economies' (Shahini 2004: 28). A delegate from communist Romania proposed the idea that the UN host a women's world conference in 1975, which Mexico volunteered to host and the Soviets threw themselves behind (Ghodsee 2010: 5). They wanted the conference to be a forum where women could debate neo-colonialism, capitalism, apartheid, racism, Zionism and poverty. The USA wanted to limit the agenda to questions of women's legal equality in education, politics and so forth, fearing 'anti-American speeches and resolutions' (Ghodsee 2010: 5). As Kristen Ghodsee points out, in the year of USA withdrawal from Vietnam, Article 29 of the Mexico women's conference document reads like a critique of US military intervention in states turning to communism:

> Peace requires that women as well as men should reject any type of intervention in the domestic affairs of States, whether it be openly or covertly carried on by other States or by transnational corporations. Peace also requires that women as well as men should also promote respect for the sovereign right of a State to establish its own economic, social and political system without undergoing political and economic pressures or coercion of any type. (United Nations 1975: Article 29)

The Soviet position on this, and economic questions, appealed to many women from countries in the developing world which had grievances against the USA.

Thus international women's politics remained a difficult arena for US intervention during the Cold War. The isolation of US feminists at the 1975 conference was not helped by a dictate from the State Department that the US delegation at the official conference should not speak to women from the Eastern Bloc, even informally (Ghodsee 2010: 5–6). After the Soviets again led resolutions at the 1980 international Women's Conference in Copenhagen condemning Zionism as racism and praising centrally planned economies for their achievements in advancing women's participation in economic development and public life, US government representatives put extra effort into their preparation for the 1985 Nairobi conference (Ghodsee 2010: 7–9). They worked hard to keep questions of Zionism, racism and socialism off the agenda in Nairobi, providing financial assistance to Kenya for the costs of hosting the conference and appointing the president's daughter, Maureen Reagan, as one of the US delegates. US delegates at the official conference managed to keep the word Zionism out of the final conference document, but could not forestall resolutions and debates over the links between capitalism, imperialism and women's oppression (Ghodsee 2010: 8–9).

During the UN decade on women, international women's organizations rarely discussed sexual violence as an issue for the UN and the final documents of these three conferences do not highlight it. In March 1975 Diane Russell along with other anti-sexual violence feminists organized an International Tribunal on Crimes against Women in Brussels involving 2,000 women from forty countries as a counteraction to the 1975 UN Conference in Mexico, in which superpower politicking had dominated (Joachim 2003: 255–6). The CEDAW, another project of the UN women's bureaucracy, failed to explicitly address questions of sexual violence or violence against women, although the text underwent wide discussion by international women's NGOs before finalization. While communist countries supported women's economic advancement and participation in public life they did not back feminist attempts to politicize violence against women or sexual violence at the UN. Formerly, the Soviets opposed sexual violence and exploitation as a manifestation of capitalist oppression. The Bolsheviks had linked public and private sexual violence and exploitation, criminalizing both workplace sexual harassment and rape within marriage as early as 1922 (Attwood 1997: 100; Juviler 1977: 245). Nevertheless, by the 1970s and 1980s when feminists in the non-communist world started mobilizing around sexual violence, communists tended to dismiss such concerns as 'bourgeois', peripheral to the more 'fundamental' class struggle (Boxer 2007). Feminist anti-sexual violence politics only had an impact on domestic politics and policy outside the communist world. Protesters against the Vietnam War and against US bases in Japan, Korea and the Philippines condemned military sexual violence. Feminists also analyzed the links between the growth of sex tourism to Asia and the presence of US military bases (Brownmiller 1975; Enloe 1988; Moon 1997: 34–5, 47). Yet these political issues never made it onto the mainstream 'women's' agenda at the UN. Women's organizations could get little traction on questions of violence against women or sexual violence in the UN system. When a women's legal group put forward a proposal to study forced prostitution, the Commission on the Status of Women cautioned them that the UN did not want to pursue that issue (Barry 1979: 65). The Soviets and 'Third World' nations opposed investigations into forced prostitution as a kind of Western imperialist monitoring and argued that apartheid in South Africa presented a more serious instance of modern slavery (Barry 1979: 63). Women's organizations in the UN attempted to get a resolution at the UN General Assembly in 1985 condemning violence against women, which did not pass until reformulated as 'domestic violence' (Pietilä and Vickers 1996: 143).

International women's NGOs and women's bureaucracies in the UN had few resources or political support to document or politicize sexual violence during the Cold War. The human rights NGOs and activists did sometimes document rape alongside other forms of torture, but did not develop a gendered analysis of human rights violations. Thus, in 1971, rapes committed by Pakistani soldiers of Bengali women in Bangladesh only got attention from international feminists as an issue of abortion rights, since the topics of unwanted children and family planning fit into the development field where women's organizations had a voice (Brownmiller 1975: 80). The fields of human rights and security provided no such space for women to speak *as* women, and made no response to the rapes. In the late 1970s the Indonesian army's mass rapes of women and girls in East Timor barely registered in the UN system, although human rights monitors did record these rapes along with other atrocities (Chomsky and Herman 1979: 166). The Soviets did not use sexual violence as an issue with which to attack US foreign intervention. In the 1980s, neither Soviet women's leaders nor UN NGOs raised sexual violence issues as relevant when the USA supported the patriarchal Afghan Mujahideen against a modernizing regime which promoted women's rights (Moghadam 2005: 45). Nor did the US or pro-US feminists seek to expose Soviet hypocrisy on women's issues. They could have pointed out, for instance, that the USSR purported to defend the rights of Afghan women while members of the Red Army used prostitutes and perpetrated rapes during the conflict, and that Soviet women who served in the armed forces suffered sexual harassment and violence (Galeotti 2001: 41–2, 72).

Yet following the collapse of the Soviet Union, the USA emerged not only as a global hegemon, but posed as champion in fighting violence against women. Joachim's argument that 'the US government assumed leadership on the issue [of violence against women]' because of domestic feminist lobbying and because it 'fit the world views and beliefs of the Clinton administration which was generally supportive of women's issues' (Joachim 2003: 259) neglects to analyze how the issue fit with the US security agenda in the post-Cold War era. The question remains as to why only after 1989 'trafficking in women', wartime rape and domestic violence became important to the women's sector of the UN under US global hegemony. The following section argues that violence against women emerged as an international security issue after the Cold War because of its framing within new wars discourse as a reason for international policing and surveillance. In this context Resolution 1325 passed as a response to the tension produced by embedding opposition to violence against women within the militarized projects of political and economic transformation which characterize the new wars.

VIOLENCE AGAINST WOMEN AND US GLOBAL HEGEMONY

International policing of sexual violence forms part of the global democratic policing stance adopted by the USA and its allies since the collapse of the Soviet Union and the reorientation of global security discourse. North Atlantic Treaty Organization (NATO) security analysts criminalize their military targets in the post-Cold War order with 'new wars' doctrine, which pits alliances of democratic state and non-state actors against militia that control populations through rape and other forms of bodily atrocity.[2] Speaking of the 'new wars', Kofi Annan commented that: 'A disturbing characteristic of these conflicts is the practice of deliberately targeting civilian populations – the majority being women and children' (Annan 2002: ix). A UN gender training manual reminds military peacekeepers that in post-conflict situations: 'Women with the loss of their male family members, are vulnerable to discrimination and are subject to human rights violations' (DPKO 2001: 20). In new wars discourse, the notion of 'women's human rights' typically refers to women's right to bodily integrity, rather than broader notions of social or economic rights. Thus, in post-Cold War security discourse the term 'human rights violations' typically means bodily violation and signifies a lack of democracy.

Since 1989 the UN, NATO, the International Monetary Fund, World Bank, EU, the Organization for Security and Cooperation in Europe and humanitarian NGOs have assumed links between security, democracy and capitalist development: such consensus on the economic foundations of democracy would have been impossible in the Soviet era (Paris 2003: 446). This theory of democratic peace posits that democratic states do not go to war with each other and a democratic world would be a peaceful world (Bellamy et al. 2004: 30–1). NATO and its allies support a 'democracy building' approach to security and discuss their military actions as 'peace support', securing broader 'peacekeeping' efforts usually co-ordinated by the UN. Peacekeeping operations have proliferated since 1989: between 1989 and 2010 more than forty new operations were deployed, compared with only sixteen between 1948 and 1988. These post-1989 operations attempt to oversee fundamental economic and political transformation, including attention to 'women's human rights' (Chappell and Evans 1997: table 1; Bellamy et al. 2004: Appendix).

Post-Cold War peacekeeping and democracy building introduces precisely the kind of Western surveillance of developing countries' domestic affairs that the Soviets opposed at the UN when they scorned international action against trafficking in women. Violations of women's human rights, in the sense of bodily violation, have become an international security concern subject to monitoring and intervention. The Security Council first mentioned sexual violence in December 1992, declaring itself 'appalled by reports of the massive, organized and systematic detention and rape of women, in particular Muslim women, in Bosnia and Herzegovina' (UNSC 1992). This observation fuelled the case for military intervention and reports of rape now routinely accompany foreign military intervention or calls for intervention. The Clinton administration ordered that State Department human rights reports document violations of women's human rights, a practice that continues (Joachim 2003: 260). The UN also began monitoring violence against women and in 1994 the UN General Assembly created a new post of special rapporteur to research gender-based violence, while the UN system began producing information on violence against women around the globe.[3] Following this trend, regional powers now also monitor and intervene in the gender relations of their neighbors. For example, in the Pacific, the Australian and New Zealand police run training programs for police from Tonga, Samoa, the Cook Islands and Kiribati on dealing with domestic violence and they include domestic violence as an issue in their meetings with police from the region (Australian Federal Police [AFP] 2010; PPDVP 2010).

The reemergence of 'trafficking in women' as a 'violence against women' issue facilitated policing of the new illegal trade and migration routes in Europe and Central Asia that opened after the collapse of the Soviet Union. The USA and EU began pushing for a new International Convention on Transnational Organized Crime in the early 1990s. In 1995 Hilary Clinton met anti-trafficking activists at the UN Beijing Women's Conference and began championing the issue. With Madeleine Albright, she co-chaired the President's Interagency Council on Women to ensure that the Convention would include a protocol to address trafficking in women (Harrington 2010: 148). Following this, the USA passed the Victims of Trafficking and Violence Protection Act (US Congress 2000), which required the State Department to produce regular country reports on trafficking in persons (reports).

Such monitoring contributes to a hegemonic conflation of women's equality with 'Western' (or Northern) civilization, and women's oppression with an undeveloped 'rest', obscuring 'Western' agency in both male privilege and violence against women. Peacekeeping practices clearly manifest 'Western' male violence and domination. An Australian English language teacher in Timor Leste described how 'within the first five minutes of my landing' the expatriate head of the project told her that she had come to 'a man's world' (Appleby 2005: 165). Another noted that the gender ratio in the expatriate Dili community seemed to be 'nine men to one woman' and even men in civilian positions, such as journalists and NGO workers, liked to don 'little military outfits' (Appleby 2005: 168). She remembered her time in Timor Leste as

> probably one of the freakiest experiences of my life ... the whole bar scene, the pick up in the bars, like those World War II movies. And men, those truckloads of

> soldiers looking like predators, looking at us like predators. They'd drive past and I'd just look at them and think, when I was by myself and I'd think, thank god I'm not in one of the villages that you're liberating! (Appleby 2005: 169)

Likewise, whistleblower Ben Johnston described the private military contractor scene in Bosnia as 'such a boys' club because these guys are making so much money' (Subcommittee on International Operations and Human Rights 2002: 28). Australian women international police also talked of peacekeeping operations as a 'boys club', of displays of 'male ego and macho bull crap' in rivalry between Australian state and territory policy and the Federal police (Harris and Goldsmith 2010: 302). One woman police officer said:

> Missions have a tendency to bring out 'old' culture that, in my experience, has been greatly reduced in the AFP [Australian Federal Police], but will never cease to exist. This old culture (jobs for the boys, pack mentality, don't rat on your mates, if nobody else sees it, it didn't happen and so on) is still very much alive. (Harris and Goldsmith 2010: 302)

Studies of Nordic male military peacekeepers show that volunteers imagine going on a peacekeeping mission as a great male adventure away from the world of women and family (Tallberg 2007: 74).

Commentators frequently assume that men from 'advanced democracies' revert to the patriarchal norms of the society they aim to democratize on peacekeeping operations; again obscuring 'Western' agency in violence against women. Thus an interviewee in Afghanistan said 'Afghan culture seemed to rub off on them [male expatriates], it also made it difficult for women expats at times whilst I worked in Afghanistan. Male arrogance' (Barrow 2009: 59). Similarly, Harris and Goldsmith argue that 'distance from gendered social norms in the home country, location within a society that has different gender-based roles and expectations, and a male dominated international deployment' produced the sexist behavior of International Australian Police (Harris and Goldsmith 2010: 303). Such commentary allows the problem of peacekeeper sexism to be acknowledged, but displaced onto local cultural norms in 'non-Western' countries.

The Working Group for Women, Peace and Security, a network of women's NGOs which advocated for 1325, monitor the problem of peacekeeper violence, sexual exploitation and abuse, pointing to implementation of the Resolution as the solution (NGO Working Group on Women, Peace and Security n.d.). The Resolution's origins lie in joint UN research on 'Gender and UN Peacekeeping', consisting of a series of case studies that revealed patterns of sexism and abuse across operations and posited gender mainstreaming as the solution (Carey 2001: 51). Since passing 1325, the Security Council has continued to remain, in the words of the Resolution, 'actively seized of the matter' by issuing Presidential Statements requesting reports that review implementation (UNSC 2006, 2007, 2008, 2010a, 2010b). Implementation of

1325 depends upon country-level commitment to changes in the composition and conduct of their security services. International legal experts differ as to whether UN member states must abide by Security Council resolutions. In practice, states do not treat them as binding and it is up to feminist NGOs to hold states to the commitments they make at the UN (Tryggestad 2009: 544). In 2006, CEDAW began referencing compliance with 1325 in its country reporting sessions (Hudson 2009: 62–3). Such feminist monitoring doubtless ensures that most peacekeeping missions now incorporate gender officer positions and have sexual exploitation and abuse reporting procedures. Feminists have developed gender training resources and numerous security officials involved in peacekeeping have attended gender training sessions.

Thus, Resolution 1325 has allowed acknowledgement of peacekeeping operations' sexist culture at the highest level by representing this culture as a technically manageable problem, which the UN has a process for addressing in consultation with women's NGOs. In this way the Resolution manages the tensions created by security experts' engagement with feminist NGOs as part of new forms of peacekeeping. When feminists produce information about peacekeeper sexual violence, experts can call for more effort to implement the Resolution and the evidence of peacekeepers as sexually violent does not undermine the broader project of peacekeeping and democracy building.

CONCLUSION

Social movement theorists provide celebratory accounts of feminist transnational advocacy networks' success in putting violence against women onto the mainstream security agenda. While not denying that activist efforts made a difference, the transformed agenda of UN women's bureaucracies and NGOs in the late twentieth century largely reflects the end of Cold War superpower rivalry and the emergence of the USA as the unrivaled global hegemon fighting the new wars and championing democratization as a security issue. Within this context, women's human rights, signified by the problem of violence against women, has emerged as an integral part of the post-Cold War security agenda, with the USA, backed by international institutions and allies, adopting the pose of democratic defender of women and children. Leading global institutions and self-styled democratic states have represented the problem of global security by criminalizing their military opponents as perpetrators of bodily human rights violations against innocent civilians, especially women and children. Thus, the post-Cold War agenda of women's NGOs active in the UN system and UN women's bureaucracies reflects these broader changes in hegemonic security discourse. In this new global environment feminist activists have highlighted the contradiction between official rhetoric and peacekeeper perpetrated sexual violence, abuse, harassment and exploitation. Resolution 1325 has allowed for high-level recognition of the validity of these feminist concerns while representing peacekeeper sexism as a manageable problem and thereby avoiding information about peacekeeper sexual violence undermining the broader framework of new forms of peace-keeping as a way of fighting the 'new wars'.

Notes

1   See Americas Watch, Women's Rights Project (1992), Asia Watch, Thomas and Jones (1993), Amnesty International (1991, 1993, 1995a, 1995b, 1995c, 1995d, 1995e, 1995f) and Human Rights Watch (1993, 1994, 1995, 1996).
2   See Chappell and Evans (1997), Kaldor and Vashee (1997), Kaldor (1999), Brahimi et al. (2000) and Bellamy et al. (2004: 169–73).
3   See Pietilä and Vickers (1996: 142–5), United Nations (1993, 1994, 1996a, 1996b, 1996c) and UNHCR (1993).

References

Agee, P. 1975. *Inside the Company: CIA Diary.* Harmondsworth: Penguin.

Americas Watch, Women's Rights Project. 1992. *Untold Terror: Violence Against Women in Peru's Armed Conflict.* New York and Washington, DC: Human Rights Watch.

Amnesty International. 1991. *Women in the Front Line.* London: Amnesty International.

Amnesty International. 1993. *Bosnia-Herzegovina: Rape and Sexual Abuse by Armed Force.* London: Amnesty International.

Amnesty International. 1995a. *Women in War.* London: Amnesty International.

Amnesty International. 1995b. *It's About Time: Human Rights Are Women's Right.* New York and London: Amnesty International.

Amnesty International. 1995c. *Women in Peru: Rights in Jeopardy.* London: Amnesty International.

Amnesty International. 1995d. *Sudan-Women's Human Rights: An Action Report.* London: Amnesty International.

Amnesty International. 1995e. *Women in Colombia: Breaking the Silence.* London: Amnesty International.

Amnesty International. 1995f. *Women in the Middle East: Human Rights under Attack.* London: Amnesty International.

Annan, K. 2002. 'Forward to the Study on Women, Peace and Security', in *Women, Peace and Security: Study Submitted by the Secretary-General Pursuant to Security Council Resolution 1325 (2000)*. New York: United Nations. Available at http://www.un.org/womenwatch/daw/public/eWPS.pdf (accessed 9 September 2011).

Appleby, R. 2005. *The Spatiality of English Language Teaching, Gender and Context*. PhD Thesis, Faculty of Education, University of Technology, Sydney.

Asia Watch, Thomas, D. Q. and Jones, S. 1993. *A Modern Form of Slavery Trafficking of Burmese Women into Brothels in Thailand*. New York: Human Rights Watch.

Attwood, L. 1997. '"She was Asking for It": Rape and Domestic Violence against Women', in Buckley, M. E. A. (ed.) *Post Soviet Women: From the Baltic to Central Asia*, pp. 99–142. Cambridge: Cambridge University Press.

Australian Federal Police (AFP). 2010. 'Media Release: Police Chiefs from 18 Pacific Nations to Meet', 23 August. Available at http://www.afp.gov.au/media-centre/news/afp/2010/august/police-chiefs-from-18-pacific-nations-to-meet.aspx (accessed 1 November 2010).

Barrow, A. 2009. '[It's] like a Rubber Band'. Assessing UNSC 1325 as a Gender Mainstreaming Process', *International Journal of Law in Context* 5 (1): 51–68.

Barry, K. 1979. *Female Sexual Slavery*. New York: New York University Press.

Bellamy, A. J., Williams, P. and Griffin, S. 2004. *Understanding Peacekeeping*. Cambridge: Polity Press.

Berkovitch, N. 1999. *From Motherhood to Citizenship: Women's Rights and International Organizations*. Baltimore, MD: Johns Hopkins University Press.

Boxer, M. J. 2007. 'Rethinking the Socialist Construction and International Career of the Concept "Bourgeois Feminism"', *The American Historical Review* 112 (1): 131–58. Available at http://www.historycooperative.org/journals/ahr/112.1/boxer.html (accessed 4 September 2009).

Brahimi, L., Atwood, B., Granderson, C., Hercus, A., Monk, R., Naumann, K., Shimura, H., Shustov, V., Sibanda, P. and Sommaruga, C. 2000. *Report of the Panel on United Nations Peace Operations*. New York: General Assembly, A/55/305-S/2000/809.

Brownmiller, S. 1975. *Against Our Will: Men, Women and Rape*. New York: Fawcett Columbine.

Carey, H. F. 2001. 'Women and Peace and Security: The Politics of Implementing Gender Sensitivity Norms in Peacekeeping', *International Peacekeeping* 8 (2): 49–68.

Carpenter, R. C. 2007. 'Setting the Advocacy Agenda: Theorizing Issue Emergence and Nonemergence in Transnational Advocacy Networks', *International Studies Quarterly* 51 (1): 99–120.

Chappell, D. and Evans, J. 1997. *The Role, Preparation and Performance of Civilian Police in United Nations Peacekeeping Operations*, International Centre for Criminal Law Reform and Criminal Justice Policy. Available at http://www.icclr.law.ubc.ca/Publications/Reports/Peacekeeping.pdf (accessed 21 June 2011).

Chomsky, N. and Herman, E. S. 1979. *After the Cataclysm, Postwar Indochina and the Reconstruction of Imperial Ideology*. Boston, MA: South End Press.

Connors, J. 1996. 'NGOs and the Human Rights of Women at the United Nations', in Willetts, P. (ed.) *'The Conscience of the World': The Influence of Non-governmental Organisations in the UN System*, pp. 147–80. London: Hurst and Company.

DPKO. 2001. *Gender and Peacekeeping Operations In-Mission Training.* New York: Training and Evaluation Service, Military Division, Department of Peacekeeping Operations, United Nations.

Enloe, C. 1988. *Does Khaki Become You? The Militarization of Women's Lives.* London: Pandora Press.

Friedman, E. 1995. 'Women's Human Rights: The Emergence of a Movement', in Peters, J. and Wolper, A. (eds) *Women's Rights, Human Rights: International Feminist Perspectives*, pp. 18–35. London: Routledge.

Galeotti, M. 2001. *Afghanistan: The Soviet Union's Last War.* New edition. edition. London: Routledge.

Ghodsee, K. 2010. 'Revisiting the United Nations Decade for Women: Brief Reflections on Feminism, Capitalism and Cold War Politics in the Early Years of the International Women's Movement', *Women's Studies International Forum* 33 (1): 3–12.

Harrington, C. 2010. *Politicization of Sexual Violence: From Abolitionism to Peacekeeping.* London: Ashgate.

Harris, V. and Goldsmith, A. 2010. 'Gendering Transnational Policing: Experiences of Australian Women in International Policing Operations', *International Peacekeeping* 17 (2): 292–306.

Hudson, N. F. 2009. 'Securitizing Women's Rights and Gender Equality', *Journal of Human Rights* 8 (1): 53–70.

Human Rights Watch. 1993. *Seeking Refuge, Finding Terror: The Widespread Rape of Somali Women Refugees on North Eastern Kenya.* New York: Human Rights Watch.

Human Rights Watch. 1994. *Rape in Haiti: A Weapon of Terror*, 1 July. Available at http://www.unhcr.org/refworld/docid/3ae6a7e18.html (accessed 30 July 2010).

Human Rights Watch. 1995. *The Human Rights Watch Global Report on Women's Human Rights.* New York: Human Rights Watch.

Human Rights Watch. 1996. *Shattered Lives: Sexual Violence During the Rwandan Genocide and Its Aftermath.* New York: Human Rights Watch.

Joachim, J. M. 2003. 'Framing Issues and Seizing Opportunities: The UN, NGOs, and Women's Rights', *International Studies Quarterly* 47 (2): 247–74.

Juviler, P. H. 1977. 'Women and Sex in Soviet Law', in Dallin, A., Atkinson, D. and Lapidus G. W. (eds) *Women in Russia*, pp. 243–66. Stanford: Stanford University Press.

Kaldor, M. 1999. *New and Old Wars: Organized Violence in a Global Era.* Cambridge: Polity Press.

Kaldor, M. and Vashee, B. (eds). 1997. *Restructuring the Global Military Sector 1, New Wars.* London: Pinter.

Keck, M. E. and Sikkink, K. 1998. *Activists Beyond Borders: Advocacy Networks in International Politics.* Ithaca, NY: Cornell University Press.

Laville, H. 2002. *Cold War Women: The International Activities of American Women's Organisations.* Manchester: Manchester University Press.

Moghadam, V. M. 2005. *Globalizing Women: Transnational Feminist Networks*. Balti-more, MD: JHU Press.

Moon, K. H. S. 1997. *Sex among Allies: Military Prostitution in US – Korea Relations*. New York: Columbia University Press.

NGO Working Group on Women, Peace and Security. n.d. 'About Us'. Available at http://www.womenpeacesecurity.org/about/ (accessed 30 July 2010).

Paris, R. 2003. 'Peacekeeping and the Constraints of Global Culture', *European Journal of International Relations* 9 (3): 441–73.

Pietilä, H. and Vickers, J. 1996. *Making Women Matter: The Role of the United Nations*. 3rd edition. London: Zed Books.

PPDVP. 2010. 'Welcome to the Pacific Prevention of Domestic Violence Programme (PPDVP) Website'. Available at http://www.ppdvp.org.nz/ (accessed 1 November 2010)

Shahini, L. R. 2004. 'The UN, Women and Development: The World Conferences on Women', A. S. Fraser and I. Tinker (eds), *Developing Power: How Women Trans-formed International Development*, pp. 26–36. New York: The Feminist Press.

Subcommittee on International Operations and Human Rights. 2002. 'Hearing before the Subcommittee on International Operations and Human Rights of the Committee on International Relations. 2002. House of Representatives, One Hundred Seventh Con-gress, Second Session, April 24, 2002, Serial No. 107 – 85', *The UN and the Sex Slave Trade in Bosnia: Isolated Case or Larger Problem in the UN System?* Washington, DC: US Government Printing Office. Available at http://commdocs.house.gov/committees/intlrel/hfa78948.000/hfa78948_0f.htm (accessed 9 September).

Tallberg, T. 2007. 'Bonds of Burden and Bliss: The Management of Social Relations in a Peacekeeping Organization', *Critical Perspectives on International Business* 3 (1): 63–82.

True, J. 2008. 'Global Accountability and Transnational Networks: The Women Leaders' Network and Asia Pacific Economic Cooperation', *The Pacific Review* 21 (1): 1–26.

Tryggestad, T. 2009. 'Trick or Treat? The UN and Implementation of Security Council Resolution 1325 on Women, Peace, and Security', *Global Governance* 15 (4): 539–57.

UNHCR. 1993. *Executive Committee of the High Commissioner's Programme*. Sub-Committee of Whole on International Protection. Note on Certain Aspects of Sexual Violence against Refugee Women, EC/1993/SCP/CRP.2, 29 April.

United Nations (UN). 1975. 'World Conference of the International Women's Year 1975 Declaration of Mexico on the Equality of Women and Their Contribution to Development and Peace, Adopted at the World Conference of the International Women's Year Mexico City, Mexico. 19 June – 2 July 1975'. Available at http://www.un-documents.net/mex-dec.htm (accessed 2 October 2010).

United Nations (UN). 1993. *Economic and Social Council Commission on Human Rights*. Rape and Abuse of Women in the Territory of the Former Yugoslavia. Report of the Secretary-General. E./CN.4/1994/5.

United Nations (UN). 1994. *Economic and Social Council Commission on Human Rights*. Preliminary Report Submitted by the Special Rapporteur on Violence against

Women, Its Causes and Consequences, Ms. Radhika Coomaraswamy, in Accordance to Commission on Human Rights Resolution 1994/45, E/CN.4/1995/42.

United Nations (UN). 1996a. *Economic and Social Council Commission on Human Rights*, Report of the Special Rapporteur on Violence against Women, Its Causes and Consequences, Ms. Radhika Coomaraswamy, Submitted in Accordance with Commission on Human Rights Resolution 1995/85, E/CN.4/1996/53.

United Nations (UN). 1996b. *Economic and Social Council Sub-Commission on Prevention of Discrimination and Protection of Minorities.* Contemporary Forms of Slavery: Preliminary Report of the Special Rapporteur on the Situation of Systematic Rape, Sexual Slavery and Slavery-Like Practices During Periods of Armed Conflict, Ms. Linda Chavez, E/CN.4/Sub.2/1996/26, 16 July.

United Nations (UN). 1996c. *General Assembly*, Human rights Questions: Human Rights Situation and Reports of Special Rapporteurs and Representatives: Rape and Abuse of Women in the Areas of Armed Conflict in the Former Yugoslavia: Report of the Secretary-General, A/51/557, 25 October.

UNSC (United Nations Security Council). 1992. 'Resolution 798. Adopted by the Security Council at Its 3150th Meeting on 18 December 1992'. S/Res/798. Bosnia and Herzegovina. Available at http://daccess-dds-ny.un.org/doc/UNDOC/GEN/N92/828/82/IMG/N9282882.pdf?OpenElement (accessed 21 June 2011).

UNSC (United Nations Security Council). 2000. 'Women Peace and Security Resolution 1325. Adopted by the Security Council at Its 4213th Meeting, on 31 October 2000'. S/Res/1325. Available at http://daccess-dds-ny.un.org/doc/UNDOC/GEN/N00/720/18/PDF/N0072018.pdf?OpenElement (accessed 21 June 2011).

UNSC (United Nations Security Council). 2006. 'Statement by the President of the Security Council', S/PRST/2006/42, 8 November. Available at http://daccess-dds-ny.un.org/doc/UNDOC/GEN/N06/588/65/PDF/N0658865.pdf?OpenElement (accessed 21 June 2011).

UNSC (United Nations Security Council). 2007. 'Statement by the President of the Security Council'. S/PRST/2007/40, 24 October. Available at http://daccess-dds-ny.un.org/doc/UNDOC/GEN/N07/560/22/PDF/N0756022.pdf?OpenElement (accessed 21 June 2011).

UNSC (United Nations Security Council). 2008. 'Statement by the President of the Security Council', S/PRST/2008/39, 29 October. Available at http://daccess-dds-ny.un.org/doc/UNDOC/GEN/N08/576/39/PDF/N0857639.pdf?OpenElement (accessed 21 June 2011).

UNSC (United Nations Security Council). 2010a. 'Statement by the President of the Security Council', S/PRST/2010/22, 26 October. Available at http://daccess-dds-ny.un.org/doc/UNDOC/GEN/N10/603/52/PDF/N1060352.pdf?OpenElement (accessed 21 June 2011).

UNSC (United Nations Security Council). 2010b. 'Statement by the President of the Security Council', S/PRST/2010/8, 27 April. Available at http://daccess-dds-ny.un.org/doc/UNDOC/GEN/N10/331/57/PDF/N1033157.pdf?OpenElement (accessed 21 June 2011).

US Congress. 2000. 'Victims of Trafficking and Violence Protection Act of 2000 Public Law 106–386 106th Congress October 28', Available at http://www.state.gov/documents/organization/10492.pdf (accessed 21 June 2011).

Weigand, K. 2001. *Red Feminism: American Communism and the Making of Women's Liberation.* Baltimore, MD: Johns Hopkins University Press.

Willetts, P. 1996. 'Consultative Status for NGOs at the United Nations', in Willetts, P. (ed.) *'The Conscience of the World': The Influence of Non-governmental Organisations in the UN System*, pp. 31–62. London: Hurst and Company.

'Women, Peace and Security': Addressing Accountability for Wartime Sexual Violence

SAHLA AROUSSI
University of Antwerp, Belgium

Abstract

This article examines the issue of accountability for wartime sexual violence within the UN agenda on women, peace and security. The study offers a unique contribution to the growing body of literature on Resolution 1325 by reviewing how the issue of accountability for sexual violence has been treated in peace agreements signed since its adoption in October 2000. The author triangulates data collected from peace agreements with interviews with elite peacemaking practitioners to establish that justice for victims of sexual violence continues to be side-lined. The central argument of this article is that the lack of attention to accountability for sexual violence is symptomatic of larger problems within the UN agenda which is underpinned by a masculinized perception of accountability limited to sanctions and punishment and a narrow focus on sexual violence as a weapon of war. The author argues that unless a holistic approach to justice and accountability and a broader concern with gender-based violence are adopted, the UN's aim of ending impunity for wartime sexual violence will remain unfulfilled.

INTRODUCTION

We are here today because ... women continue to be targeted in wars, because rape and sexual violence continue to be used as weapons of war ... Women are seldom protected from these threats. Their aggressors are not punished.

> What kind of message does this send to the people who continue to rape, exploit, torture and mutilate? (United Nations Security Council 2000a: 2)

This is the message that Noeleen Heyzer presented a decade ago, when the Security Council met for the first time to debate the agenda on women, peace and security. The prevalence of sexual violence in conflicts came to light during the 1990s following the mass atrocities committed in the former Yugoslavia and Rwanda (Melandri 2009). Yet, despite its widespread and endemic nature, wartime sexual violence has historically been met by the international community with silence and inaction. During transitional justice processes, crimes of sexual violence typically become invisible and their victims are frequently forgotten (Nowrojee 2005). Accountability for wartime sexual violence was undoubtedly one of the main concerns at the heart of the UN agenda on women, peace and security initiated with the adoption of the ground-breaking Security Council Resolution 1325 in October 2000. The issue of accountability for sexual violence was further addressed by the Security Council in Resolution 1820, adopted in June 2008. The fact that the Security Council paid specific attention to wartime sexual violence perpetrated against women in conflicts ought, without doubt, to be celebrated not least because of the conservative nature of the Council. However, the task of securing justice for women requires a broad and holistic approach to justice capable of adequately responding to victims' needs. This necessarily entails a break from the traditionally militaristic and masculinized Security Council's strategies of sanctions and punishment. A decade after the adoption of Security Council Resolution 1325, it is important to examine how and to assess whether the promises of accountability for sexual violence made in New York translate into actions in war-torn countries around the world.

This study critically examines the treatment of accountability for sexual violence in the UN Security Council Resolutions 1325 and 1820 and argues that unless a holistic approach to justice and a broader focus on gender-based violence are adopted, the UN will be unable to respond adequately to victims' needs. In developing this argument, the author uses all available peace agreements since the adoption of Resolution 1325 to the end of 2008 as a data set. The decision to use peace agreements was largely motivated by the historical marginalization of justice for women victims of wartime sexual violence within such documents, as well as the common practice of granting amnesties to perpetrators of violence in return for peace. This marginalization of issues affecting women in pre-Resolution 1325 peace agreements has been well documented (Chinkin 2002), and this study will therefore assess any changes in respect to post-Resolution 1325 agreements. The author has employed quantitative and qualitative content analysis techniques to analyse a total of 111 peace agreements relevant to thirty-five countries. Content analysis is commonly used in feminist scholarship to investigate women's representation and gender issues in various documents (Sarantakos 2005: 290). The peace agreements studied represent all the agreements available in English or French that were signed between October 2000 and the end of December 2008. The research utilized Bell's (2008) broad definition of peace agreements. Bell labels peace agreements as all 'documents produced after discussion with some or all of the conflict's protagonists that address military violent conflict with a view to ending it' (Bell 2008: 53). Thus, the agreements studied include pre-negotiation, substantive and implementation agreements. The original texts of the agreements used in this investigation are available on the UN peacemaker website. The study found that while twenty peace agreements have addressed issues of gender-based violence only five agreements included provisions on justice and accountability for gender-based violence. In this article, the author examines the provisions coded from the five peace agreements and argues that the UN agenda on women, peace and security has not led so far to the inclusion of real commitments to justice for women in peace agreements. The issue of accountability for sexual violence in peace agreements is further explored, using qualitative telephone interviews conducted with six elite practitioners (UN officials and senior diplomats) with significant experience in formal peace negotiations and knowledge of the UN agenda on women, peace and security.

This article is divided into four sections. The first part discusses the issue of accountability for wartime sexual violence. The second section examines the way in which Resolutions 1325 and 1820 address the issue of accountability for crimes of wartime sexual violence. The article then assesses the issue of accountability for sexual violence in peace agreements. The final section of this article critically reflects on the limitations of the current UN agenda on women, peace and security in dealing with wartime gender-based violence.

DEFINING JUSTICE FOR VICTIMS OF SEXUAL VIOLENCE IN A TRANSITIONAL CONTEXT

Transitional justice as defined by the UN comprises 'the full range of processes and mechanisms associated with a society's attempts to come to terms with a legacy of large-scale past abuses, in order to ensure accountability serves justice and achieves reconciliation' (United Nations Security Council 2004: 4). The past two decades have seen major normative legal developments in international criminal law aimed at providing justice for victims of sexual violence. Most notable of these was the recognition, prosecution and punishment of sexual crimes committed in the Former Yugoslavia and Rwanda by the International Criminal Tribunal for Yugoslavia (ICTY) and the International Criminal Tribunal for Rwanda (ICTR), respectively. In these tribunals, rape was found to constitute a war crime, a crime against humanity, genocide and a grave breach of the Geneva Conventions (Askin 1999; Campanaro 2001; De Brouwer 2005). The findings of the tribunals added legal significance to the strategic rape theory, whereby wartime rape is no longer considered a simple by-product of war, but rather a planned and targeted policy perpetrated as part of the wider strategic objectives (Askin 2003; Buss 2009). Another significant development in this struggle against impunity for wartime sexual violence is the establishment of the permanent International Criminal Court (ICC). The ICC statute recognizes rape, sexual slavery, enforced prostitution, forced pregnancy, enforced sterilization or any other forms of sexual violence of comparable gravity as crimes against humanity, war crimes and grave breaches of the Geneva Conventions and allows for their prosecution wherever committed (Campanaro 2001). The legal developments at the international level have a direct bearing on transitional justice processes in national contexts. This is because the principle of complimentarity gives jurisdiction to the ICC when national courts are unable or unwilling to prosecute (Jurdi 2010).

Despite these noteworthy achievements in international law, the project of dispensing justice for victims of wartime sexual violence has remained largely unfulfilled (Nowrojee 2005; Melandri 2009). One of the shortcomings of the current strategies for transitional justice revolves around how justice for sexual violence is perceived and pursued. While the goal of holding the perpetrators accountable cannot be under-estimated, this on its own is not enough to fulfil women victims' needs for a meaningful form of justice. Criminal prosecutions, as Cahn (2005) points out, are almost exclusively focused on the perpetrators' actions, guilt or innocence, while the victims are assigned to the periphery of the witness stand. In these adversary processes, the legal meta-narrative of 'women as victims' reinforces gender and cultural essentialism, and disempowers women by undermining their agency (Mertus 2004). Henry (2010) argues that, because of taboos and the social stigma surrounding sexual violence, the experience of providing testimony in rape trials has the counter-productive effect of re-traumatising the victims. The stigma attached to rape often prevents victims from disclosing their experiences in criminal tribunals for fear of retaliation, rejection, social ostracism and reputational damage (Ross 2003; Borer 2009). Transitional justice processes also treat cases of sexual violence in isolation or as a one-off occurrence and fail to take into account the continuum of violence and the structural and social causes behind it (Okello and Hovil 2007; Ni Aolain 2009). It can also be the case that in conflicts, where mass atrocities were committed not all crimes and perpetrators can be prosecuted, partly due to limited judicial capacities. In these circumstances, transitional justice mechanisms become highly selective, prioritising which perpetrators to hold accountable and what kind of crimes to prosecute (Haskell 2009). As a rule gender-based harm generally struggles to gain a space in this hierarchy (Ni Aolain 2009). Consequently, the structures set by international law with the purpose of ensuring justice for raped women become instead a source of new forms of alienation and subordination for women in general (Haskell 2009: 39).

Moreover, the narrow and masculinized concept of justice limited to prosecution and punishment as employed in transitional justice processes is not very useful for women victims (Cahn 2005). Wartime sexual violence often has detrimental and far-reaching consequences for women. This is especially true, given that the concepts of 'shame' and 'honour' associated with the rape of women in peacetime continues for the sexual violence committed in conflicts (McGinn 2000). Raped women and girls are frequently disowned by husbands and families and unmarried girls are considered 'spoiled' (Melandri 2009). Sexual violence also has numerous socio-economic and health consequences. Women victims are often faced with the difficulties of providing for themselves and their children without support and as a result become vulnerable to further exploitation and violence. Victims often contract sexually transmitted diseases including HIV/AIDS and suffer from sexual mutilations and other permanent and life-threatening injuries (Cahn 2005; De Brouwer 2007). Women continue to suffer from the consequences of the violence even when perpetrators are successfully caught and punished. Increasingly, the emerging scholarship on adequate responses to gender-based violence in conflict has been calling for a holistic and broad approach to justice that goes beyond the traditional boundaries of how justice is perceived (Cahn 2006; Borer 2009). Höglund (2003: 350) contends that in this quest for justice for sexual violence, a revised feminist ethics of care is needed and that gender justice can only be achieved through the merging of values derived from ethics of care with those associated with the ethics of justice. Gender justice as such entails bringing the victims back to the centre and thinking creatively about strategies that best respond to their needs.

THE UN AGENDA ON WOMEN, PEACE AND SECURITY AND ACCOUNTABILITY FOR SEXUAL VIOLENCE

During the Security Council debate that preceded the adoption of Resolution 1325, sexual violence against women emerged as a common concern among member states requiring an immediate response. The UN Secretary General opened the debate by referring to the need to ensure that 'women and girls in situations of armed conflicts are adequately protected, that perpetrators of violence against women in conflict are brought to justice' (United Nations Security Council 2000a: 3). Sexual violence is one of the key issues addressed by Resolution 1325. The resolution acknowledges in its preamble that 'women and children account for the vast majority of those adversely affected by armed conflict' and recognizes that they are being targeted for sexual violence. Paragraph 11 of the resolution specifically tackles the issue of accountability for sexual violence:

> Emphasizes the responsibility of all states to put an end to impunity and to prosecute those responsible for genocide, crimes against humanity, and war crimes including those relating to sexual and other violence against women and girls, and in this regard stresses the need to exclude these crimes, where feasible from amnesty provisions. (United Nations Security Council 2000b: 3)

However, because paragraph 11 only called for the exclusion of these crimes from amnesty provisions 'where feasible', the resolution's commitment to accountability has remained rhetorical allowing those involved in the negotiation of peace agreements to easily side-line justice for women.

The years that followed the passage of Resolution 1325 have seen a renewed interest in the issue of sexual violence with the adoption of Resolution 1820 in June 2008 almost exclusively dedicated to this issue. Resolution 1820 explicitly recognizes the use of sexual violence as a weapon of war and stresses in its first operative paragraph that sexual violence as a war strategy represents a threat to international peace and security. Resolution 1820 uses stronger language regarding impunity than that used by Resolution 1325 (Cook 2009) and explicitly recognizes that sexual violence can constitute a breach of international law. Resolution 1820 rectifies Resolution 1325's stand on amnesty in peace agreements by stressing in paragraph 4 'the need for the exclusion of sexual violence crimes from amnesty provisions in the context of conflict resolution processes' (United Nations Security Council 2008: 3). In Resolution 1820, the Security Council takes an even firmer position on the issue of accountability for gender-based violence by expressing in its operative paragraphs its readiness and intention to take measures, including sanctions against parties that perpetrate sexual violence against women and girls.

However, it must be noted that despite these significant achievements, the UN agenda on women, peace and security in relation to accountability did not deliver anything new to women in conflict that has not been previously established elsewhere within the UN system. What the two resolutions did was to reiterate already established principles of international law and to bring all of these issues within the power and authority of the Security Council, which cannot be underestimated (Cook 2009). How these commitments made by the Security Council actually impact on peace agreements will be examined in the section below.

ACCOUNTABILITY FOR SEXUAL VIOLENCE IN PEACE AGREEMENTS

Transitional justice mechanisms are often the result of compromises achieved during the negotiation of peace agreements between the various protagonists to the conflict and the peace mediator. This study analyses 111 peace agreements signed between the adoption of Security Council Resolution 1325 in October 2000 and the end of December 2008 and finds that only five agreements included provisions linked to accountability for gender-based violence. These are the Darfur Peace Agreement (DPA) of Sudan (2006), the Agreement on Accountability and Reconciliation (2007) and the Annexure to the Agreement on Accountability and Reconciliation of Uganda (2008), the Inter-Congolese Negotiations, the Final Act of the Democratic Republic of the Congo (DRC) (2003) and the regional Pact on Security, Stability and Development in the Great Lakes Region (2006).[1] The coded provisions consist of commitments to investigate, enquire into, hear and prosecute crimes of violence against women; establishing separate police counters for women victims of sexual violence and providing gender sensitive rules of procedures that involve and protect women in the process of pursuing justice. The first part of the analysis below will closely examine the provisions on accountability for sexual violence and briefly situate these within the context in which they were adopted. In order to triangulate some of the peace agreements data, the second part of this section will include qualitative interview material collected from six elite participants with significant experience in peacemaking.

The first agreement discussed in this study is the DPA. The conflict in Darfur was one where sexual violence and other grave human rights violations against women were endemic (Schneider 2007). The Darfur agreement was concluded at a time when the ICC was already involved in Darfur to investigate crimes of an international nature committed in the area (Kastner 2007). The peace agreement provides for the investigation, prosecution and punishment of crimes against women, stating that:

> In areas of Government of Sudan (GoS) control, the GoS Police shall investigate all crimes, including those committed against women and children, and ensure the prosecution of the perpetrators and the protection of the victims. They shall give the African Union Mission in Sudan (AMIS) Civilian Police unimpeded access and information to monitor these activities. (DPA 2006, paragraph 277)

In addition, paragraph 278 of the DPA provides for the establishment of separate police counters by the GoS and AMIS police staffed with women police personnel and dedicated to the reporting of gender-based violence. While these two provisions are welcomed, arguably these pledges are closer to rhetoric than reality. To start with, the agreement calls on the police of the GoS to investigate, prosecute and punish the crimes. However, accounts from victims point to the fact that not only are rape and sexual assaults in Darfur condoned by the state, but also frequently committed by government forces alongside the government-backed Janjaweed militia (Schneider 2007). Moreover, the setting of separate police counters for reporting sexual violence while a welcome step is very unlikely to be successful in the case of Sudan, in light of evidence that the GoS exerted pressure on women not to report their attacks (Schneider 2007). The government's pressure alongside the social and religious taboos surrounding rape, mean that women are unlikely to come forward to report their rapes. Most importantly, the DPA provisions are rhetorical because the agreement itself lacks legitimacy. The negotiation of the DPA suffered from heavy international involvement and was marked by an absolute lack of local ownership (Nathan 2006). The DPA was rejected by two of the main factions, the Sudan Liberation Army, as well as the Justice for Equality Movement (Kastner 2007). The DPA did not end the conflict in Darfur and talks are still on going about the possibility or the desirability of renegotiating it if a satisfactory and viable political settlement to the conflict can to be achieved (Kastner 2007).

The Ugandan agreements relate to the conflict in Northern Uganda. Violence against women was widespread during this conflict and was perpetrated by the Lord's Resistance Amy (LRA) and the government's Uganda People's Defence Forces (UPDF) (Okello and Hovil 2007). In 2000, the government of Uganda offered amnesty and protection to the rebel leaders if they disarmed and returned from the bush yet the amnesty was rejected by the rebel forces who continued to commit atrocities in the region (Hanlon 2006; Apreotesei 2009). This prompted the government of Uganda to recommend the matter to the ICC on December 2003 (Apreotesei 2009). However, shortly afterwards, the LRA leaders declared their willingness to enter peace negotiations and the government renewed the offer for amnesty. But the involvement of the ICC, supported by donor countries, has meant that amnesty is no longer possible and the government of Uganda was caught between the promises of peace or prosecuting the LRA leaders. In an effort to underscore the ICC involvement, the government of Uganda organized national criminal prosecution for massive violations of human rights by the LRA leaders and justice mechanisms acceptable by international legal standards as an alternative to the ICC prosecution (Kastner 2007; Apreotesei 2009). The two Ugandan agreements discussed below represent an attempt to bring justice into the jurisdiction of Uganda and vitiate the ICC warrants (Apuuli 2008).

The first Ugandan agreement to be examined here is the Agreement on Accountability and Reconciliation (2007) which specifically deals with transitional justice measures and includes some impressive gender sensitive provisions. The agreement in its preamble provides for commitments to redress and prevent impunity in accordance with the requirements of the ICC statute. Such adherence to international standards and to the ICC in particular, necessarily entails prosecuting sexual violence. Articles 3 and 10 of the agreement include commitments to adopt gender sensitive rules of procedure in the transitional justice process that ensure the protection of victims of sexual violence. Article 11 includes a section, under the sub-heading 'women and girls', whereby the parties agree to:

> (i) Recognise and address the special needs of women and girls. (ii) Ensure that the experiences, views and concerns of women and girls are recognised and taken into account. (iii) Protect the dignity, privacy and security of women and girls. (Agreement on Accountability and Reconciliation 2007, paragraph 11)

The second Ugandan agreement is the Annexure to the Agreement on Accountability and Reconciliation (2008). This peace accord establishes a framework for implementing the agreement on Accountability and Reconciliation and reiterates the commitments of the parties to prosecute the crimes committed during the conflict in accordance with international legal standards acceptable to the ICC. In terms of accountability for gender-based violence, the agreement establishes a body, which, among its responsibilities is:

> (c) to inquire into human rights violations committed during the conflict, giving particular attention to the experiences of women and children; (e) to make provision for witness protection, especially for children and women; (f) to make special provisions for cases involving gender based violence. (Annexure to the Agreement on Accountability and Reconciliation 2008, paragraph 4)

The composition of this body, according to paragraph 6, should 'reflect gender balance and the national character' (Annexure to the Agreement on Accountability and Reconciliation 2008). In paragraph 25, the annexure agreement emphasizes further that due regards is paid to gender balance in all the institutions envisaged by the agreement. The agreement also requires criminal investigations to '(c) give particular attention to crimes and violations against women and children committed during the conflict' (Annexure to the Agreement on Accountability and Reconciliation 2008, paragraph 13). The agreement additionally states that 'all bodies implementing the agreement shall establish internal procedures and arrangements for protecting and ensuring the participation of victims, traumatised individuals, women, children, persons with disabilities and victims of sexual violence in proceedings' (Annexure to the Agreement on Accountability and Reconciliation 2008, paragraph 24). The agreement also requires the government in consultation with the relevant interlocutors to consider the role and impact of pursuing traditional justice on women and children.

However, while the provisions included in the Ugandan agreements are gender sensitive, doubts exist as to Uganda's ability and commitments to implement them (Apuuli 2008). Okello and Hovil (2007: 3) argue that the Ugandan agreements, while representing an opportunity to address injustices that happened during the course of the conflict in Uganda as a whole, in substance only relate to the conflict in Northern Uganda. The implication of this is that violations suffered by women in other parts of the country and particularly during displacement are not covered by the agreements. Moreover, the agreements do not include or refer to the violations committed by the UPDF. Thus arguably, the agreements' provisions on accountability for sexual violence are contradicted by the hidden dynamics of these abuses. Henry (2010) has argued that because of the taboos and social stigma surrounding sexual violence in Uganda very few women admit to being raped. Finally, it must be noted as well, that the LRA leaders, fearing the ICC prosecution, refused to sign the final peace agreement, which led the whole process into political impasse (Apuuli 2008).

The fourth peace agreement that provided for accountability for gender-based violence is the Inter-Congolese Negotiations Final Act agreement (2003). During the conflict in the DRC, sexual violence was a defining feature, being committed by the rebel groups, as well as the armed forces and police (Meger 2010). The Final Act agreement sets up a power-sharing agreement, whereby the rebel leaders gain access to impressive positions of powers within the transitional government. In relation to accountability for wartime violence, rather than agreeing to criminal prosecution, the parties resolve that a 'National Truth and Reconciliation Commission is empowered to hear any person involved in the crimes and large-scale violation of human rights, including the rape of women and girls in times of war' (The Final Act agreement 2003, Resolution 33). However, this commission, which was eventually set up in 2004, has suffered from critical problems. This is because its composition included representatives of groups known to have committed egregious human rights violations and who have been in some cases directly involved in the perpetration of serious abuses. Therefore, the composition of this commission represented a real impediment for pursuing accountability. As a result, the commission's mandate ended in 2006 without investigating a single case of human rights violations (Davis and Hayner 2009: 23).

The final agreement that includes provision for accountability for gender-based violence is the Pact on Security, Stability and Development in the Great Lakes Region (2006). This agreement was conceived and designed to set up the legal framework for the implementation of the Dar Es Salaam Declaration agreement. The pact is a far reaching ambitious attempt by the Great Lakes region countries to establish the necessary conditions for achieving peace and stability (Beyani 2007). The coded provision calls on state parties to 'combat sexual violence against women and children by combating, criminalising and punishing acts of sexual violence, both in times of peace and in times of war in accordance with national laws and international criminal law' (Pact on Security, Stability and Development in the Great Lakes Region 2006, Article 11). The pact does not specifically prescribe any transitional justice measures in the countries of the Great Lakes region, but rather provides a general legal framework for pursuing justice for victims. The pact is more of a declaration of principles and real commitments to implementation are yet to be seen.

To conclude, provisions on justice for victims of sexual violence remain very scarce in peace agreements and the UN agenda on women, peace and security has not so far impacted on peace agreements. One glaring omission from all the peace agreements examined is the absence of any forms of reparations or other forms of redress for victims of wartime sexual violence. Finally, looking at the five peace agreements above, it seems that agreements that have included significant gender-sensitive provisions on transitional justice, particularly the two Ugandan agreements and the DPA, have been characterized by a very high level of international involvement along with the presence of the ICC in the country. This international involvement while it may have facilitated the inclusion of model provisions on justice for gender-based violence, both in the cases of Uganda and Sudan has created significant threats to the peace process and resulted in peace agreements that carry very little hope of implementation.

The silences surrounding accountability for wartime sexual violence in peace agreements was put to a number of elite peacemaking practitioners to explore their perspectives on the issue. The resultant interview data provide insight into the problem of addressing justice for sexual violence in peace agreements.

Interviewees generally argued that sexual violence is 'an invisible crime' surrounded by social taboos and stigma and therefore raising it, in a peace-making context, very difficult. Because of the nature of these crimes, often the peacemakers involved in the process are not made fully aware of the prevalence of sexual violence in a particular conflict area. This often leads to the lack of emphasis on crimes of sexual violence in peace agreements.

In relation to accountability, all interviewees agreed that peace agreements should include general commitments to justice for victims of gender-based crimes and particularly exclude blanket amnesties for crimes of an inter-national nature from peace agreements. It was widely recognized that so far this has not been the case. For instance, in a typical response, one interviewee stated, 'serious sexual crimes can no longer be subject to amnesty; that should be officially enshrined in every peace agreement'.[2]

Most interviewees, however, argued that the details of how justice should be carried out and through which mechanisms should be decided later at the post-conflict stage. For instance, the UN Secretary General Special Representative stated, 'with regards to justice you can have a general clause but the actual system itself would be put up at later date'.[3]

The research participants suggested that there are many reasons why provisions on accountability for gender-based violence remain absent from peace agreements. First, some interviewees expressed concerns that insisting on prosecution for wartime crimes of gender-based violence may endanger the peace process. A senior Norwegian diplomat argued that simply by insisting on prosecution you may end up without a peace agreement. The interviewee explained that the Juba peace process of Northern Uganda (discussed above) went into a deadlock over the issue of ICC indictments against the LRA leaders for crimes against humanity.[4]

Similarly, a Swedish diplomat also claimed that addressing issues of accountability for gender-based violence in peace agreements is not possible, arguing:

> Who has the say in the peace agreement? It is the perpetrators. So do you really expect that they will accept and say yes we will be prosecuted, and for sexual vio-lence! I mean they don't do it for sexual violence but they don't do it for murder or torture. So from my point of view in that context, sexual violence is another very, very serious offence but it is not the only one. I think that the point is that you can't have a peace deal until you have the belligerents signing it. You might simply not get your peace deal.[5]

Some of the interviewees argued that people's priorities in conflict situations are generally peace first and then justice and expressed concerns that the current focus on justice within the international community is not helpful for peacemaking. For instance a senior Swedish diplomat stated:

> One of the main problems of peace agreements is, do you insist on justice now ... very often at the expense of having a peace agreement? ... Justice in Chile took twenty-five years, and in Spain it only came out fifty years later or more. Now, we are insisting that justice should be done more or less simultaneously at the peace table and I don't think this is right.[6]

A senior Irish diplomat also underlined the necessity of postponing accountability for wartime sexual violence:

> In most of these countries where you have got high level conflict, the justice system has collapsed [...]. You need a functioning justice system, you need a functioning prison system, you need a functioning policing system and you need a functioning accountability system to make sure that those things will work.[7]

Finally, on the issue of justice and accountability, some of the interviewees questioned the universality of the retributive approach to justice championed by Western countries through the ICC and its suitability for non-Western societies in transition. They argued that the decision of how to deal with the past should be left to the local population and not imposed by the international community during the peace talks. For instance, a senior Irish diplomat said:

> In Northern Uganda, the ICC indicted Kony but nobody or the vast majority of Northern Ugandans don't understand what the ICC is and they see it as a white man court in Europe ... That to the guy, who had suffered in Northern Uganda at the hands of the LRA, means nothing at all. To them they want to see those guys face their jury system or face traditional reconciliation mechanisms.[8]

Interviewees also contended that in a post-conflict context, justice is 'a very complex issue' that cannot be solved through criminal prosecution. A senior Norwegian diplomat compared the enormous financial cost of international tribunals like the ICTR to what has been invested for the surviving victims and argued that this money would have been better spent on health care and reparations for the victims.[9]

REFLECTIONS ON THE UN AGENDA ON WOMEN, PEACE AND SECURITY AND THE QUESTION OF SEXUAL VIOLENCE

More than 10 years have passed since the adoption of Resolution 1325 and accountability for wartime sexual violence continues to be inadequately addressed in peace processes. The marginalization of justice for women in peace agreements while perhaps related to the difficulties in dealing with transitional justice issues at the peace negotiation stage is symptomatic of the limitations of the current agenda on the approach of the women, peace and security agenda to sexual violence and its inability to help victims on the ground.

First of all, the UN agenda is rooted in a very narrow concept of justice focused on criminal prosecution. Both Resolutions 1325 and 1820 are silent on victims' needs of reparation, compensation, restoration and restitution. Resolutions 1325 and 1820 confirm and reiterate concepts of justice developed by international law and in so doing reproduce the limitations of this framework in dealing with crimes against women.

Justice for wartime sexual violence cannot be dissociated from the issues of reparation, restitution and restoration. De Brouwer (2007: 208) argues that because of the physical, psychological, economic and social consequences of sexual violence, female survivors deserve a separate consideration when it comes to reparation. Cahn (2006) suggests adopting the concept of 'social services justice' as the way to ensure justice for women in post-conflict societies. Social services justice according to Cahn (2006: 339) 'provides another dimension to concepts of justice by focusing on the social, economic, medical and psychological components of providing justice to victims'. The current focus of the UN agenda on women, peace and security on accountability, narrowly construed according to scholars and practitioners, is neither helpful for peacemaking nor useful for the victims. For the agenda on women, peace and security to be effective a broader focus on gender justice that takes into considerations women's needs must be adopted.

Another problem with Resolutions 1325 and 1820 is in their use of the concept of rape as a weapon of war. While rape as a weapon of war is widely accepted in the scholastic literature with incontrovertible evidence as to its existence, the strategic rape theory at its root is rather problematic. This theory coupled with the UN's narrow focus on women instead of gender has very serious repercussions not only in terms of access to justice but also in relation to humanitarian protection in times of emergencies. Rape as a weapon of war creates a multi-layered hierarchy of victims. The first hierarchical distinction is between victims of sexual violence as a targeted strategy and victims of random rape, making access to justice for victims of equally vicious attacks being dependent on the perpetrators' intent. The second hierarchy is between victims of sexual violence and those affected by other forms of violence. For instance, Resolution 1820 in paragraph 3 calls for the 'evacuation of women and children under imminent threat of sexual violence to safety' (United Nations Security Council 2008: 3). But what about women facing imminent threats from non-sexual wartime violence, such as a bomb attack, or men at risk of sexual violence? The final layer within this hierarchy is between men and women. Making gender-based violence synonymous with sexual violence against women clearly obscures all other types of violations and the multiple identities of victims and perpetrators. This hierarchical stratification of victims, in the context of peace and security, may have detrimental consequences in terms of civilian protection (Carpenter 2005; Otto 2009). For instance, while the international community for many years has been focused on violence against women in Afghanistan, the traditional practice of 'Bacha Bazi' or 'Boy Play' which involves the sexual exploitation and enslavement of young boys was only recently uncovered (Quraishi 2010).

While the representation of rape as a weapon of war might have been necessary to convince the Security Council to treat it seriously, arguably, this militaristic and masculinized perception of rape only leads to equally masculinized and militaristic responses. Resolutions 1325 and 1820 fail to acknowledge the link between violence and inequality that increases the vulnerability of certain groups to being victims of violence. The UN agenda is focused on accountability, military discipline and prosecutions, but strategies that empower the victims are marginalized and silenced. The agenda is consequently unable to challenge or transform the power structures underpinning the violence and its continuation. Rape within the agenda on women, peace and security becomes a masculine problem that can only be solved through the masculine solutions of military discipline or threat of punishment from a masculinized state (Otto 2009).

Finally, the UN resolutions on women, peace and security arguably represent additional instruments that reinforce the supremacy of the Security Council and the authority of its nation states. Resolution 1325 gives legitimacy to Western countries to intervene in the name of women in peace processes around the world and dictate the form of justice that they deem acceptable for the local population. These interventions are often detrimental to peace-building efforts and generally detached from the daily realities of women victims (Glasius 2009). Ni Aolain (2009: 1058) argues that 'once entangled with a transitional society, the international community of decision-makers who arrive after a conflict on a mission of "good will" play a complex role in compounding gender inequality and unaccountability'. Resolution 1820 further empowers the Security Council to take actions and impose sanctions on countries that perpetrate sexual violence. However, as often is the tradition with the Security Council, the measures stipulated by the UN agenda are in essence only meant to apply outside the core nation states of the international order. Because of the dynamics of the Security Council such measures are not only incapable of providing redress to victims, but they may also have serious implications for countries in conflict and increase the vulnerability of the civilian population. Haskell (2009), writing on justice for women victims of rape through the Security Council and international law, warns that we should not be naïve about the intention of the grand narrative of international law since 'the very concepts that we so often hold up to battle "injustice" [are actually] a postscript to colonialism, tainted with its imagination and harnessed by its imperialist relationships of power' (Haskell 2009: 69–83).

As such, we have to be careful that the grand project of dispensing justice for women victims does not become a political cover-up for interventionist policies that have nothing to do with women's wellbeing.

CONCLUSION

A decade after the adoption of Resolution 1325, women continue to suffer at the hands of their abusers in conflict and post-conflict societies and their quest for justice and accountability remains marginalized. While the attempts made by the UN Security Council to address the issue within the agenda on women, peace and security are welcomed, the Council's choice of strategy and framework are, to say the least, questionable. The agenda endorses the international criminal law hierarchy between crimes of 'international nature' and other crimes and as such continues to restrict the victim's right to justice for rape irrelevant of the circumstances in which it was committed. The agenda adopts a narrow concept of justice focused on sanctions and prosecutions, but fails to envisage strategies that respond to victims' needs. The UN agenda also adopts a narrow conception of sexual violence as a weapon used to wage war, but ignores the multiple causal factors behind rape, the complex identities of its victims and its continuation in the aftermath of conflicts. As such, the UN agenda remains trapped in a conservative and masculinized worldview that renders it incapable of helping the majority of victims in war-torn societies. The key argument of this article is that combating impunity for sexual violence requires broadening the way we think about accountability and drawing on non-legal remedies that deliver real justice for victims. It also requires looking much more broadly at sexual violence in conflicts and its causes and consequences. The project of ending impunity can neither be dissociated from the broader agenda of achieving gender equality nor from the aim of ending militarism and wars in the first place.

Notes
1   The full texts of these agreements are available on the UN peacemaker website, which requires a subscription to enter.

2   Senior Irish diplomat, interview with the author, June 2009.
3   UN Secretary General Special Representative, interview with the author, October 2009.
4   Senior Norwegian diplomat, interview with the author, July 2009.
5   Senior Swedish diplomat, interview with the author, September 2009.
6   Senior Swedish diplomat, interview with the author, September 2009.
7   Senior Irish diplomat, interview with the author, June 2009.
8   Senior Irish diplomat, interview with the author, September 2009.
9   Senior Norwegian diplomat, interview with the author, July 2009.

Acknowledgements

I thank Nicola Pratt, Sophie Richter-Devroe, Carmel Roulston, Ian Somerville and the two anonymous reviewers for their helpful comments on previous drafts.

References

Apreotesei, A. I. 2009. 'The International Court at Work: The First Cases and Situations', *Eyes on the ICC* 5 (1): 1–22.

Apuuli, P. K. 2008. 'The ICC's Possible Deferral of the LRA case to Uganda', *Journal of International Criminal Justice* 6 (4): 801–13.

Askin, K. D. 1999. 'Sexual Violence in Decisions and Indictments of the Yugoslav and Rwandan Tribunals: Current Status', *American Journal of International Law* 93 (1): 97–123.

Askin, K. D. 2003. 'Prosecuting War Time Rape and Other Gender-related Crimes under International Law: Extraordinary Advances, Enduring Obstacles', *Berkeley Journal of International Law* 21 (1): 288–349.

Bell, C. 2008. *On the Law of Peace, Peace Agreements and the Lex Pacificatoria.* New York: Oxford University Press.

Beyani, C. 2007. 'Introductory Note on the Pact on Security, Stability and Development in the Great Lakes Region', *International Legal Materials* 46 (2): 173–5.

Borer, T. A. 2009. 'Gendered War and Gendered Peace: Truth Commissions and Post-conflict Gender Violence: Lessons from South Africa', *Violence Against Women* 15 (10): 1169–93.

Buss, D. E. 2009. 'Rethinking Rape as a Weapon of War', *Feminist Legal Studies* 17 (2): 145–63.

Cahn, N. R. 2005. 'Beyond Retribution: Responding to War Crimes of Sexual Violence', *Stanford Journal of Civil Rights & Civil Liberties* 1 (1): 217–70.

Cahn, N. R. 2006. 'Women in Post-conflict Reconstruction: Dilemmas and Directions', *William & Mary Journal of Women and the Law* 12 (1): 335–76.

Campanaro, J. 2001. 'Women War and International Law: The Historical Treatment of Gender-based War Crimes', *Georgetown Law Journal* 89 (1): 2557–70.

Carpenter, C. 2005. '"Women, Children and Other Vulnerable groups" Gender, Strategic Frames and the Protection of Civilians as a Transnational Issue', *International Studies Quarterly* 49 (2): 295–334.

Chinkin, C. 2002. 'Gender, Human Rights and Peace Agreements', *Ohio State Journal on Dispute Resolution* 18 (3): 267–886.

Cook, S. 2009. 'Security Council Resolution 1820: On Militarism, Flashlights, Raincoats, and Rooms with Doors. A Political Perspective on Where it Came from and What it Adds', *Emory International Law Review* 23 (1): 125–40.

Davis, L. and Hayner, P. 2009. *Difficult Peace, Limited Justice: Ten Years of Peacemaking in the DRC*. New York: International Center for Transitional Justice.

De Brouwer, A. M. 2005. *Supranational Prosecution of Gender Based Violence: The ICC and the Practice of the ICTY and the ICTR*. Antwerp: Intersentia.

De Brouwer, A. M. 2007. 'Reparation to Victims of Sexual Violence: Possibilities at the International Criminal Court and at the Trust Fund for Victims and their Families', *Leiden Journal of International Law* 20 (1): 207–37.

Glasius, M. 2009. 'What is Global Justice and Who Decides? Civil Society and Victim Responses to the International Criminal Court's First Investigations', *Human Rights Quarterly* 31 (2): 496–520.

Hanlon, K. 2006. 'Peace or Justice: Now that Peace is Being Negotiated in Uganda, Will the ICC Still pursue Justice?', *Tulsa Journal of Comparative and International Law* 14 (1): 295–338.

Haskell, J. D. 2009. 'The Complicity and Limits of International Law in Armed Conflict Rape', *Boston College Third World Law Journal* 29 (1): 35–84.

Henry, N. 2010. 'The Impossibility of Bearing Witness: Wartime Rape and the Promise of Justice', *Violence Against Women* 16 (10): 1098–119.

Höglund, A. T. 2003. 'Justice for Women in War? Feminist Ethics and Human Rights', *Feminist Theology* 11 (3): 346–61.

Jurdi, N. 2010. 'The Prosecutorial Interpretation of the Complementarity Principle: Does It Really Contribute to Ending Impunity on the National Level?', *International Criminal Law Review* 10 (1): 73–96.

Kastner, P. 2007. 'The ICC in Darfur – Savior or Spoiler?', *ISLA Journal of International & Comparative Law* 14 (1): 145–88.

McGinn, T. 2000. 'Reproductive Health of War-Affected Populations: What Do We Know?', *International Family Planning Perspective* 26 (4): 174–80.

Meger, S. 2010. 'Rape of the Congo: Understanding Sexual Violence in the Conflict in the Democratic Republic of Congo', *Journal of Contemporary African Studies* 28 (2): 119–35.

Melandri, M. 2009. 'Gender and Reconciliation in Post-conflict Societies: The Dilemmas of Responding to Large-scale Sexual Violence', *International Public Policy Review* 5 (1): 4–27.

Mertus, J. 2004. 'Shouting from the Bottom of the Well, the Impact of International Trials for Wartime Rape on Women's Agency', *International Feminist Journal of Politics* 6 (4): 110–28.

Nathan, L. 2006. 'No Ownership, No Peace: The Darfur Peace Agreement', *LSE Crisis States Working Papers* 2 (5): 1–20.

Ni Aolain, F. 2009. 'Women, Security and the Patriarchy on Internationalized Transitional Justice', *Human Rights Quarterly* 31 (1): 1055–85.

Nowrojee, B. 2005. 'Making the Invisible War Crime Visible: Post Conflict Justice for Sierra Leone Rape Victims', *Harvard Human Rights Law Journal* 18 (1): 86–105.

Okello, M. C. and Hovil, L 2007. 'Confronting the Reality of Gender-based Violence in Northern Uganda', *The International Journal of Transitional Justice* 1 (1): 1–11.

Otto, D. 2009. 'The Exile of Inclusion: Reflections on Gender Issues in International Law over the Last Decade', *Melbourne Journal of International Law* 10 (1): 11–26.

Quraishi, N. 2010. 'Frontline: The Dancing Boys of Afghanistan'. Available at http://www.pbs.org/wgbh/pages/frontline/dancingboys/ (accessed 2 August 2010).

Ross, F. C. 2003. 'On having a Voice and Being Heard: Some After-effects of Testifying before the South African Truth and Reconciliation Commission', *Anthropological Theory* 3 (3): 325–41.

Sarantakos, S. 2005. *Social Research*. Hampshire: Palgrave Macmillan.

Schneider, M. D. 2007. 'About Women, War and Darfur: The Quest Continuing for Gender Violence Justice', *North Dakota Law Review* 83 (1): 915–96.

United Nations Department of Political Affairs (UNDPA). 2006. 'UN Peacemaker'. Available at http://peacemaker.unlb.org/index1.php (accessed 17 June 2011).

United Nations Security Council. 2000a. 'Women and Peace and Security'. A/55/S/PV.4208. Available at http://daccess-dds-ny.un.org/doc/UNDOC/PRO/N00/705/89/PDF/N0070589.pdf?OpenElement (accessed 17 June 2011).

United Nations Security Council. 2000b. 'Security Council Resolution 1325 on Women, Peace and Security'. S/RES/1325. Available at http://daccess-dds-ny.un.org/doc/UNDOC/GEN/N00/720/18/PDF/N0072018.pdf?OpenElement (accessed 17 June 2011).

United Nations Security Council. 2004. 'Report of the Secretary General on the Rule of Law and Transitional Justice in Conflict and Post-conflict Societies'. S/2004/616. Available at http://daccess-dds-ny.un.org/doc/UNDOC/GEN/N04/395/29/PDF/N0439529.pdf?OpenElement (accessed 17 June 2011).

United Nations Security Council. 2008. 'Security Council Resolution 1820 on Women, Peace and Security'. S/RES/1820. Available at http://daccess-dds-ny.un.org/doc/UNDOC/GEN/N08/391/44/PDF/N0839144.pdf?OpenElement (accessed 17 June 2011).

Configurations of Post-Conflict: Impacts of Representations of Conflict and Post-Conflict upon the (Political) Translations of Gender Security within UNSCR 1325

LAURA McLEOD
University of Manchester, UK

Abstract

UNSCR 1325 is a Security Council Resolution designed to operate in post-conflict contexts. 'Post-conflict' is a discourse with contested temporal and spatial aspects, raising questions about how different perspectives towards 'post-conflict' has affected interpretations of UNSCR 1325 on the ground. Given the contestability of 'post-conflict', surprisingly little research has focused upon how what is identified as the 'post-conflict problem' shapes responses to UNSCR 1325. To address this gap, I contrast configurations of 'post-conflict' within three different initiatives in Serbia that have drawn upon UNSCR 1325. The constructions of 'post-conflict' are understood through an analytical strategy concerned with the representation of conflict and post-conflict reconstruction within each initiative. Making explicit antagonisms at the heart of 'post-conflict' demonstrates how the logic of gender security as it relates to UNSCR 1325 is shaped by the specific problematization of 'post-conflict'. This article outlines new empirical research on the utilization of UNSCR 1325 within three different political contexts in Serbia to assert the importance of realizing the contestability of 'post-conflict' contexts in shaping how we might respond to UNSCR 1325, and indeed, any international policy or ambition intended as a response to post-conflict situations.

INTRODUCTION

United Nations Security Council Resolution 1325 (UNSCR 1325) on Women, Peace and Security is a resolution primarily designed to deal with gender matters in post-conflict situations. Yet, 'post-conflict' is a discourse with contested temporal and spatial aspects: not least because lines between conflict and post-conflict can be fuzzy. How we understand and position these lines reflect a particular representation of conflict and post-conflict. This is not to say that a conflict did not occur, but rather, that 'we have thought the specific configuration of the conflict into existence' (Zalewski 2006: 481). Conflict, and post-conflict, is a state of existence crafted in particular highly politicized ways, where certain problems are thrown into focus and others downplayed (Vaughan-Williams 2006). This article offers a reflection upon how configurations and problematizations of 'post-conflict' have affected interpretations of gender security in relation to UNSCR 1325.

The notion of 'gender security' relies upon links being made between discourses of security and discourses of gender. Conceptualizations of both gender and security rest upon a particular set of logics (Shepherd 2010: 5, 2008: 294). I understand logics as 'the ways in which various concepts are organized within specific discourses' (Shepherd 2008: 294). That is, the specific logic of 'gender security' represented is reliant upon how concepts – including gender and/or security – are arranged, as well as the 'the assumptions that inform [these representations], and the policy prescriptions that issue from them' (Shepherd 2008: 294). There is no single logic of what 'gender security' might look like, but each vision of gender security is underpinned by a set of political considerations governing policy choices made. The following analysis highlights different logics of gender security represented in programmes and initiatives aiming to implement or utilize UNSCR 1325.

To investigate how logics of gender security are connected to configurations of 'post-conflict', this article will examine initiatives in Serbia that claim to incorporate, implement or respond to UNSCR 1325. The first part outlines Serbia's problematic relationship to 'post-conflict' to provide the necessary context for analysis. In the second part, attention will turn to an examination of three different sites claiming political authority over UNSCR 1325 in Serbia. First, a programme with its origins within a UN agency; second, a project operated by a grassroots NGO; and finally, a proposed National Action Plan (NAP) for the implementation of UNSCR 1325, co-ordinated by a government department. These contrasting case studies are based upon research carried out in Serbia during 2008 and 2009. The analytical centre is a document outlining the action, and I draw out various representations of conflict and post-conflict within the initiative. These documents are contextualized by interviews, policy reports, publicized responses and website sources. By contrasting three initiatives in Serbia that in some way respond to UNSCR 1325, it is clear that very different logics of gender security are represented. This article concludes by evaluating the case studies to reveal how antagonisms at the heart of discourses about 'post-conflict' and 'gender security' shape the political translation of UNSCR 1325.

PROBLEMATIZING POST-CONFLICT

Serbia has a problematic association with conflict, a difficulty spilling over into the post-conflict period. These difficulties enable space for various representations of conflict and post-conflict to be configured. Critically, 'post-conflict' is a representation that can be crafted in various ways, shaping political responses to UNSCR 1325. This section explores how post-conflict is represented and problematized in Serbia.

Dominant perceptions of post-conflict refer to a period when combatants are no longer engaging in 'official' war, accompanied by an apparent cessation of violence. However, these definitions belie the difficulties of pinpointing precisely when a conflict period becomes a post-conflict period. For many feminists, post-conflict periods are characterized by violence, insecurity and militarization, even where official peace treaties have been signed (Enloe 1993, 2010: 211–25; Cockburn and Zarkov 2002; Handrahan 2004: 430–36). 'Post-conflict' can also be tricky to define spatially, a point that is particularly pertinent to Serbia. In the case of Serbia, the state was not officially at war with another state, and little war-related fighting took place within the borders of Serbia (not including Kosovo). And yet, the Serbian state experienced many social, economic and political problems associated with war. Furthermore, Serbia is perceived as a key perpetrator of the violence that took place in ex-Yugoslavia during the 1990s. This article highlights how an understanding of a moment or area as 'post-conflict' reflects particular temporal and spatial assumptions.

These complexities about post-conflict take on unique characteristics where Serbia is concerned, in part because of Serbia's complex relationship to the conflicts of the 1990s. Wars in Croatia, Bosnia-Herzegovina and Kosovo attracted much international coverage as the Yugoslavian state disintegrated in conflicts, featuring systematic rape, genocide and ethnic hatred. For Serbia, the 1990s were characterized by heavy political repression under the dictatorship of Slobodan Milošević, who many point to as the main protagonist of Serb nationalism underpinning the wars. Perspectives about the connections between the Serbian state and the extent of Serbian responsibility for ethnic violence committed during the conflicts of the 1990s continue to shape Serbian politics (Obradović-Wochnik 2009). Thus, for some, Serbia's present post-conflict concern is to accept responsibility for the crimes committed by the Serbian state during the 1990s.

In addition, Serbia faced a number of social and economic problems that can be related to war and conflict. Many in Serbia experienced the wars through friends or family who became refugees or soldiers (Obradović-Wochnik 2009: 71). During the 1990s, nationalized media coverage of the wars was relentless (Obradović-Wochnik 2009: 62), and a combination of international economic sanctions, military spending and hyperinflation (1993–4) had a devastating economic impact upon many individuals. Kosovo remained a site of intense nationalism, resulting in fundamental human rights violations attributed to Milošević's pro-Serb policies. In response to atrocities in Kosovo, NATO countries took the step of bombing much of the infrastructure in Serbia and Kosovo between March and May 1999, a strategy that continues to cause resentment in Serbia today.

These events outlined in the previous paragraphs place Serbia in a problematic and complex location in relation to the wars in the region during the 1990s. The 'wartime' story of the Serbian state is replete with complexities and confusions: Serbia is simultaneously inside, outside and at the margins of the wars in the region. Unsurprisingly, these tensions spill over into the 'post-conflict' period, reflecting a specific image of the type and extent of the post-conflict problem that exists, or does not exist.

The spatial and temporal assumptions that make, or do not make, Serbia a 'post-conflict zone' matter because it affects how political actors – including international institutions, NGOs and government bodies – present policy responses, apply for funding, or, in the case of international institutions, their operational mandates. The very contestability of the Serbian state's trajectory to war, conflict and war-related violences make Serbia an intriguing case study for how 'post-conflict' is conceptualized, and how these conceptualizations have affected political translations of UNSCR 1325. How actors imagine Serbia's relationship to the wars of the 1990s identify very different post-conflict problems to be addressed. That is; 'different solutions result from a specific form of problematization' (Foucault, cited in Glynos and Howarth 2007: 167). In essence, the problems identified by actors in Serbia's post-conflict present – influenced by perceptions of the past and hopes for the future – shape responses to UNSCR 1325.

As Cockburn and Zarkov (2002) urge us, when considering 'a society affected by war', we 'should not hear this as referring only to a country that has participated in the fighting, or on whose territory the war was fought' (p. 9). Attention should be paid to understanding how actors think about, relate to, and perceive, conflict, and post-conflict. In this article, the analytical strategy utilized is concerned with the representation of conflict and post-conflict. These representations are embedded in discourses about the past conflict, perceived problems in the post-conflict present, and hopes for future post-war reconstruction. Pasts, presents and futures of conflict and post-conflict integrate to craft a particular image of 'post-conflict', shaping notions about how UNSCR 1325 could be implemented in Serbia.

SITES CLAIMING POLITICAL AUTHORITY OVER UNSCR 1325

This section investigates three different initiatives responding in some way to UNSCR 1325, highlighting how the resolution is framed within various measures designed as responses to post-conflict gender security concerns in Serbia.[1] The analysis pivots upon appreciating the representations of 'post-conflict' within each initiative, then seeks to grasp the specific vision of 'gender security' within each programme. By drawing upon the dominant discursive representations of gender security and post-conflict, I make explicit how the political interpretation of 'gender security' within UNSCR 1325 depends upon how 'post-conflict' is thought about.

The UN System

The first site of claimed political authority over UNSCR 1325 examined in this article relates to the UN system in Serbia. The 'intervention' of UNSCR 1325 into the functioning of the UN was the intended aim of the resolution: parts of the document call for actions to be taken by actors within the UN system (Cohn 2008: 189). The primary 'intervention' that UNSCR 1325 calls for is the place of women's rights, gender concerns and gender mainstreaming within post-conflict processes (Cohn 2008: 189). The stated aim is to develop 'effective institutional arrangements' that guarantee female participation in peace processes to improve the ability of the UN in achieving its primary aim of maintaining international peace and security (Hudson 2010: 44–7). More critically, UNSCR 1325 can be seen as one articulation of what is represented as a growing concern within the UN system about global gender mainstreaming and gender security.

With the existence of UNSCR 1325, the UN system in post-conflict zones claimed to include gender security considerations. For instance, the Department of Peacekeeping Operations (DPKO) has been successful in increasing women's participation and representation within DPKO efforts in a number of post-conflict zones since 2000 (Hudson 2010: 54–60). The United Nations Development Programme (UNDP) has also been proactive in utilizing the gender security framework of UNSCR 1325 within its Crisis Prevention and Recovery programme (BCPR).[2] Echoing much of the gender security language within UNSCR 1325, the BCPR issued an 'Eight Point Agenda' (8PA) for 'practical, positive outcomes for girls and women in crises' (BCPR 2006). Central to the achievement of the 8PA is 'full implementation' of UNSCR 1325 (BCPR 2006). The 8PA was issued to all UNDP agencies in early 2007, along with the recommendation that 10–15 per cent of the budget was dedicated to gender issues.[3] It can be said that UNSCR 1325 (re)produced a framework of concerns about women and security that is beginning to trickle across parts of the UN system.

One agency partially supported and mandated by the UNDP is SEESAC.[4] The primary mission of SEESAC is to develop the capacity to 'control and reduce the proliferation and misuse of SALWs, and thus contribute to enhanced stability, security and development in South Eastern and Eastern Europe' (SEESAC n.d.). The agency was established as a response to a perceived post-conflict problem in South-Eastern Europe: that of the proliferation of small arms during and after the wars. In 2007, following the recommendations made in the 8PA, funds were made available to carry out work connecting gender and small arms. A gender strategy was publicized in June 2007, reasserting SEESAC's commitment to engaging with UNSCR 1325 (SEESAC 2007). Following the development of a gender strategy, a report titled *Firearms Possession and Domestic Violence in the Western Balkans: A Comparative Study of Legislation and Implementation Mechanisms* was commissioned (Dokmanović 2008). While this action is not a direct response to UNSCR 1325 per se, it is a response to the gender and security frameworks articulated in the resolution. That is, UNSCR 1325 is a critical part of the discursive terrain encouraging the main-streaming of gender security concerns within the UN system in post-conflict zones.

The SEESAC report made a connection between the (ab)use of SALW in domestic violence and the easy access to SALW in the post-conflict era. The representation of conflict and post-conflict within the report stresses an image of violence and disorder continuing long after the conflict has ended. This depiction is highlighted in the opening paragraph of the report, which states that:

> The countries of the Western Balkans face high levels of violence, crime and human insecurity as a legacy of recent conflicts, political turbulence and econ-omic crises. The war in the former Yugoslavia increased the proliferation and easy availability of small arms and light weapons ... contributing to a rise in violent behaviour not only in the public space, but also within the family. (Dokmanović 2008: i)

Post-conflict is represented as a period of continued violence and insecurity as a result of conflict. The increase of SALW (ab)use in domestic violence is attributed to the instability caused by the consequences of conflict. It is stressed that the 'countries of the Western Balkans' have all experienced 'violence, crime and human insecurity'. In other words, Serbia is not distinguished as having a *different* post-conflict problem in the context of SALW compared with other countries in the region. Serbia's post-conflict problematization represented in the SEESAC report emphasizes violence and insecurity following a conflict.

Furthermore, the post-conflict violence and insecurity is represented as a problem that can be resolved. The report insists that 'responses to domestic vio-lence must address the issue of SALW control in policies, strategies and measures aimed at prevention and protection of victims' (Dokmanović 2008: i). SALW concerns are represented as especially relevant to post-conflict situations, where the problem is best addressed by preventive and legislative measures carried out by governments and civil societies (Dokmanović 2008: i–ii, 31–46). The envisaged solution for future post-conflict reconstruction and development rests upon a perception that 'victims' of the post-conflict problem require legal solutions and targeted help and support.

Curiously, while the report reproduces assumptions that the victims are women, the victimized subject is rarely explicitly stated as a woman. The intricacies of 'gender' are flagged up (Dokmanović 2008: 3–5), but inscriptions of a biologically female victimized subject is present within the subtext of the document. For example, the image on the cover of the report depicts a young woman holding a baby, with a man in the background cleaning a gun. This image is reflective of the gender assumption within the initiative, where gender is synonymous with women (Carver 1996). This in itself is not surprising: scholars have long recognized that international organizations tend to equate gender with women. However, the key actors involved in the production of the report were aware of the complexities of gender.[5] Why did they choose to represent a gender logic drawing upon portrayals of women as victims of violence and insecurity following a conflict?

In part, this is because enduring gender essentialisms are (often accidently) drawn upon. When asked why SEESAC had chosen to focus on domestic violence in their attempts to include gender concerns in their work, the response was that,

> It's difficult in heavy work like destruction and stop power management to include gender, so of course we would focus on the softer side of awareness and violence prevention.[6]

Within this response, there is an implicit conflation of gender with women, who apparently hold 'softer' and more peaceable qualities: a logic which not only constrains images of victimhood, but also the possibilities of introducing a gender perspective to processes normally thought of as gender-neutral, like weapons destruction. Additionally, the focus upon women throughout the SEESAC report reinforces perceptions that considering women will significantly increase peace and security: a gender perspective echoing and supporting the aims of the UN system. As highlighted earlier, UNSCR 1325 is thought of as a contribution to the central ambition of the UN system to secure international peace and security. Within the SEESAC initiative, UNSCR 1325 is referred to as part of a range of UN documents mandating the report and subsequent actions. Making the connection between SALW and domestic violence was a programme conceived as a means of considering gender: it was a response to the gender-inclusion demands of the 8PA and the gender security framework of UNSCR 1325. Working from a perspective that Serbia's post-conflict problem is increased violence and security, where victims need to be specifically protected, SEESAC represented a logic of gender security suggesting that women (because gender means women) require specific measures for their security.

Within the SEESAC initiative, UNSCR 1325 is politically translated as a resolution designed to protect women, producing a useful interpretation of 'gender security' for some actors. The report was designed as a capacity-building initiative, supporting concrete research to legitimize future actions.[7]

For some feminist civil society actors in Serbia, the opportunities offered by SEESAC during 2008 opened the way for a bigger campaign on the connections between domestic violence and SALW. A previous attempt to raise the same issue during 1999 was not pursued because of a lack of resources.[8] Since the publication of the report, feminist civil society actors have sought to raise awareness of the connections between SALW (ab)use and domestic violence, campaigning for legislative changes to the Criminal Code of Serbia to tighten gun ownership laws.[9] While interpretations of 'post-conflict' and 'gender security' have operated to craft a representation of UNSCR 1325 as a resolution designed to protect vulnerable women, this political translation of the resolution has opened up opportunities for political action.

Women's and Feminist Organizations

While UNSCR 1325 is a document that primarily aims to alter the practice of the UN's peacekeeping processes, many feminist and women's non-governmental organizations (NGOs) have enthusiastically seized upon the opportunities opened up by invoking UNSCR 1325 (Cohn 2004, 2008: 190–1). This is unsurprising given that it was the international women's movement that pushed for the formulation of a Security Council resolution on women and security in post-conflict contexts (Hill et al. 2003). The second site of claimed political authority over UNSCR 1325 in Serbia investigated in this article places the spotlight upon Women in Black, one Serbian feminist antiwar initiative. The Women in Black network in Serbia is part of a transnational complex of pacifist organizations sharing values about feminism, antimilitarism, peace and peaceful protest (Cockburn 2007: 51–3, 79–105). Each Women in the Black group highlights localized concerns, and the Serbian group is no exception: one of its core values remains an insistence upon responsibility.

The issue of political responsibility remains a sensitive and controversial social and political topic in Serbia (Duhaček 2006; Fridman 2006; Obradović-Wochnik 2009). The concept of responsibility derives from debates in post-World War II Germany about how to manage the legacy of the Holocaust (Duhaček 2006: 207–12). Within the Serbian context, the central question in relation to political responsibility is the extent to which Serbian state and society is responsible for the war crimes committed during the 1990s. These war crimes include the massacre at Srebrenica, where at least 7,000 Bosnian Muslim men and boys were executed after the Srebrenica enclave, in northern Bosnia, fell to Bosnian Serb forces in July 1995. For Women in Black, political responsibility refers to the perspective that in the post-war, post-Milošević era, Serbian institutions and society needs to resist the denial of war crimes committed in the name of Serbia during the 1990s and deal with militarized violence that remains embedded in society (Zajović 2007: 31–8). Accepting responsibility and facing the past is a necessary path to take for Serbia to successfully achieve post-conflict reconstruction and reconciliation (Zajović

2007). Women in Black have connected their post-conflict critiques of the Serbian state to their visions for future reconstruction, utilizing UNSCR 1325 to legitimize and support their views.

Women in Black have invoked UNSCR 1325 in many ways (Women in Black 2010: 10–14). I focus upon their advocacy campaigns, reasserting perspectives about political responsibility, which the group sees as a necessary achievement for successful post-conflict transformation. Since 2005, Women in Black has presented to the Serbian Parliament a Draft Resolution outlining how they think UNSCR 1325 could be implemented in Serbia. Reverberating through the Draft Resolution is an emphasis upon making the social and institutional changes that would signal a significant move towards accepting political responsibility. For Women in Black, lasting and meaningful peace and security can only be achieved by giving 'special attention to social justice and the protection of victims of the previous period marked by war and war profiteers' (Women in Black 2007: 188). The Draft Resolution lists specific and localized recommendations that would establish the principle of political responsibility in Serbia. These recommendations include revoking a law providing for financial assistance to war criminals indicted by The Hague,[10] and criminalizing the denial of war crimes committed during the 1990s, including the genocide in Srebrenica. Women in Black insist that to fully implement UNSCR 1325 in Serbia, issues surrounding the political responsibility project need to be addressed.

The emphasis upon political responsibility within the Draft Resolution arises out of the critique of militarism at the heart of Women in Black's ideology. For Women in Black, UNSCR 1325 has the potential to be used as 'a tool for developing a new kind of security'.[11] For many feminist-pacifists, UNSCR 1325 is problematic as the resolution itself does not challenge the existing structures and assumptions of the war system (Cockburn 2007: 147–52; Cohn 2008: 194–200). However, this does not limit the possibility of UNSCR 1325 being used to support activism condemning the war system or the processes of militarization that antiwar activists criticize. For Women in Black, militarism, and associated processes, fosters insecurity (Zajović 2007: 49). The evasion of the post-conflict political responsibility agenda in Serbia is viewed as a manifestation of militarism, and there are 'security risks [in] not confronting the criminal past' (Women in Black 2010: 3). These perspectives arise out of a feminist standpoint understanding that 'women close to militarization and war are observant of cultures . . . in societies before, in and after conflicts' (Cockburn 2010: 149). Women in Black observed that the dominant culture of militarism in Serbia is rendered more problematic by the evasion of political responsibility, an attitude prevalent within institutions and society. The group uses UNSCR 1325 as a means of promoting their 'new kind of security', which challenges the dominance of militarism.[12]

The gender logics underpinning Women in Black's response to UNSCR 1325 draws upon an explicitly feminist standpoint analysis of war, which understands conflict as a consequence of deeper problems in society. Hence, post-conflict security requires transformation of social attitudes to enable constructive change and growth (Höglund and Kovacs 2010: 372). Embedded in this notion of post-conflict transformation, Höglund and Kovacs (2010) point out, is 'a strong sense of justice ... [where] social and legal justice is not only a precondition for peace, but the essence of the peace concept' (p. 373). Thus, for Women in Black, security is best achieved through altering dominant social values in contemporary Serbian society: values produced by and productive of the nationalist civil war. These gender security logics emphasize 'an idea of security that is people-centred and process-orientated', typical of much women's activism surrounding women, peace and security frameworks and actions (Hudson 2010: 37). Through a feminist standpoint perspective about war and militarism, Women in Black see the achievement of gender security through a reconceptualization of security, shifting the object to be secured away from the liberal-democratic state and highlighting conditions for long-term reconciliation and transformation.

The co-ordinator of Women in Black, Stasa Zajović, believes that UNSCR 1325 is useful because the resolution is a language accepted by formal political institutions.[13] By reinterpreting UNSCR 1325 and formulating a critical feminist conceptualization of security, Women in Black have utilized the resolution to provide an element of international legitimacy to support visions of how future gender security can be achieved. The push for a more critical conceptualization of security draws upon a gender logic insisting that gender security can be achieved through long-term reconciliation programmes, inspired by the perspective that the post-conflict problem is embedded in the cultural norms of society. To challenge these cultures of violence and militarism that affect women, UNSCR 1325 is politically translated as a resolution with the potential to support and legitimize a critical reconceptualization of security.

State Institutions

Since 2002, the Security Council has encouraged member states to develop NAPs for the implementation of UNSCR 1325 as a means of developing strategies, goals and timetables for member states to integrate gender perspectives in all peacekeeping and post-conflict processes (Gumru and Fritz 2009: 214). UNSCR 1889 (October 2009) reinforces the Security Council's support for the creation of NAPs to implement UNSCR 1325. Gumru and Fritz (2009) argue that NAPs 'can be a way of co-ordinating existing initiatives (local, national and international) and adding ones to deal with identified gaps' (p. 214). The final site of claimed political authority investigated in this article concentrates upon the processes of making recommendations towards a NAP implementing UNSCR 1325 in Serbia.

A NAP was accepted by the Serbian Parliament in December 2010.[14] Prior to this, a series of consultations took place. The analysis in this article is based upon a report produced by working groups co-ordinated by the BFPE and the Ministry of Defence in Serbia to formulate recommendations for a draft NAP (Belgrade Fund for Political Excellence (BFPE) 2010). BFPE is an NGO operating training programmes for key social and political actors to support development of skills for the 'democratic transformation of society and participation in European and Euro-Atlantic structures' (Belgrade Fund for Political Excellence (BFPE) n.d.). Between May – November 2009, the BFPE and the Serbian Ministry of Defence convened four working groups, including politicians, civil society actors and civil servants (Belgrade Fund for Political Excellence (BFPE) 2009: 2). These groups dealt with different elements of the proposed draft NAP: the role of women in decision-making processes, the role of women in conflict and post-conflict situations, legal protection of women and human security, and gender issues in the Serbian armed forces (BFPE 2010: 10 – 11). A set of proposals and recommendations for the Serbian NAP was publically presented for discussion during March 2010.[15] Investigating the early stages of negotiations towards a NAP reveals the aspirations actors have for the NAP. Critically, these aspirations are a product and productive of how Serbia's relationship to 'post-conflict' is thought about, shaping subsequent interpretations of UNSCR 1325.

The recommendations presented embody multiple visions of post-conflict, in part because the draft was made available to several voices in the public consultation. However, very little of the document focuses upon 'Serbia as a post-conflict country undergoing transition' (BFPE 2010: 7); although issues related to refugees and internally displaced persons (IDPs) are highlighted as post-conflict problems. Rather, the dominant representation of Serbia's relationship to conflict and post-conflict emphasizes Serbia's future participation as part of external peacekeeping forces. Hence, the post-conflict problem relates to Serbia's external operations. This is a positioning of Serbia as a country with a part to play on the world stage and it is revealing that a document designed to promote gender equality uses the opportunity to do this. Passing a NAP is viewed as a way of confirming 'that Serbia, as a UN member country, wants to contribute actively to the processes of peacebuilding, stability and security' (BFPE 2010: 6). Within the recommendations, the need for international legitimacy is inscribed, suggesting a desire to escape connotations with a post-conflict past. UNSCR 1325 is used as a way to 'show' the world that Serbia is a progressive and forward-thinking state that has dealt with the bulk of problems caused by the conflicts of the 1990s.

The perception that formulating a NAP to implement UNSCR 1325 is a progressive move is reinforced by Ministry of Defence press releases, which reassert with pride that Serbia is 'the first country in the region which is on the verge of adopting the resolution' (Ministry of Defence 2010). The notion that enthusiasm for UNSCR 1325 is partly a public relations exercise to demonstrate that Serbia is undergoing a successful democratic transition was expressed by some involved in the NAP process. One person said:

> They [the Ministry of Defence] got interested in representing women in security institutions primarily because it is very easy to communicate this change to ordinary people because you see women instead of men.[16]

It is commendable that Serbia is adopting a NAP to implement UNSCR 1325. However, some actors are concerned that in the rush to represent Serbia as a modernized, liberal-democratic state which has moved on from the problems arising from the conflicts of the 1990s, there is little questioning about what it means to achieve gender security, and whether it is necessary to push for a deeper transformation.

Connected with these progressive assumptions is the notion that instrumental equality is a way of achieving gender security. In essence, the gender logic of the recommendations for the draft NAP emphases measurable, quota-based indicators of the participation and involvement of women in the Serbian defence sector (BFPE 2010: 15–16). Some participants in the working groups suggested the focus upon instrumental equality is a result of the involvement of the Ministry of Defence. Co-operation with the Ministry of Defence requires compromises about how gender security is thought about: security means quantitative equality rather than a new definition of security.[17] The dominant perception of gender security within the draft NAP stresses the importance of 'the protection of fundamental human rights of women' and their inclusion in state security processes: 'security entails security of the state, and thus, the involvement of all its citizens, including women, in articulation of policies, strategies and directions for actions' (BFPE 2010: 9). Equating gender security with state security *processes* stresses that instead of shifting the meaning and subject of security, gender security is about inclusion of groups currently not involved in security processes.

The NAP positions itself as necessary for Serbia's future position on the world stage.

> The adaptation of the National Action Plan and the implementation of the UN SC Resolution 1325 on women, peace and security would confirm Serbia's intention to *contribute actively* to the processes of peace-building, stability and security, above all, in the immediate environment of the Southeast European region, as well as in entire Europe through a *comprehensive process of European integrations* and the world at large through its *participation in peace support operations*. (BFPE 2010: 8. My emphasis)

To craft this position on the world stage, it is necessary to shed the image of Serbia as a post-conflict country. As a consequence, Serbia's post-conflict problematization is the state's future participation in peace support operations. This particular representation of post-conflict is secured through the achievement of a gender security logic that stresses instrumental equality. The document, drafted with the involvement of the Ministry of Defence, stresses the importance of numerical gender equality, and so its reinterpretation of UNSCR 1325 highlights ways of improving the representation of women within the Serbian defence and military structures. The dominant logic of gender security that arises from the configuration of post-conflict as an external issue suggests that women can be secured through equalizing opportunities,

GENDER, GOVERNANCE AND INTERNATIONAL SECURITY

suggesting that if women are formal political actors they will be secured. UNSCR 1325 is politically translated as a document designed to reinforce a liberal notion of gender equality.

CONCLUSIONS

In Serbia, UNSCR 1325 has been utilized and interpreted in different ways by various sites claiming political authority in relation to the resolution, producing very different visions of gender security. Each perception of gender security presents different ways of resolving the 'gender problem', either through equality, reconceptualization or inclusion. This article concludes by drawing together insights from each case study to highlight antagonisms at the heart of 'post-conflict' and/or 'gender security' discourse, shaping political translations of UNSCR 1325.

As a brief reminder, SEESAC places discursive emphasis upon perceptions that Serbia continues to suffer from the effects of war and conflict. Serbia's successful post-conflict reconstruction depends upon provision of support for capacity-building and development. The logic of gender security represented stresses the need to *include* women's problems to secure future (international) peace and security. In contrast, Women in Black suggest Serbia's post-conflict progress depends upon the acceptance of responsibility for the past conflict. The gender security logic emphasized by Women in Black calls for a radical *reconsideration* of who, and what, should be secured in the future. The final initiative investigated, the NAP recommendations, downplays Serbia's direct relationship to conflict. The post-conflict vision focuses upon Serbia's role as an external actor in peacekeeping. Gender security is represented as something that can be achieved through application of liberal notions of *equality*. Each initiative represents very different notions of both 'post-conflict' and 'gender security', all conveying hopes about Serbia's future.

The antagonisms at the heart of 'post-conflict' intersect with, and shape, normative ambitions for 'gender security', with implications for political action. The initiative making connections between SALW (ab)use and domestic violence has not been publically opposed, as the problematization of post-conflict crafted stresses increased insecurity for women, a vision which does not present a significant challenge to debates about Serbia's relationship to conflict and post-conflict. In contrast, the NAP initiative has been criticized by Women in Black for stripping the radical potential from UNSCR 1325.[18] The NAP recommendations are viewed as supporting a militarized vision of security that fails to account for the 'security risks of not confronting the criminal past [or] condemning the genocide in Srebrenica' (Women in Black 2010: 3). Yet, many involved with the NAP working groups felt that Women in Black's critiques were not relevant to successful implementation of UNSCR 1325.[19] Debates about how to interpret 'gender security' in Serbia's NAP are tangled with, and reflective of, how political actors describe Serbia's relationship to conflict, and ambitions for the direction of Serbia's post-conflict reconstruction.

This opens up questions about the connections between representations of gender and configurations of post-conflict. Zalewski (2006) has argued that how gender is thought about not only 'performs significant but cloaked functions in the constitution of representations of the conflict' (p. 485). That is, the way we think about gender affects how conflict and post-conflict is represented, and the issues thrown to the forefront. Simultaneously, representations of conflict and post-conflict shape what is identified as a gender concern. Thus, representations of gender are a product and productive of configurations of post-conflict. Connections between configurations of post-conflict and gender security logics are apparent in the examples provided in this article: for instance, where the concern is with post-conflict insecurity, violence and crime – like the UNDP and its agencies – then the gender problems identified respond to these concerns. Alternatively, where the (post-)conflict focus is upon critiques of militarization and its processes – like Women in Black – then the gender concerns include aims to dismantle processes of militarism. However, if the post-conflict problem relates to external participation of the armed forces, then the gender perspective emphasizes the need for numerical equality within the armed forces. The normative ambition for gender security intersects with visions for the future direction of post-conflict reconstruction, shaping political translations of UNSCR 1325.

Foregrounding the role of UNSCR 1325 within three different sites of political action has demonstrated the variety of conceptualizations about 'gender security' that exist. Evidently, 'gender security' in Serbia can be multifarious and contradictory. Like Wibben (2011), I believe that creating space for multiple security narratives to 'exist alongside each other' is enabling, and the 'contradictions can be seen as enriching, rather than as a problem to be transcended' (p. 39). These contradictory visions of security are enriching because they make us ask different questions: *how* and *why* do different visions of 'gender security' in relation to UNSCR 1325 exist? In beginning to respond to these questions, it is critical to see the connections between personal-political identities about the future of post-conflict reconstruction, the objectives of the gender mainstreaming project, and how UNSCR 1325 is politically translated. In making these connections, we can see that the resolution serves to *legitimize* (often pre-existing) post-conflict visions: from the belief held by Women in Black that Serbia should accept political responsibility, or the dominant ambition of the NAP working groups to craft Serbia as a progressive liberal democracy that has moved on from the conflicts of the 1990s.

Antagonisms at the heart of 'post-conflict' are productive in opening up spaces and choices for a variety of perceptions about what the achievement of gender security means. All of the programmes and measures discussed in this article are important, as they each embody some vision of gender equality. These tensions and debates make up politics: without these debates, we do not push and test the boundaries of politics and political change. The potential for debate and challenge is perhaps the greatest potential of UNSCR 1325. In 2004, Helen Kinsella argued that the potential of UNSCR 1325 in shaping conceptions of women and of gender was significant (Cohn et al. 2004: 136). Looking at how UNSCR 1325 has been politically translated into programmes in Serbia, Kinsella's words still ring true as alternative interpretations of gender security can be identified within various initiatives inspired by UNSCR 1325. I believe these tensions to be eventually productive of greater gender equality by opening up possibilities for equality at all levels and in all ways.

Notes

1   There are other initiatives using UNSCR 1325 in Serbia: this article discusses the most prominent ones.
2   The Bureau for Crisis Prevention and Recovery is no longer operating in Serbia.
3   Interview, small arms and light weapons (SALW) Awareness officer, South-Eastern European Small Arms Clearinghouse (SEESAC), Belgrade, 11 April 2008. In English.
4   Until February 2008, SEESAC was mandated by the UNDP and the Stability Pact for South-Eastern Europe (SP). The SP was succeeded by the Regional Cooperation Council.
5   Interview, SALW Awareness officer, SEESAC, Belgrade, 11 April 2008. In English.
6   Interview, SALW Awareness officer, SEESAC, Belgrade, 11 April 2008. In English.
7   Interviews, SALW Awareness officer, SEESAC, Belgrade, 11 April 2008; SEESAC Project Manager, Belgrade, 18 September 2009. In English.
8   Interview, Director, Victimology Society, Belgrade, 10 July 2008. In English.
9   Interviews, Mirjana Dokmanović, International Gender Consultant, Subotica, 3 June 2009; Jasmina Nikolić, Victimology Society, Belgrade, 18 September 2009. In English.
10   Official Gazette 30 March 2004.
11   Interview, Staśa Zajović, Coordinator of Women in Black: Serbia, Belgrade, 18 September 2009. In English and Serbian.
12   Interview, Staśa Zajović, Coordinator of Women in Black: Serbia, Belgrade, 18 September 2009. In English and Serbian.
13   Interview, Staśa Zajović, Coordinator of Women in Black: Serbia, Belgrade, 18 September 2009. In English and Serbian.

14 Email correspondence with Belgrade Fund for Political Excellence (BFPE), 14 February 2011.
15 These proposals are recommendations made in collaboration with the Ministry of Defence: they do not form the final NAP document.
16 Interview, off the record, Belgrade, September 2009. In English.
17 Interviews, UNIFEM Serbia representative, Belgrade, 15 September 2009; Director Civil-Military Relations, Belgrade, 17 September 2009. All in English.
18 Interview, Staśa Zajović, Coordinator of Women in Black: Serbia, Belgrade, 18 September 2009. In English and Serbian.
19 Interview, Programme Coordinator BFPE, Belgrade, 8 June 2009. In English.

Acknowledgements

The research for this article was made possible by an ESRC Postgraduate Studentship Award (PTA-031-2005-00220). Field research was carried out in Serbia during February–August 2008, June 2009 and September 2009. I am indebted to all the people I interviewed for their valuable contributions, and can only hope that this does their work some justice. I am grateful to Georgina Waylen for her insightful and encouraging feedback on an early draft of this article, to the anonymous reviewers for their constructive comments and to Gordana Radaković, Aleksander Skundric and Adam Hardie for their supportive and efficient research assistance. Any mistakes that I have made are my own.

References

Belgrade Fund for Political Excellence (BFPE). 2009. Program: Implementation of UNSCR 1325 in Serbia. Belgrade, May.
Belgrade Fund for Political Excellence (BFPE). 2010. *United Nations Security Council Resolution 1325 in Serbia – On Women, Peace and Security: Recommendations for drafting National Action Plan for implementation of UN Security Council Resolution 1325 in Serbia*. Belgrade.
Belgrade Fund for Political Excellence (BFPE). n.d. 'About BFPE'. Available at http://www.bfpe.org/bfpe/indexENG.php (accessed 5 June 2010).
Carver, T. 1996. *Gender is Not a Synonym for Women*. Lynne Rienner: London.
Cockburn, C. 2007. *From Where We Stand: War, Women's Activism and Feminist Analysis*. London: Zed Books.
Cockburn, C. 2010. 'Gender Relations as Causal in Militarization and War: A Feminist Standpoint', *International Feminist Journal of Politics* 12 (2): 139–57.
Cockburn, C. and Zarkov, D. (eds). 2002. *The Postwar Moment: Militaries, Masculinities and International Peacekeeping*. London: Zed Books.
Cohn, C. 2004. 'Feminist Peacemaking: In Resolution 1325, the United Nations Requires the Inclusion of Women in All Peace Planning and Negotiation', *The Women's Review of Books* 21 (5): 8–9.

Cohn, C. 2008. 'Mainstreaming Gender in UN Security Policy: A Path to Political Transformation?, in Rai S. M. and Waylen, G. (eds) *Global Governance: Feminist Perspectives*, pp. 185–206. Basingstoke: Palgrave.

Cohn, C., Kinsella, H. and Gibbings, S. 2004. 'Women, Peace and Security: Resolution 1325', *International Feminist Journal of Politics* 6 (1): 130–40.

Dokmanović, M. 2008. *Firearms Possession and Domestic Violence in the Western Balkans: A Comparative Study of Legislation and Implementation Mechanisms.* Belgrade: SEESAC.

Duhaček, D. 2006. 'The Making of Political Responsibility: Hannah Arendt and/in the Case of Serbia', in Lukić, J., Regulska, J. and Zaviršek, D. (eds) *Women and Citizenship in Central and Eastern Europe*, pp. 205–21. Aldershot: Ashgate.

Enloe, C. 1993. *The Morning After: Sexual Politics at the End of the Cold War.* Berkley, CA: University of California Press.

Enloe, C. 2010. *Nimo's War, Emma's War: Making Feminist Sense of the Iraq War.* Berkley, CA: University of California Press.

Fridman, O. 2006. 'Alternative Voices in Public Urban Space: Serbia's Women in Black', *Ethnologia Balkanica* 10: 291–303.

Glynos, J. and Howarth, D. 2007. *Logics of Critical Explanation in Social and Political Theory.* London: Routledge.

Gumru, F. B. and Fritz, J. M. 2009. 'Women, Peace and Security: An Analysis of the National Action Plans Developed in Response to UN Security Council Resolution 1325', *Societies Without Borders* 4 (2): 209–25.

Handrahan, L. 2004. 'Conflict, Gender, Ethnicity and Post-Conflict Reconstruction', *Security Dialogue* 35 (4): 429–45.

Hill, F., Aboitiz, M. and Poehlman-Doumbouya, S. 2003. 'Nongovernmental Organizations' Role in the Buildup and Implementation of Security Council Resolution 1325', *Signs: The Journal of Women in Culture and Society* 28 (4): 1255–69.

Höglund, K. and Kovacs, M. S. 2010. 'Beyond the Absence of War: the Diversity of Peace in Post-settlement Societies', *Review of International Studies* 36 (2): 367–90.

Hudson, N. F. 2010. *Gender, Human Security and the United Nations: Security Language as a Political Framework for Women.* Abingdon: Routledge.

Ministry of Defence. 2010 'Roundtable: Women, Peace and Security'. Available at: http://www.mod.gov.rs/novi_eng.php?action=fullnews&id=2396 (accessed 12 February 2011).

Obradović-Wochnik, J. 2009. 'Knowledge, Acknowledgement and Denial in Serbia's Responses to the Srebrenica Massacre', *Journal of Contemporary European Studies* 17 (1): 61–74.

SEESAC. 2007. 'SEESAC Strategy for Gender Issues in SALW control and AVPP Activities'. Available at http://www.seesac.org (accessed 14 July 2010).

SEESAC. n.d. 'About SEESAC'. Available at http://www.seesac.org (accessed 13 July 2010).

Shepherd, L. J. 2008. '"To Save Succeeding Generations from the Scourge of War": The US, UN, and the Violence of Security', *Review of International Studies* 34 (2): 293–311.

Shepherd, L. J. 2010. 'Sex or Gender? Bodies in World Politics and Why Gender Matters', *Gender Matters in Global Politics: A Feminist Introduction to International Relations*, pp. 3–16. London: Routledge.

United Nations Development Programme: Crisis Prevention and Recovery [BCPR]. 2006. 'The Eight Point Agenda: Practical, Positive Outcomes for Girls and Women in Crisis'. Available at http://www.undp.org/cpr/we_do/8_pa.shtml (accessed 12 July 2010).

Vaughan-Williams, N. 2006. 'Towards a Problematisation of the Problematisations that Reduce Northern Ireland to a "Problem"', *Critical Review of International Social and Political Philosophy* 9 (4): 513–26.

Wibben, A. T. R. 2011. *Feminist Security Studies: A Narrative Approach*. London: Routledge.

Women in Black 2007. 'Draft Resolution', in Zajović, S., Perković, M. and Urošević, M. (eds) *Women for Peace*, pp. 187–89. Belgrade: Women in Black.

Women in Black. 2010. 'Women in Black Activities and Important Documents Related to the Implementation of the Resolution 1325' (Response document to the draft National Action Plan). Available at: http://www.zeneucrnom.org (accessed 26 July 2010).

Zajović, S. 2007. *Always Disobedient*. Belgrade: Women in Black.

Zalewski, M. 2006. 'Intervening in Northern Ireland: Critically re-thinking representations of the conflict', *Critical Review of International Social and Political Philosophy* 9 (4): 479–497.

Feminist Knowledge and Emerging Governmentality in UN Peacekeeping

PATTERNS OF CO-OPTATION AND EMPOWERMENT

AUDREY REEVES
University of Bristol, UK

Abstract

Since the 1970s, gender expertise has achieved a high degree of salience in global governance processes in general, and, over the last decade, within institutions concerned with international peace and security in particular. This study addresses the question of what happens when feminist knowledge is incorporated into the discourse of security institutions. It draws on Michel Foucault's concept of governmentality to examine the contingent encounters of feminist discourses with the liberal peace paradigm and traditional conceptions of security in the context of United Nations multidimensional peacekeeping operations over the period 1999–2010. Throughout these encounters, political rationalities of peacekeeping tend to subjugate feminist objectives to the broader goal of conflict resolution. Simultaneously, feminists and women's rights activists who engage with mainstream peacekeeping rationalities are turning into potentially influential 'gender experts', who contest and redefine traditional meanings of peace and security. As bureaucratic machineries become involved in the collection of data on post-conflict gender dynamics, such as violence against women and girls, women's formal political participation and acts of sexual violence committed by peacekeepers, feminist knowledge increasingly informs technologies of population management in post-conflict settings. In the process, certain gendered and racialized identities are normalized, and certain rationales for military intervention in the post-colonial world are put forward, thus contributing to creating new marginalities and consolidating existing ones.

Since the 1970s, gender expertise has achieved a high degree of salience in global governance processes (Prügl 2009). This increasing importance attached to gender expertise stems in part from the expansion of transnational women's movements and related scholarship. Another factor is the adoption of gender mainstreaming as *the* way to promote gender equality, an outcome of the Fourth World Conference on Women (Beijing, 1995). Gender mainstreaming was then defined as 'a strategy for making women's as well as men's concerns and experiences an integral dimension of the design, implementation, monitoring and evaluation of policies and programmes ... so that women and men benefit equally and inequality is not perpetuated' (ECOSOC 1997 Chapter IV, Section AIA).

Less than a decade after the Beijing call for the mainstreaming of a gender perspective through all United Nations policy-making processes, its impact was judged far-reaching in international organizations (Hafner-Burton and Pollack 2002: 339–40). The adoption of UN Security Council Resolution (UNSCR) 1325 (2000), which called for the consideration of the special needs of women and girls at all stages of conflict management and post-conflict reconstruction, marked a defining step in extending gender mainstreaming to peace and security institutions.

The institutionalization of certain forms of 'feminist knowledge' in global governance has led some observers to argue that feminists 'have gained authority' (Prügl 2009: 18) and that 'they now walk the halls of power' (Halley 2008: 21). However, gender mainstreaming has also been criticized by scholars and activists who problematize the tensions emerging from the encounter between a 'feminist discourse' which seeks 'gender equality' as its ultimate goal, on the one hand, and a 'neoliberal discourse' which identifies efficiency and market-driven economic growth as normative goods, on the other hand (True 2003: 371). As gender perspectives become mainstreamed, some consider that feminist goals are 'co-opted' by other agendas, as gender is turned into a technocratic tool and thus stripped of its critical content (Whitworth 2004: 17; Squires 2005: 374).[1]

Notwithstanding the intellectual and normative value of these criticisms, they fail to conceptualize adequately what appears to be the paradox of the simultaneous 'empowerment' and 'co-optation' of feminist intellectual resources. This holds true especially in the field of international peace and security, where high-level consideration of gender issues only started in the past ten to fifteen years.[2] In this study, I seek to shed new light on the integration of feminist knowledge in security governance by using the Foucauldian concept of *governmentality*. My project contains a double-argument: first, I argue that one can make sense of the co-optation/empowerment paradox by examining gender mainstreaming in peacekeeping as a product of the merging of feminist knowledge with 'mainstream' rationalities of government, a process that gives way to *simultaneous* processes of co-optation and empowerment. Second, as a result of the merging of these discourses, hybrid forms of feminist knowledge increasingly inform programmes geared towards the management of populations from a distance, which in turn creates new marginalities through the normalization of certain gendered and racialized identities and the (re)production of rationales for military intervention in the post-colonial world.

The article is structured in four parts. The first section introduces a conceptual and methodological framework drawing on Foucault's concept of governmentality in relation to UN peacekeeping. The second and third sections examine patterns of 'co-optation' and 'empowerment' in the political rationalities and governmental technologies of peacekeeping. The last section suggests possible directions for future research.

A FOUCAULDIAN APPROACH TO GENDER AND PEACEKEEPING

Scholars and observers have described post-Cold War peacekeeping operations as increasingly frequent and interventionist (see, for instance, Bellamy *et al.* 2009). Critical theorists have associated this new peacekeeping model with the exportation of liberal market democracy 'from the core to the periphery of the international system' (Paris 2002: 638), which Mark Duffield (2001) termed the 'liberal peace project'. In this study, the liberal peace project and its growing integration of gender-related knowledge are considered through a governmentality approach.

Michel Foucault used the term 'government' to refer to the activity of governing populations, or 'any more or less calculated and rational activity, undertaken by a multiplicity of authorities and agencies, employing a variety of techniques and forms of knowledge, that seeks to shape conduct by working through our desires, aspirations, interests and beliefs' (Dean 2006: 11). Governing practices embed themselves in a web of knowledges and meanings that inform what is interpreted as the greater good and the means to achieve it, which constitute governmentality. *Liberal* governmentality privileges managing populations 'at a distance' over direct intervention (Foucault 2004 [1977– 8]: 360). However, it does not exclude coercive disciplinary mechanisms, but reactivates them in new configurations (Foucault 2004 [1977–8]: 110–11). From a governmentality perspective, peacekeeping can thus be seen as an assemblage of more or less coercive techniques of government with the objective of transforming 'abnormal states' into responsible, peaceful, democratic and predictable elements of the international system (Zanotti 2006). Proliferating 'mechanisms of international knowledge and control' include the statistical specification of populations, as well as training, monitoring and reporting that target the host state's population (Zanotti 2006: 152) in addition to troop- and police-contributing states and peacekeeping personnel.

As high-level security institutions have started incorporating elements of gender-related knowledge into their security governance discourse, technologies of government deployed by these institutions have increasingly turned into conscious (though often incomplete) attempts at transforming gender relations in the host-country. For instance, since 2005, UN peacekeeping has sought to 'effectively target female ex-combatants and women associated with fighting forces' in the context of its Disarmament, Demobilization and Reintegration (DDR) programmes (DPKO 2005: 8), breaking with the previous practice of DDR centred on male ex-combatants (Worthen *et al.* 2010). Gender mainstreaming, in DDR contexts, has meant compiling gender-disaggregated data of beneficiaries; changing eligibility criteria for access; advocating the integration of female ex-combatants in regular military and police forces; ensuring the availability of reproductive health care for women and providing female personnel to screen female ex-combatants and separate transit and disarmament sites for male and female combatants (DPKO 2005: 9; UNIFEM and DPKO 2010: 34).[3]

'Governmentalized peacekeeping' also involves reshaping national and local security institutions to encourage post-conflict states to comply with certain gender-related standards, such as an improved gender balance in legal and security institutions, the prosecution of perpetrators of sexual violence and the prevention and punishment of practices judged harmful for or discriminatory against women. UN agencies are thus undertaking training and other 'capacity-building' activities mainly targeting police, justice and political institutions. For instance, in 2010, in seven UN peacekeeping missions, 'UN police divisions have helped create national specialized units that investigate and assist victims of gender-based and sexual violence' (United Nations 2010a: 18). In Afghanistan, the UN mission's gender unit has looked into the expansion of the number of women shelters (DPKO 2005: 23). These techniques and procedures through which the UN seeks to achieve certain gender equality objectives constitute *technologies of government* developed around webs of knowledge and abstract concepts, or *rationalities of government* (Rose and Miller 2010: 273) drawn from the 'liberal peace' paradigm with which feminist knowledge has become increasingly enmeshed. Such technologies of government are not deployed smoothly: they encounter resistance and are not always effective. However, in this study, the question of the impact on post-conflict societies is bracketed in order to focus on the problematization of the particular ways in which gender knowledge is governmentalized in peacekeeping contexts. As they pragmatically negotiate the mobilization of resources to pursue what they interpret as gender equality, gender advisers contribute to shaping the way gender analysis is introduced in neoliberal rationalities of government. While peacekeeping language describes advisers' work as 'technical assistance' provided by 'experts' in the transmission of society management skills, this idea of a neutrally determined and thus appropriate management of international security downplays the political nature of the transformative processes at work (Väyrynen 2004: 126–31). Thus, the questions this study seeks to answer are: How has the merging of feminist knowledge with neoliberal rationalities of government influenced peacekeeping discourse and practices? In what ways does this merging provoke the co-optation (i.e. use of feminist discursive resources to promote normative goals which are implicitly or explicitly identified as superior to gender equality) or empowerment (i.e. increase of discursive space and resources dedicated to the promotion of gender equality) of feminist knowledge?[4]

In order to answer these questions, I proceed through a diachronic study of the evolution of gender components in UN peace operations since their emergence in 1999 to 2010. While these are likely to show only a part of the larger picture of peace and security governmentalism in the post-Cold War world, they are nonetheless significant, as peacekeeping has been identified early on as the area where 'the most significant progress in the implementation of resolution 1325 (2000) has been made' (UN Secretary-General 2004: 7). While acknowledging the difficulties inherent to the progressive integration of a gender perspective in peacekeeping, I focus on the impact of the emergence of a new 'gender and peacekeeping' discourse on the UN as an organization (internal disciplinarity), rather than on the host states (external disciplinarity). Through different examples, I illustrate the simultaneous occurrence of 'co-optation' and 'empowerment' processes and show how they can be understood as episodes of a continuous and open-ended negotiation between feminist discourses and mainstream neoliberal rationalities. Sources include donor reports, internal UN 'gray literature', press reports and semi-structured interviews with eight gender experts who have worked as gender advisers or consultants for the UN Department of Peacekeeping Operations (DPKO).

PATTERNS OF CO-OPTATION AND CONSTRAINT: GENDER MAINSTREAMING FOR THE SAKE OF 'OPERATIONAL EFFECTIVENESS'

As gender knowledge has been integrated into peacekeeping, the realization of sustainable peace has increasingly been described as 'inextricably linked to equality between women and men' (UN General Assembly 2000: 13). However, there is an overwhelming tendency in the emerging UN 'gender and security' discourse to subordinate the ideal of gender equality to that of sustainable peace. The full participation of women and a targeted response to their specific needs is considered necessary for missions to succeed in bringing an end to conflict. Gender advisers pragmatically use such arguments, which are then reclaimed by official UN discourse. This section introduces examples of 'co-optation' drawn from advocacy and training contexts, in addition to an instance of how feminist knowledge can be marginalized, when issues first framed as gender-related are reframed as non-gender.

Achieving Gender Balance among Peacekeepers: Recruiting Women to Improve 'Operational Effectiveness'

The objective of improving gender balance among peacekeeping personnel has been voiced by the UN as early as 1994 (Mazurana 2002: 43). However, the UN does not have control over the percentage of women deployed in peacekeeping missions, as it is the prerogative of the states contributing to the operation. The UN has thus deployed technologies of government to target troop- and police-contributing states. Notably, it publishes statistical records of the percentage of female peacekeepers deployed by each contributing state. Rankings are publicized in public information material, as well as during workshops and seminars attended by representatives of member states (see, for instance, UN Secretary-General 2005: 4).

Following the deployment of these strategies, the proportion of female soldiers serving on peacekeeping missions has followed a slow but steady rise, reaching 2.61 per cent of military personnel in May 2011 (United Nations 2011), from 0.1 per cent in 1989 (UN 1995 in Olsson 2000: 2). This low proportion can partly be explained by the limited presence of women in the armed forces of many of the major troop-contributing countries and by the fact that many armed forces are reluctant to send women into combat zones (the percentage of women in contributing countries' armed forces averaged 8.77 per cent in 2006 (DPKO 2006: 10)). The call for women in uniforms has been more effective with civilian police officers, potentially because the presence of women in police forces is usually better accepted in troop- and police-contributing countries. The proportion of policewomen deployed in peacekeeping has more than doubled in ten years, reaching 10.09 per cent of police personnel (United Nations 2011), and DPKO aims to reach 20 per cent women by 2014 (United Nations 2009).

Arguments aimed at convincing reluctant member states to deploy more female peacekeepers often reflect the 'co-optation' of gender-related technologies to pursue objectives implicitly considered more important than gender equality per se. The typical arguments supporting the inclusion of more female peacekeepers rely on posited differences between men and women: women should be peacekeepers, not because they can and should have the opportunity to do whatever men do, but because their fundamentally different way of being peacekeepers is needed for mission success. UN Secretary-General Ban Ki-Moon, while urging member states to contribute more female troops to peacekeeping missions, insisted that 'the point is not to achieve gender parity for its own sake', but 'to draw on the unique and powerful contribution women can make'. The 'typically feminine' qualities and skills of female peacekeepers most frequently mentioned are their 'conciliatory nature', resulting in a greater 'ability to defuse potentially violent situations'; their communication skills, especially when engaging with local women; and their empathy, translating into a greater commitment to the inclusion of all voices and a stronger interest in issues of sexual violence, as well as in a 'greater access to vulnerable communities' in general and to women in particular (UN gender advisers quoted by Pearson Peacekeeping Centre 2009: 3–7). Therefore, as gender advisers pragmatically argue for the integration of women among peacekeeping personnel, feminist arguments find themselves co-opted in the reproduction of a discourse where women are portrayed as the instruments of political goals which are still mainly defined by and for men.

Moreover, these discursive frames also entail contradictory power dynamics with regard to the (re)construction of gendered identities. On one hand, gender advisers create a discursive space where female peacekeepers are portrayed positively. New ways of 'doing peacekeeping' are valorized and 'feminine' traits such as empathy and cultural sensitivity are framed as productive and positive in peacekeeping. On the other hand, female and male peacekeepers remain constrained in a certain range of behaviours deemed acceptable for each gender. Not all female peacekeepers are 'naturally' good listeners, or communicators; yet they are expected to be, according to the gendered standards that now apply to them. Moreover, an insistence on female peacekeepers in uniform as being more apt at communicating with local women and better confidants for victims of rape is likely to reinforce the assimilation of police-women to 'social workers' – common in many parts of the world, as indicated by Tilly Stroosnijder (2010), a former gender adviser for the United Nations Civilian Police Force in Kosovo – and undermine their demands for the same opportunities as their male counterparts. Finally, the 'militarized masculinities' (Higate and Henry 2004: 484) performed by many male peacekeepers in uniforms are left unproblematized. The hyper-masculine subcultures of the military are left in place as female peacekeepers are expected to provide the social skills the men are not encouraged to perform.

Training Peacekeepers on Gender: Learning to 'Harness' Women's Peacebuilding Efforts

Resolution 1325 invited member states to incorporate elements of gender awareness 'into their national training programmes for military and civilian police personnel in preparation for deployment'. DPKO has made gender training available for troop-contributing countries (Mazurana 2002: 47) and, already in 2003, had conducted 'training of trainers' to over 350 training officers from member states (Guéhenno 2003). The countries which, by 2004, had reported to have taken measures to integrate gender in pre-deployment training include Canada, the United Kingdom, Argentina, Australia, Germany and Switzerland (UN Secretary-General 2004: 8). Peacekeepers also follow courses online and in peacekeeping schools, notably in Bangladesh and South Africa (Bastick and de Torres 2010).

In addition, the provision of in-mission gender training has been increasingly systematized. According to Angela Mackay (2010), in 2002, in Kosovo, gender training was 'very erratic'. However, in 2006, former Under-Secretary General for Peacekeeping Operations Jean-Marie Guéhenno estimated that 75 to 90 per cent of peacekeeping personnel had received gender training (Guéhenno 2006). It has now become a norm in several missions for all incoming peacekeepers, military or civilian, to go through gender training upon their arrival (Lyytikäinen 2007). However, with gender training courses lasting between one hour and two days and considering the problem of language barriers, it is unclear to what extent they actually influence peacekeepers' behaviour and attitudes (Pearson Peacekeeping Centre 2009: 5).

Co-optation processes similar to the ones characterizing the advocacy for gender balance among peacekeepers also occur as gender is integrated in training material. DPKO insists that 'gender mainstreaming is in the interest of the mission: it is necessary to take gender issues into consideration to effectively fulfil the mandate' (Lamptey and DPKO 2004). This discursive move is informed by the tactical advocacy of gender experts encountering security institution personnel unfamiliar and often unreceptive to arguments based on women's rights and gender equality as normative goods. As Tilly Stroosnijder (2010) indicated, 'when we [gender advisers] talk like feminists, we shut the door in front of us'. A more effective way of opening a dialogue, she argued, was to suggest that military and police units need to integrate women 'in intelligence units, because they can get different kinds of information' as they establish connections with local women who share information about their security environment that is often different from what the men may share.

This type of instrumental justification has been incorporated into official discourse of high-level advocates of gender mainstreaming processes. For instance, Guéhenno (2003) argued that women can have an 'enormous, positive impact ... when their knowledge, skills and motivation are harnessed in the name of peace and rebuilding a country'. In a statement to the Security Council, he also mentioned that, of the 21,000 women who were demobilized as a result of DDR programmes in Liberia, many 'contributed important information on where arms caches were hidden' (Guéhenno 2005). Just like the female peacekeepers, local women tend to be presented as an 'untapped resource', which, if put to better use, could help achieve sustainable peace (Cohn 2008).

Simultaneously, the UN 'women, peace and security' discourse tends to reify the conflict-affected woman as an individual who is not predisposed to harm (and is therefore inherently peaceful) and requires protection. Such generalizations are at odds with many arguments widely shared among feminist activists and scholars, as they obscure how some women do fuel conflict and perpetrate violence, rely on a conception of gender roles as static, present violence as a natural and therefore legitimate characteristic of male behaviour, obscure differences between conflict-affected women in terms of age, class, ethnicity, religion, marital status, sexual orientation and disabilities[5] and reinforce a hierarchical binary between lifestyles, values and priorities of women from the North as compared to those from the post-colonial world (Marchand and Parpart 1995: 255). Nevertheless, gender advisers sometimes resort to these frames in advocacy contexts where they pragmatically expect to achieve better short- to middle-term results by using them. For instance, Tilly Stroosnijder (2010) indicated she preferred not to use the term 'gender' when interacting with traditional and religious authorities in the Middle

East or in Indonesia. In such contexts, addressing the topic in 'the western way', she argued, would only 'build a wall' between her and her interlocutor. Instead, she would use the key words 'vulnerable groups', which she knew to be already accepted as a valid topic of concern in the cultural environment she was operating in. By pragmatically deploying certain discursive strategies for tactical purposes, gender advisers find themselves caught in a double movement of empowerment and co-optation of feminist knowledge. Their use of conservative discursive frames contributes to the reproduction of these very frames. Yet, they also allow for the creation of spaces of discussion where they can inform policy, establish partnerships, collect crucial information and eventually redefine accepted meanings and related social practices.

Tackling Sexual Exploitation and Abuse and the Spread HIV/AIDS among Peacekeepers: Ungendering 'Problematic' Sexual Encounters

While the above examples illustrate how elements of feminist discourse can be 'co-opted' to support other goals, the merging of discourses can also result in the 'marginalization' of feminist knowledge, as is the case for sexual exploitation and abuse (SEA) and the spread of HIV/AIDS among peacekeepers.

Feminists have long argued that in some cases, the deployment of peacekeeping forces has led to an increase of insecurity, notably for women and girls. This was emphasized following the mediatization of (sometimes widespread) acts of sexual violence committed by peacekeepers (Whitworth 2005; Quénivet 2007: 659–60). In reaction, a peacekeepers' Code of Conduct was established in 1998, requesting peacekeepers not to 'indulge in immoral acts of sexual, physical or psychological abuse or exploitation of the local population or United Nations staff, especially women and children' (United Nations 2010b). However, some have raised concerns that even cases of sexual intercourse between mutually consenting peacekeepers and 'local women' are not unproblematic. In the past they have led to the rise of prostitution and the spread of sexually transmitted diseases, including AIDS, and put women at risk of being ostracized and victims of violence in their own community (Whitworth 2004: 13). In 2003, the UN thus established a zero tolerance policy towards sexual encounters between peacekeepers and the local population (United Nations 2003). In 2006, a 'conduct and discipline' unit was established at DPKO Headquarters (Guéhenno 2006). Conduct and discipline officers, as well as telephone hotlines, were set up in the field (Netherlands, Norway, United Kingdom 2006: 7). The investigation process, however, is neither easy to understand for victims, nor transparent. Moreover, the presumed aggressor's superiors often try to intervene and insist on addressing the problem informally. If action is taken, it often consists of repatriation of the presumed aggressor without any prosecution (Quénivet 2007). Nonetheless, a number of disciplinary measures are typically undertaken to prevent sexual encounters between peacekeepers and the local population. As of 2010, awareness-raising is realized through training material made available to troop-contributing countries. The centralized collection of data and information on allegations of misconduct and investigations is also a significant development.

Similar developments have occurred with regard to the spread of HIV/AIDS among peacekeepers. In 2003, HIV/AIDS policy officers were present in four UN missions (Guéhenno 2003). The following year, such officers or focal points were present in all peacekeeping operations (UN Secretary-General 2004: 8). These officers conducted four training workshops on HIV/AIDS, human rights and gender in 2003 in Sierra Leone and provided free testing and counselling in Timor Leste. In 2004, training and testing facilities had been systematically established throughout missions (UN Secretary-General 2004).

Feminist authors and activists have played an important part in highlighting SEA and the spread of HIV/AIDS in peacekeeping contexts as valid concerns for the international community. However, these issues tend to be framed in ways that make it difficult for critical gender knowledge to be taken into account when addressing them in policy. For instance, while peacekeepers do receive training on SEA, this topic tends to be addressed separately from other 'gender issues' (Lyytikäinen 2007). Moreover, SEA perpetrated by peacekeeping personnel is typically addressed by conduct and discipline units rather than by gender units.

There are valid reasons to address these issues separately. In the case of SEA, it avoids reducing the integration of gender perspectives to questions of misconduct by peacekeepers and makes it easier for gender advisers to work with peacekeepers on other gender questions. Simultaneously, reframing SEA and HIV/AIDS as issues of 'conduct and discipline' and 'health' involves a risk of placing them out of reach of political debate informed by a gender perspective, which seems paradoxical considering all the attention drawn to SEA following the adoption of UNSCRs 1820 (2008) and 1888 (2009) on sexual violence in conflict. For instance, it makes it difficult for gender experts to challenge the idea that acts of sexual exploitation perpetrated by peacekeepers might not be 'a failure of traditional military values', but rather a problem that precisely has to do with the hegemonic representations of masculinity that are cultivated in military environments and that often entail 'an explosive mix of misogyny, racism, and homophobia' (Whitworth 2005). Current approaches to prevention of SEA and HIV/AIDS remain 'containment' strategies based on disciplinary mechanisms such as 'restriction of movement, curfews, requiring soldiers to wear uniforms outside barracks, designating off-limits areas, non-fraternization policies, increased patrols around high risks areas and decentralization of [conduct and discipline] personnel into locations with a potentially high risk of misconduct' (UN Conduct and Discipline Unit 2010). Such a 'containment' strategy leaves untouched the idea that 'boys will be boys' and does not engage with conceptions of sexuality as socially constructed. Similarly, there is little institutional space to engage with criticisms of the zero-tolerance policy, such as its possibly over-inclusive definition of SEA, which includes consensual sex between peacekeepers and local people (Otto 2007: 260).

PATTERNS OF EMPOWERMENT: THE OPENING OF NEW DISCURSIVE SPACES

The examples quoted above can be interpreted as instances where feminist arguments are either 'constrained' or 'co-opted' to promote a broader neoliberal agenda. However, it is important to keep a view of 'constraint' and 'co-optation' as only one facet of a broader phenomenon: the merging between two discursive formations – feminist interpretations of insecurity and violence and the 'liberal peace paradigm'.

As this merging takes place, feminist discourse is bound to be transformed and to some extent diluted. 'Co-optation' may be more easily observable than 'empowerment' from a feminist perspective. However, even dominant rationalities of government are by definition porous, to some extent unstable and bound to be contested and transformed. As gender is becoming recognized as an important dimension of peacekeeping, gender experts increasingly find themselves in a position where they can 'make their arguments and calculations the obligatory mode of operation for the network as a whole' (Rose and Miller 2010: 286). This section examines three developments through which 'empowerment' can be observed: the development of resources dedicated to the promotion of gender equality; the reinterpretation of core security concepts; and the collection of gender-related data.

Development of Resources Dedicated to the Promotion of Gender Quality

The mandate of peacekeeping missions' gender units is to diffuse information about gender-sensitivity and mainstream the integration of gender perspectives throughout all peacekeeping activities (Bouta *et al.* 2005: 21). Their continuous development over the last decade is thus a crucial element to take into account with regard to the 'empowerment' of feminist knowledge. First, the pool of staff dedicated to gender issues has dramatically increased. In 1999, two UN peacekeeping missions, in Kosovo and East Timor, had dedicated gender units, which lacked financing, expertise, policy, accountability and staff and suffered from delays in filling key gender-related positions (Mazurana 2002: 42; Olsson 2009: 107). These difficulties pervaded all newly formed gender units until the mid-2000s. For instance, according to Angela Mackay (2010), in 2002, the human resources of the gender unit of the UN Mission in Kosovo were 'questionable at best', as 'no one seemed interested in being part of the gender team'. Before 2004, there was no gender capacity at

DPKO Headquarters either, only ad hoc gender mainstreaming (Peacewomen 2004). In 2004 and 2005, however, gender advisers were appointed 'to every new multidimensional peacekeeping operation', as well as in DPKO Headquarters (DPKO 2005: 1). As of the time of writing, the gender component at Headquarters is a four-member team (UN Secretary-General 2010: 67). As for field missions, of the sixteen DPKO-led missions,[6] ten missions have full-time gender advisory capacity[7] and six have a 'gender focal point'[8] (a staff member who takes on gender in addition to other tasks). In total, 118 full-time gender positions in the field were budgeted for the year 2009–10 (UN Secretary-General 2010: 67).

Second, statements of gender advisers and mission staff indicate that there have been substantial developments in how gender advisers perceive their own capacity to influence peacekeeping policy and programming. According to Angela Mackay (2010), gender advisers in Kosovo in 2002 had 'no financial resources, no strategic planning, no advisory function to any other unit, no seat at the [decision-making] table, no support or any backup resources from Headquarters in New York'. In 2005, there was a general agreement across UN agencies that gender advisers appointed by DPKOs were 'a major capacity-development achievement' in the implementation of gender mainstreaming requirements, but that their expertise was 'underutilized' and too often cut from senior officials (UN Secretary-General 2005: 9). In contrast, in 2010, a gender adviser described the African Union–UN Hybrid Mission in Darfur (UNAMID)'s gender unit's access to resources as 'so far, so good'.[9] For the budgetary year 2010–11, she expected the unit to receive USD100,000–150,000, essentially for training purposes, an amount that she judges commensurate with the unit's advisory mandate, but which counts for only 1 per cent of the UNAMID budget. However, whenever a project requiring additional funds is organized, it is 'very easy' to find funding by creating partnerships with other components of the mission, who are 'more than happy' to associate themselves with the gender unit over specific projects. Moreover, 'high leadership is now more likely to ask gender advisers for advice and are more and more conscious [of the importance of integrating gender]' (Anonymous A 2010). For another gender adviser based in the Democratic Republic of the Congo (DRC) since 2002, 'gender is going fast' and 'practices are now established' (Anonymous B 2010). Comfort Lamptey (2010), gender adviser at DPKO Headquarters since 2004, agreed, arguing that 'people are starting to think of [gender] as central and not as something marginal' and that, consequently, the consultation of gender advisers has become more systematic. 'Nobody is questioning the relevance [of addressing gender in peacekeeping] any more'. Carole Doucet (2010), a senior gender adviser in Liberia since 2008, agrees that it has become almost impossible for peacekeeping staff 'to do [their] work without paying some attention to the gender dimensions in peacekeeping operations whether they fall under the civilian, military or police component'. This is in part due to new human resources planning which includes gender as a mandatory requirement. Staff performance is evaluated on whether they engage with gender and there are specific gender-related requirements to fulfil when recruiting new staff.

This is not to say that the implementation of these policies is not marked by shortcomings. Different circumstantial conditions still have an important impact on gender advisers' capacity to deploy their knowledge and influence social practices. These include the sensitivity to gender issues demonstrated by senior members of the mission, as well as the location of the gender unit in the organizational structure of the mission (Bouta *et al.* 2005: 20). Moreover, while governmental technologies seem to have had an impact on behaviour, there are still doubts as to whether they effectively 'colonize the minds'. As the UNAMID gender adviser (Anonymous A 2010) argues, 'they [peacekeeping staff] get to act [on gender issues], but I am not sure whether they do so with conviction'. Moreover, according to Clare Hutchinson (2010), gender units remain 'terribly under-resourced', as their advisory status grants them meagre financial resources compared to programmatic sections. However, as Tilly Stroosnijder (2010) argues, this needs to be put in the perspective of the general lack of resources that characterizes UN missions: 'everyone suffers, not only the gender [staff]'. Despite the many remaining difficulties, it is important to recognize that a significant shift has occurred with regard to the availability of resources that makes a change in social practices conceivable.

Reinterpretation of Core Security Concepts

The greater capacities of gender staff are directly connected to another important example of 'empowerment' of feminist knowledge. As it becomes increasingly accepted that gender expertise is essential to mission success, gender experts achieve a position where they can challenge traditional conceptions of 'peace' and 'mission success' in favour of more gender-sensitive definitions.

Feminist authors and activists have long argued that, as far as women are concerned, 'it is meaningless to make a sharp distinction between peace and war, prewar, and postwar' (Cockburn 2004: 43). In post-conflict settings, violence against women tends to *increase* due to the continuation of forms of violence left unaddressed by peace settlements negotiated primarily by men and for men and of new forms of violence that become particularly acute in the aftermath of conflict, such as domestic violence and human trafficking (Pankhurst 2008).

However, a conception of peace that is blind to the types of violence that mainly affect women is increasingly challenged. The 2009 Secretary-General Report on women, peace and security recognized that 'after conflict has ended, high levels of sexual and gender-based violence tend to persist' (UN Secretary-General 2009). Moreover, already in 2005, DPKO stated that gender mainstreaming 'in all operational activities' was considered 'vital for institutionalizing the principle of equal rights for women and men within the framework of reconstruction' (DPKO 2005: 2). Many gender advisers take an active part in this struggle as they challenge conventional definitions of core security concepts such as peace, security and 'mission success' to make these concepts inclusive of gender equality ideals. These transformations are reflected in official UN discourse, this being epitomized by Guéhenno's (2003, emphasis added) statement that '[o]nly [by listening to women's voices], can we understand how best to help women and girls, and foster an *equitable peace*'.

Importantly, 'co-optation' and 'empowerment' of feminist knowledge in peacekeeping discourse occur simultaneously; specific enactments of both processes are even often performed by the same actors. They are the product of contingent negotiations in the context of the merging between two discursive fields, a dynamic encounter that necessarily results in tensions and struggles, visible in the discourses of individuals and institutions.

Collection of Gender-Related Data: 'Counting' Gender to Make It Count

The definition of gender equality as a normative ideal to strive for in post-conflict contexts creates a need to measure it, which opens a space where gender expertise is valued and empowered. Early in the process of gender mainstreaming peacekeeping, the UN started to collect data and information on 'the impact of armed conflict, the impact of interventions of peace operations on women and girls and the roles and contributions of women and girls in conflict situations' (UN Secretary-General 2002). Common 'gender indicators' include the involvement of women in formal political processes, the number of reported and prosecuted acts of 'gender-based violence' and initiatives to counter human trafficking (DPKO 2005: 11).

Following the adoption of UNSCR 1889 (2009), which requested the Secretary-General to submit 'a set of indicators for use at the global level to track implementation of its resolution 1325 (2000)', a formidable effort of research and consultation was launched through which 2,500 gender indicators were identified and shortlisted to a set of twenty-six (UNIFEM 2010). After much political debate, the Security Council committed to 'take forward' the global indicators (UN Security Council 2010).

The identification of indicators to assess and measure the participation of women in politics and peace processes and the prevention and response mechanisms to various forms of gender-based violence is an important aspect of the governmentalization of feminist knowledge. Such collection of data, when situated in 'abstract theories of social processes', allows for regulatory controls inherent to the management of populations 'at a distance' as privileged by liberal governmentality (Dean and Hindess 1998 in Lui 2004: 122). The collection of gender-related data is seen by many as a way to attract attention and resources and provide ground for accountability mechanisms. However, these technologies of government also have marginalizing effects: they produce a

137

difference between liberal subjects who can be governed 'at a distance' and those who require more coercive forms of management, a distinction usually articulated in 'historicist, developmental and gendered terms' (Hindess 2004: 28). What is presented as an unfair treatment of foreign women by foreign men has often been used throughout colonial and post-colonial history to build a hierarchical binary contrasting the 'civilized white man' against the 'barbaric brown man'. This discursive performance is part of a process of othering which produces a conception of foreign men as unable to care for themselves and 'their' women and therefore legitimizes (military) intervention. In contemporary global governance, gender-based dis-crimination and sexual violence have hence become indicative of the inability of a state to manage the interests of its population (Prügl 2010). Moreover, as the UN develops 'specific programmes that address the healing of women from trauma' (UN General Assembly 2000: 13) resulting from sexual violence, peacekeepers acquire the identity of healers of victims and prosecutors of per-petrators of sexual violence, thus legitimizing their presence and the violence they may perpetrate in the name of liberal peace (Harrington 2006).

CONCLUSION

Despite the development of gender mainstreaming strategies in peacekeeping, many criticisms made by feminist scholars remain valid: gender mainstream-ing is often restricted to 'add women and stir' (Harding 1995), without recon-sidering how peacekeeping is conceived and enacted, and without critically reflecting on how gender inequalities were produced in the first place, or how 'women' might be a problematic category. Gender questions remain framed as 'women's issues', leaving unaddressed how certain forms of mascu-linities and femininities are both productive of certain patterns of violence and necessary for them to take place, and as a result influence prospects for peace (Whitworth 2005; Cohn 2008). Moreover, gender issues which are not specifically women's issues, such as sexual violence perpetrated against men and boys, remain absent from peacekeeping political rationalities and policies.[10]

However, in a context where acting on gender relations becomes a moral responsibility, individuals endowed with access to the data, analytical skills and knowledge necessary to provide explanations of gendered phenomena and remedies to identified problems gain in influence (Prügl 2010). As gender experts have grown in number and gained in influence over the last decades, they have become better positioned to challenge accepted meanings and methods. The 'co-optation' of gender knowledge in the context of peacekeeping and peacebuilding activities thus comes with some degree of 'empowerment'.

The findings derived from the examination of gender mainstreaming in UN peacekeeping operations raise questions for further study. First, gender mainstreaming has been adopted as a technology of government following the efforts of women's groups who were resisting a hegemonic order and therefore positioned themselves as 'anti-hegemonic'. However, as gender knowledge becomes governmentalized, feminists increasingly participate 'in constructing technologies of power' (Prügl 2010: 6). Moreover, there is a broad tendency in global governance for 'gender experts' to be western-educated, elite women to whom institutions grant a voice and institutional power which is superior to that of women living in conflict-affected areas, who are only rarely considered experts of their own condition. The question remains open as to how these realities stand in the way of feminists' emancipatory goals and could be overcome. Second, this article has bracketed the question of the gendered impact of peacekeeping operations and their gender component on host societies. Field work would be necessary to assess the impacts of the development of an explicitly gendered discourse of security and of the (lack of) implementation of gender sensitive policies in peacekeeping operations, both in terms of the likelihood of new episodes of violent conflict and of the differentiated impacts on levels of (in)security of women, men, boys and girls.

Notes

1 Gender mainstreaming was also accused of shifting attention and resources away from programmes targeting women and empowering a few gender 'experts' but not women at the grassroots (Alvarey 1999 in True 2003).

2 The 'engendering' of international security agendas happened following post-Cold War discursive openings, whereby new conceptions of security (notably human security) took precedence, creating a space for addressing gender in peace and security discourse (Väyrynen 2004: 131).

3 However, DDR programmes remain to a large extent built on the assumption of fundamental differences between men and women (Shepherd 2010: 154). For instance, in Sierra Leone, fewer vocational skills were deemed appropriate for female beneficiaries (MacKenzie 2009). Moreover, linkages between the use of weapons, the perpetration of violent acts and constructions of gender remain addressed in very limited ways, if at all (Dzinesa 2008; Theidon 2009; Shepherd 2010).

139

4   I take into account that, considering that a 'discourse is a system or structure with variably open boundaries between itself and other discourses' (Purvis and Hunt 1993: 489) one can hardly conceive of a 'pure' feminist or neoliberal discourse. Rather, in this study, I treat them as relatively persistent 'discursive formations' in the Foucauldian sense.

5   This was suggested to me by Gwendolyn Beetham, gender consultant at DPKO in 2006.

6   This number comprises both multidimensional and conventional peacekeeping operations.

7   These are Kosovo, the Democratic Republic of the Congo, Liberia, Cote d'Ivoire, Haiti, Sudan, Timor Leste, Darfur, Central African Republic/Chad and Afghanistan. Former missions which had gender advisers were Burundi, Bosnia and Herzegovina and Sierra Leone.

8   These are the missions in Cyprus, India and Pakistan, the Middle East, Syria, Lebanon and Western Sahara; completed missions which used to have a gender focal point include missions in Ethiopia and Eritrea and Georgia.

9   The UNAMID gender unit is the largest one of all missions; it counts thirty-five staff positions, thirty of which were filled as of 2010.

10 While a well-known case has been made about the mass rapes which occurred in the context of the wars in the former Yugoslavia, it is almost never mentioned that acts of sexual violence against both men and women were systematic and widespread (Zarkov 2001).

Acknowledgements

I would like to thank Keith Krause, Elisabeth Prügl, Timo Walter, Aiko Holvikivi, and two anonymous readers for providing advice and comments on earlier drafts of this project, as well as Karin Grimm, Kathrin Quesada, Daniel de Torres and Kristin Valasek for putting me in contact with most of the interviewees quoted in these pages. A scholarship from the Fonds de recherche du Québec - Société et culture has enabled me to conduct part of this research.

Notes on contributor

Audrey Reeves is pursuing an MPhil/PhD in politics at the University of Bristol. She holds a BSc from Université de Montréal and a Master's degree from the Graduate Institute of International and Development Studies in Geneva. Her work focuses on peacebuilding practices and how they affect gender relations in post-conflict contexts. She has been a research assistant at the Geneva Centre for the Democratic Control of Armed Forces' Gender and Security Programme, at Université de Montréal's political science department and at the Swiss Campaign to Ban Landmines' Gender and Mine Action Programme.

References

Bastick, M. and de Torres, D. 2010. *Implementing the Women, Peace and Security Resolutions in Security Sector Reform*. Geneva: DCAF.

Bellamy, A. J., Williams, P. and Griffin, S. 2009. *Understanding Peacekeeping*. Cambridge: Polity Press.

Bouta, T., Frerks, G. and Hughes, B. 2005. *Gender and Peacekeeping in the West African Context*. The Hague: Netherlands Institute of International Relations.

Cockburn, C. 2004. "The Continuum of Violence: A Gender Perspective on War and Peace", in Giles, W. and Hyndman, J. (eds) *Sites of Violence: Gender and Conflict Zones*, pp. 24–44. Berkeley, CA: University of California Press.

Cohn, C. 2008. "Mainstreaming Gender in UN Security Policy: A Path to Political Transformation?", in Rai S. M. and Waylen, G. (eds) *Global Governance: Feminist Perspectives*, pp. 185–206. Basingstoke: Palgrave Macmillan.

Dean, M. 2006. *Governmentality: Power and Rule in Modern Society*, 1st edn. London: Sage.

DPKO. 2005. *Gender Mainstreaming in Peacekeeping Operations: Progress Report*. New York: United Nations.

DPKO. 2006. *Enhancing the Operational Impact of Peacekeeping Operations: Gender Balance in Military and Police Services Deployed to UN Peacekeeping Missions*. New York: United Nations.

Duffield, M. R. 2001. *Global Governance and the New Wars: The Merging of Development and Security*. London: Zed Books.

Dzinesa, G. 2008. 'The Role of Ex-Combatants and Veterans in Violence in Transitional Societies'. Paper presented at Violence and Transition Project Roundtable, Johannesburg, May.

ECOSOC. 1997. *Report of the Economic and Social Council for 1997*. New York: United Nations General Assembly.

Foucault, M. 2004. [1977–1978]. *Sécurité, territoire, population: Cours au Collège de France (1977–1978)*. M. Senellart, F. Ewald and A. Fontana (eds). France: Seuil/Gallimard.

Guéhenno, J. M. 2003. 'Statement of Mr Jean-Marie Guéhenno, Under-Secretary General for Peacekeeping Operations, during the Open Meeting of the Security Council on Women, Peace and Security'. Available at http://www.peacewomen. org/assets/file/Resources/UN/dpko_statementonwomenpeaceandsecurity_2003.pdf (accessed 11 July 2011).

Guéhenno, J. M. 2005. 'DPKO Under-Secretary General Policy Statement on Gender Mainstreaming'. Available at http://www.peacekeepingbestpractices.unlb.org/PBPS/Library/policystatementrvs.pdf (accessed 6 February 2010).

Guéhenno, J. M. 2006. 'Remarks of Jean-Marie Guéhenno, Under-Secretary-General for Peacekeeping Operations to the Special Committee on Peacekeeping Operations'. Available at http://www.peacewomen.org/assets/file/Resources/UN/dpko_remarks guehennoc34_2006.pdf (accessed 11 July 2011).

Hafner-Burton, E. and Pollack, M. A. 2002. 'Mainstreaming Gender in Global Governance', *European Journal of International Relations* 8 (3): 339–373.

Halley, J. 2008. *Split Decisions: How and Why to Take a Break from Feminism.* Princeton, NJ and Woodstock: Princeton University Press.

Harding, S. 1995. 'Just Add Women and Stir?', in Gender Working Group of the United Nations Commission on Science and Technology for Development *Missing Links: Gender Equity in Science and Technology for Development*, pp. 295–307. London, New York and Ottawa: International Development Research Centre, Intermediate Technology Publications, UNIFEM.

Harrington, C. 2006. 'Governing Peacekeeping: The Role of Authority and Expertise in the Case of Sexual Violence and Trauma', *Economy and Society* 35: 346–380.

Higate, P. and Henry, M. 2004. 'Engendering (In)security in Peace Support Operations', *Security Dialogue* 35 (4): 481–498.

Hindess, B. 2004. 'Liberalism – What's in a Name?', in Larner, W. and Walters, W. (eds) *Global Governmentality: Governing International Spaces*, pp. 23–39. New York: Routledge.

Lamptey, C. and DPKO. 2004. 'Gender Resource Package Presentation'. Available at http://www.peacekeepingbestpractices.unlb.org/PBPS/Pages/PUBLIC/ViewDocument.aspx?docid=564&cat=22&scat=0&menukey=_7_10 (accessed 4 March 2010).

Lui, R. 2004. 'The International Government of Refugees', in Larner, W. and Walters, W. (eds) *Global Governmentality: Governing International Spaces*, pp. 116–135. New York: Routledge.

Lyytikäinen, M. 2007. *Gender Training for Peacekeepers: Preliminary Overview of United Nations Peace Support Operations.* Santo Domingo: UN INSTRAW.

MacKenzie, M. 2009. 'Empowerment Boom or Bust? Assessing Women's Post-Conflict Empowerment Initiatives', *Cambridge Review of International Affairs* 22 (2): 199–215.

Marchand, M. and Parpart, J. 1995. *Feminism, Post-modernism, Development.* Abingdon: Routledge.

Mazurana, D. 2002. 'International Peacekeeping Operations: To Neglect Gender Is to Risk Peacekeeping Failure', in Cockburn, C. and Zarkov, D. (eds) *The Postwar Moment: Militaries, Masculinities and International Peacekeeping*, pp. 41–50. London: Lawrence and Wishart.

Netherlands, Norway, United Kingdom. 2006. 'Multi Donor Review of Implementation of Security Council Resolution 1325 on Women, Peace and Security in United Nations Mission in Democratic Republic of the Congo (MONUC), Liberia (UNMIL), Sierra Leone (UNIOSIL) and Kosovo (UNMIK)'. Available at http://www.peacekeepingbestpractices.unlb.org/pbps/Pages/Public/Download.aspx?docid=855 (accessed 11 July 2011).

Olsson, L. 2000. 'Mainstreaming Gender in Multidimensional Peacekeeping: A Field Perspective', *International Peacekeeping* 7 (3): 1–16.

Olsson, L. 2009. *Gender Equality and United Nations Peace Operations in Timor Leste.* Leiden, Netherlands: Koninklijke Brill NV.

Otto, D. 2007. 'Making Sense of Zero Tolerance Policies in Peacekeeping Sexual Economies', in Munro V. E. and Stychin C. F. (eds) *Sexuality and the Law: Feminist Engagements*, pp. 259–282. Oxon: Routledge Cavendish.

Pankhurst, D. 2008. *Gendered Peace: Women's Struggles for Post-War Justice and Reconciliation.* New York: Routledge.

Paris, R. 2002. 'International Peacebuilding and the "Mission Civilisatrice"', *Review of International Studies* 28: 637–656.

Peacewomen. 2004. 'Brief History of the Position of DPKO Gender Adviser'. Available at http://www.peacewomen.org/publications_enews_issue.php?id=87 (accessed 11 July 2011).

Pearson Peacekeeping Centre. 2009. *UNSCR 1820: A Roundtable Discussion with Female UN Police Officers Deployed in Peacekeeping Operations*. New York: Pearson Peacekeeping Centre.

Prügl, E. 2009. 'Gender Expertise and the Transformation of Masculine Domination'. Paper presented at the European Consortium for Political Research Conference, Potsdam, September.

Prügl, E. 2010. 'Antinomies of Feminist Struggle'. Paper presented at the Annual Convention of the International Studies Association, New Orleans, February.

Purvis, T. and Hunt, A. 1993. 'Discourse, Ideology, Discourse, Ideology, Discourse, Ideology. . .', *British Journal of Sociology* 44 (3): 473–499.

Quénivet, N. 2007. 'The Dissonance between the United Nations Zero-Tolerance Policy and the Criminalisation of Sexual Offences on the International Level', *International Criminal Law Review* 7: 657–676.

Rose, N. and Miller, P. 2010. 'Political Power beyond the State: Problematics of Government', *British Journal of Sociology* 43 (2): 271–303.

Shepherd, L. J. 2010. 'Women, Armed Conflict and Language – Gender, Violence and Discourse', *International Review of the Red Cross* 92 (877): 143–159.

Squires, J. 2005. 'Is Mainstreaming Transformative? Theorizing Mainstreaming in the Context of Diversity and Deliberation', *Social Politics* 12 (3): 366–388.

Theidon, K. 2009. 'Reconstructing Masculinities: The Disarmament, Demobilization, and Reintegration of Former Combatants in Colombia', *Human Rights Quarterly* 31: 1–34.

True, J. 2003. 'Mainstreaming Gender in Global Public Policy', *International Feminist Journal of Politics* 5 (3): 368–396.

UN Conduct and Discipline Unit. 2010. 'Prevention'. Available at http://cdu.unlb.org/UNStrategy/Prevention.aspx (accessed 11 July 2011).

UN General Assembly. 2000. *Report of the Ad Hoc Committee of the Whole of the Twenty-Third Special Session*. New York: United Nations.

UNIFEM. 2010. 'UNIFEM Welcomes UN Security Council Support for Comprehensive Set of Indicators on the Implementation of Resolution 1325'. Available at http://www.unifem.org/news_events/story_detail.php?StoryID=1076 (accessed 11 July 2011).

UNIFEM and DPKO. 2010. *Addressing Conflict-Related Sexual Violence: An Analytical Inventory of Peacekeeping Practice*. New York: United Nations.

United Nations. 2003. *Secretary-General's Bulletin: Special Measures for Protection from Sexual Exploitation and Abuse*. New York: United Nations.

United Nations. 2009. 'United Nations in Global Effort to Increase Number of Female Police in Peacekeeping Operations'. Available at http://www.un.org/News/Press/docs/2009/pko218.doc.htm (accessed 11 July 2011).

United Nations. 2010a. 'United Nations Peace Operations 2009: Year in Review'. Available at http://www.un.org/en/peacekeeping/publications/yir/yir2009.pdf (accessed 11 July 2011).

United Nations. 2010b. 'Ten Rules: Code of Personal Conduct for Blue Helmets'. Available at http://cdu.unlb.org/UNStandardsofConduct/TenRulesCodeofPersonal ConductForBlueHelmets.aspx (accessed 11 July 2011).

United Nations. 2011. 'Gender Statistics'. Available at http://www.un.org/en/ peacekeeping/resources/statistics/gender.shtml (accessed 11 July 2011).

United Nations Security Council. S/RES/1325/2000. 31 October 2000.

United Nations Security Council. S/RES/1820/2008. 19 June 2008.

United Nations Security Council. S/RES/1888/2009. 30 September 2009.

United Nations Security Council. S/RES/1889/2009. 5 October 2009.

UN Secretary-General. 2002. *Report of the Secretary-General on Women, Peace and Security (2002)*. New York: United Nations.

UN Secretary-General. 2004. *Report of the Secretary-General on Women, Peace and Security (2004)*. New York: United Nations.

UN Secretary-General. 2005. *Report of the Secretary-General on Women, Peace and Security (2005)*. New York: United Nations.

UN Secretary-General. 2009. *Report of the Secretary-General on Women, Peace and Security (2009)*. New York: United Nations.

UN Secretary-General. 2010. *Rejustification of Posts Financed by the Support Account for Peacekeeping Operation for the Period 1 July 2009 to 30 June 2010. Administrative and Budgetary Aspects of the Financing of the United Nations Peacekeeping Operations*. New York: United Nations.

UN Security Council. 2010. 'Statement by the President of the Security Council'. Available at http://daccess-dds-ny.un.org/doc/UNDOC/GEN/N10/603/52/PDF/ N1060352.pdf?OpenElement (accessed 11 July 2011).

Väyrynen, T. 2004. 'Gender and UN Peace Operations: The Confines of Modernity', *International Peacekeeping* 11 (1): 125–142.

Whitworth, S. 2004. *Men, Militarism & UN Peacekeeping: A Gendered Analysis*. Boulder, CO: Lynne Rienner Publishers.

Whitworth, S. 2005. 'Militarized Masculinities and the Politics of Peacekeeping', in Booth, K. (ed.) *Critical Security Studies and World Politics*, pp. 89–106. Boulder, CO: Lynne Rienner Publishers.

Worthen, M., Veale, A., McKay, S. and Wessells, M. 2010. '"I Stand Like a Woman": Empowerment and Human Rights in the Context of Community-Based Reintegration of Girl Mothers Formerly Associated with Fighting Forces and Armed Groups', *Journal of Human Rights Practice* 2 (1): 49–70.

Zanotti, L. 2006. 'Taming Chaos: A Foucauldian View of UN Peacekeeping, Democracy and Normalization', *International Peacekeeping* 13 (2): 150–167.

Zarkov, D. 2001. "The Body of the Other Man: Sexual Violence and the Construction of Masculinity, Sexuality and Ethnicity in Croatian Media", in Moser, C. O. N. and Clark F. C. (eds) *Victims, Perpetrators or Actors? Gender, Armed Conflict and Political Violence*, pp. 69–82. London: Zed Books & Kali for Women.

Interviews

Anonymous A. 2010. *Integrating Gender Perspectives in the UN Mission in Sudan and the African Union–UN Hybrid Operation in Darfur.* Interviewed by A. Reeves [phone interview]. 9 July.

Anonymous B. 2010. *Integrating Gender Perspectives in the UN Stabilization Mission in the DRC.* Interviewed by A. Reeves [phone interview]. 21 July.

Doucet, C. 2010. *Integrating Gender Perspectives in the UN Mission in Liberia.* Interviewed by A. Reeves [phone interview]. 26 July.

Hutchinson, C. 2010. *Integrating Gender Perspectives in UN Peacekeeping.* Interviewed by A. Reeves [phone interview]. 21 June.

Lamptey, C. 2010. *Integrating Gender Perspectives in UN Peacekeeping.* Interviewed by A. Reeves [phone interview]. 7 June.

Mackay, A. 2010. *Integrating Gender Perspectives in UN Peacekeeping.* Interviewed by A. Reeves [phone interview]. 23 June.

Stroosnijder, T. 2010. *Integrating Gender Perspectives in the UN Mission in Kosovo.* Interviewed by A. Reeves [Skype interview]. 11 and 21 June.

Leveraging Change

WOMEN S ORGANIZATIONS AND THE IMPLEMENTATION OF UNSCR 1325 IN THE BALKANS

JILL A. IRVINE
University of Oklahoma, USA

Abstract

This article examines how regional and local women's organizations in Serbia, Bosnia-Herzegovina and Kosovo have used UNSCR 1325 as a tool for organizing and advocacy in three broad areas: women's inclusion in decision-making processes; regional and human security; and transitional justice. In response to perceived unwillingness by international as well as national actors to implement UNSCR 1325, women's organizations developed strategies to use this international norm to achieve their goals. They have done this, I argue, through a double 'boomerang effect'. In their seminal 1998 work, *Activists Beyond Borders*, Keck and Sikkink demonstrated how NGOs operate to produce a boomerang effect; they appeal to transnational actors to assert international pressure against national governments in order to enforce compliance with human rights norms. In attempting to implement UNSCR 1325, women's organizations have also often added a reverse dimension, mobilizing local support through grassroots campaigns and regional networks in order to force the United Nations and other international actors to comply with their own resolution concerning women, peace and security. In doing so, they have achieved some success in promoting inclusion. They have been less successful in using UNSCR 1325 as a tool for addressing structural sources of inequality including militarism and neo-liberal models of economic development.

This article examines the efforts of women's organizations in the Balkans to promote political change through the implementation of United Nations

Security Council Resolution (UNSCR) 1325 on women, peace and security. Prompted by the conflicts in the Balkans, among other factors, and reflecting years of intense global human and women's rights activism to reduce violence against women in conflict zones, UNSCR 1325 was adopted in 2000 to address the impact of conflict on women and girls and to enhance women's partici-pation in post-conflict processes of peace-building. UNSCR 1325 called for increasing women's role in the prevention of conflict, ensuring the protection of women and girls during conflict and increasing women's participation in post-conflict reconstruction.

As the first Security Council resolution to recognize women as something other than victims of armed conflict, UNSCR 1325 has been hailed as a water-shed in global feminist activism (Keating and Knight 2004; Otto 2009; Mazurana et al. 2005; Anderlini 2007, 2010; Porter 2007). Since its adoption, however, a consensus has emerged that the resolution has failed to live up to its promise. Some critics have pointed to problems of implementation including a lack of political motivation, scarcity of funds for women's organ-izations, institutional sexism, patriarchal cultural norms and resistance by the United Nations (UN) itself as obstacles to the greater inclusion of women's organizations in peace-making processes (NGO Working Group 2005; Porter 2007; Anderlini 2010). Others have questioned the basis of the resolution itself, arguing that it has come at too high a price of diluting feminist goals (Orford 2002; Charlesworth 2005; Shepherd 2008; Otto 2009). Most agree that perhaps its 'most remarkable impact' is its use as a lever for local feminist activists (Otto 2009). Based on over thirty interviews conducted in Serbia, Kosovo and Bosnia-Herzegovina from 2008 to 2011, and documentary evidence, this article aims to contribute to comparative analysis of such local activism. Although women's organizations in the Balkans have taken a variety of positions in relation to gender, war and peace, ranging from conser-vative nationalist to radical feminist, the organizations I examine here share a focus on promoting gender equality through regional cooperation. When, how and to what effect, I ask, have women's organizations and activists in the Balkans used UNSCR 1325 as a focal point of organization and advocacy? What can their experiences tell us about the usefulness of UNSCR 1325 as a means for promoting enduring change?

I begin by presenting current critiques of UNSCR 1325, highlighting what they reveal about its selective and instrumental use by the UN and other inter-national actors. I then discuss the failure of international actors to implement UNSCR 1325 in Bosnia-Herzegovina and Kosovo, and the emergence of regional women's organizations in response. I demonstrate how in attempting to leverage change through UNSCR 1325, women's organizations and activists have employed a double 'boomerang effect'. In their seminal 1998 work, *Activists Beyond Borders*, Keck and Sikkink demonstrated how NGOs operate to produce a boomerang effect; they appeal to transnational actors to assert international pressure against national governments in order to enforce compliance with human rights norms. Women's organizations in the Balkans engaged in such boomerang behavior beginning in the 1990s hoping to bring pressure to bear on their own governments to respect such norms. In attempting to implement UNSCR 1325, women's organizations have also added a reverse dimension, mobilizing local support through grassroots campaigns and regional networks in order to force the UN and other international actors to comply with their own resolution concerning women, peace and security. I conclude by considering what the experience of women's organizations in the Balkans can tell us more generally about UNSCR 1325 and its potential to effect enduring and transformative change. I argue that while women's organizations have used UNSCR 1325 to tackle the 'imperial tendencies' of the UN and other international actors involved in humanitarian missions, challenging them to comply with the norms they purport to enforce, the resolution has proved less useful as a tool for addressing structural causes of inequality such as militarism and neo-liberal models of post-conflict development.

UNSCR 1325

UNSCR 1325 has received a great deal of attention from practitioners and scholars alike who see it as providing a new framework for dealing with women in conflict and post-conflict settings, relations between civil society   women's organizations in particular   and the UN, and gender equality more generally. At the same time, a growing body of work questions the extent to which UNSCR 1325 has thus far provided a useful mechanism for achieving its aims. Critical assessments of the resolution range from those highlighting problems of implementation to those highlighting shortcomings inherent in the resolution itself.

Numerous works have pointed to the 'huge gap' between the rhetoric of UNSCR 1325 and the reality of its implementation. While the list of potential obstacles is long, most stem from a lack of political will or motivation by local populations, national governments and international actors (Cohn et al. 2004; Keating and Knight 2004; Mazurana et al. 2005; Porter 2007: 18; Chetail 2009; Anderlini 2010). Moreover, critics charge that the resolution is unmoored from over a century of international feminist peace activism. It challenges neither militarism nor the 'hegemonic use of power in a crisis' (Orford 2002; Otto 2009: 17). Equally problematically, the resolution fails to provide a mechanism for tackling structural causes of inequality and the challenges posed by post-conflict, neo-liberal models of development. Laura Shepherd equates the discursive logic of both the NGO Working Group, the dozen or so women's and human rights organizations which drafted the resolution, and UNSCR 1325 which offers 'a conventional narrative of development where "zones of conflict" are assisted by the "international community" to integrate into the global mechanisms of production and consumption thereby securing not only the conflict in question but a neoliberal world order' (Shepherd 2008: 399). Finally, the resolution raises serious issues about the impact of mainstreaming, which has resulted in the bureaucratization and dilution of transformative goals. It is a mistake, as Dianna Otto points out, to misread institutional inclusion as feminist activism (Otto 2009).

An underlying concern of all these critiques, and the focus of this article, is the UN and other international actors' selective and instrumental use of UNSCR 1325. Indeed, Otto argues that the UN Security Council (UNSC) adopted the resolution in order to bolster its legitimacy and intervention projects in the post-Cold War world (Otto 2009). Given this instrumental commitment at best to feminist principles and activism, has its adoption been worth the price? For some critics, the answer is a resounding no. Rather, UNSCR 1325 has primarily aided in creating new female subjects of intervention without unsettling the current imperialist intervention projects. Inclusion, as UNSCR 1325 envisions it, fails to imagine women playing a role in changing the rules of the game or the way in which the game is understood (Orford 2002). The danger, thus, is that through such mechanisms as UNSCR 1325, 'feminism ends up simply facilitating the existing projects and priorities of militarised economic globalization in the name of protecting and promoting the interests of women' (Orford 2002: 283).

In order to understand whether and how these problems of conceptualization and implementation have limited the potential of UNSCR 1325, it is necessary to examine the ways in which women's organizations and other activists have used it as a tool in their own contexts. To what extent have they encountered and overcome these obstacles in their own work? As we shall see, women's organizations in the Balkans have adopted strategies of promoting UNSCR 1325 that challenge the tendency of international actors to deal selectively with women's issues, even as they have found UNSCR 1325 wanting as a tool for advocacy in other areas.

THE UN AND UNSCR 1325 IN THE BALKANS

The wars in the Balkans, which began in 1991 and ended in 1999, provided a key impetus for the passage of UNSCR 1325. Through ethnic cleansing campaigns, these wars came to symbolize the dynamics of conflict in the post-Cold War world, which involved massive civilian casualties, the use of government force against its own population and brutality toward women, including the use of rape as a tool of war (Kumar 2001; Anderlini 2007; Cockburn 2007). Indeed, the conflict in the Balkans became the 'condensation point', to use Keck and Sikkink's term, for a global campaign against violence against women in conflict situations (Keck and Sikkink 1998: 181). Women's rights organizations and activists from the Balkans played an essential role in this larger global campaign as they sought to respond to the impact of war at home (Korac 1998; Cockburn 2007; Irvine 2007).

At the time that UNSCR 1325 was passed, Kosovo had been placed under an interim administration, the United Nations Mission in Kosovo (UNMIK).

This followed a 78-day bombing campaign in response to Serbian aggression and the withdrawal of Serbian forces from the area. As a result of this timing, the application of UNSCR 1325 was put to the test almost immediately in Kosovo, as well as in Bosnia-Herzegovina, a second area of the former Yugoslavia that had been under international administration since 1997.

Women's organizations were initially optimistic that the passage of UNSCR 1325 would have a positive impact in the Balkans, where despite a decade of activity in civil society, women occupied few positions of formal decision-making authority. Indeed, for many women's organizations, which had spent almost a decade fighting the nationalist policies of their respective governments, civil society remained the most hospitable arena for civic engagement. Women's organizing took different forms in the various national contexts, from opposing the 'militaristic and patriarchal' practices of the Milosevic regime in Serbia, to pressing the newly emerging political structures under international administration to pay attention to women's concerns in Bosnia-Herzegovina. In Kosovo, women organized as part of a parallel Kosovar society in opposition to Serbian authorities throughout the 1990s; they applied this experience to the task of reconstruction after 1999. Thus, after years of organizing on the international as well as national stages, women's organizations in the Balkans appeared well positioned to use UNSCR 1325 as a tool to leverage their increased participation and improve women's status in their post-conflict countries.

The initial assumption of UN officials and even activists themselves was that such leverage would be wielded primarily against recalcitrant domestic governments (Cohn et al. 2004). The UN was generally inclined to position itself as defender of gender equality against reluctant national governments and it approached its role in the Balkans with this view (Shepherd 2008). What women's rights activists in the Balkans soon discovered, however, was that UN personnel and other international actors were not necessarily concerned about enforcing gender equality in their own institutions and practices. This was immediately clear in Bosnia-Herzegovina and Kosovo, the two areas under direct UN administration. In response, and often drawing upon growing popular hostility toward international administration, women's organizations used UNSCR 1325 as a tool to pressure the UN and other international actors and to advocate for increased participation, improved security and access to transitional justice.

PARTICIPATION IN DECISION-MAKING BODIES

The inclusion of women 'at all decision-making levels in national, regional and international institutions and mechanisms for the prevention, management and resolution of conflict' and 'consultation with local and international women's groups' are highlighted in the language of UNSCR 1325; and women's groups saw these as the centerpiece of their own implementation efforts (United

Nations Security Council 2000). Despite the official rhetoric of international actors in Bosnia concerning gender equality, women's organizations had long complained of their lack of access to decision-making bodies controlled by these actors. The Dayton Peace Accords (DPA), which set forth the post-war settlement in Bosnia-Herzegovina, was the first major peace agreement negotiated after the adoption of the Platform for Action (PFA) at the 4th World Conference on Women in Beijing, and activists had hoped the DPA's architects would incorporate the goals of the contemporaneous and well-publicized PFA. They were soon disappointed, however, as the DPA completely disregarded the PFA. Not one woman from the region participated in the conference, and the resulting accord took a 'gender neutral' approach that failed to address the specific needs of women and girls in post-conflict settings (Lithander 2000).

This failure set the tone for the international administration of Bosnia-Herzegovina, as administrators consistently argued that they had more pressing matters to deal with than gender concerns; no women were appointed among the deputy high commissioners or other positions of authority during the ensuing months (Žene Ženama 2007). When the first elections in 1996 resulted in a mere 2.4 per cent of women elected to the House of Representatives of the Parliamentary Assembly (representing both entities), women's organizations launched a campaign for the introduction of gender quotas. These were dismissed as 'undemocratic' by the chairman of the electoral law drafting commission, Francois Froement-Meurice, though as Bosnian women 'stressed (decisively)' such quotas were being adopted at the same time in his home country of France (Borić 2004). The Office of the High Commissioner, which was invested with supreme authority in Bosnia-Herzegovina, proved particularly resistant to granting access to women's groups and activists, dismissing gender concerns as 'the responsibility of the [Bosnian] state' (Žene Ženama 2007: 38).

Like the international administrators in Bosnia-Herzegovina, UNMIK did not appear very responsive to women's issues or voices after their arrival in Kosovo. After the war, women's organizations immediately became involved in the reconstruction process but, according to Igballe Rogova, Director of the Kosovo Women's Network (KWN), 'we were not recognized because our initiatives were not under UNMIK or OSCE' (Rogova 2008). Few women were appointed to the decision-making bodies set up by UNMIK in the security or political sectors. Indeed, as the UNMIK administration became more established, women actually began to feel as if they had less power than before (Kosova Women's Network 2009: 46). According to activist Lumnije Deqani, '[w]hen UNMIK came and employed women, employment was never based on a gender perspective but based only on whether she was beautiful [and] knows a little bit of English ... We have many women professionals. We have many educated generations [of women], but UNMIK was never based on this' (Kosova Women's Network 2009: 46).

As women's frustration grew at their exclusion from peace-making processes in the ensuing months, they turned to UNSCR 1325 as a tool to pressure the UN bodies shaping the post-war order in Bosnia-Herzegovina and Kosovo to live up to the stipulations of the UN's own resolution. In June 2001, when UNMIK refused them permission to meet with a visiting UNSC delegation, women activists 'noted that UNSCR 1325 gave them the right to meet with the delegation' (Kosova Women's Network 2009: 42). As a result, the delegation agreed to meet with the women after the scheduled events of the day. This scenario was repeated in December 2002 when UNMIK failed to invite local women to meet with a visiting UNSC delegation, with the result that, after vigorous lobbying, the women were included in the regular schedule of the day (Kosovo Women's Network 2009).

Women's criticism of the UN's failure to incorporate women in post-war reconstruction in Kosovo and Bosnia-Herzegovina did not extend to all arms of the octopus-like international organization. Indeed, the UN Development Fund for Women (UNIFEM), which was charged with overseeing the implementation of UNSCR 1325, was generally perceived as supportive of local women's initiatives (Rogova 2008; Zajović 2008; Kosova Women's Network 2009: 48). Nevertheless, as the smallest UN entity, 'lacking power or access', UNIFEM had little influence over UNMIK and the highest levels of decision-making in the political and military spheres (Anderlini 2010). Moreover, although UNIFEM financially supported the efforts of local women to promote the implementation of UNSCR 1325, this support did not involve any direct acknowledgement of the failures of the UN as a whole in this respect.

With UNIFEM support, and after years of frustrating effort to pressure the UN and other international actors to implement UNSCR 1325, women's organizations decided to establish two regional organizations to increase their leverage: the Regional Women's Lobby for Peace, Security, and Justice in Southeastern Europe (RWL), composed of women leaders throughout the western Balkans formed in 2005, and the Women's Peace Coalition (WPC), comprised of a network of over 100 women's organizations affiliated with Women in Black – Serbia and the Kosova Women's Network formed in 2006. While the RWL operated primarily in the realm of formal politics, the WPC adopted a strong grassroots orientation. Nevertheless, there was overlap in their membership and strong personal ties among their members, which strengthened their ability to mount joint advocacy efforts. From the outset, RWL and the WPC understood their work as building upon cross-border cooperation that had existed throughout the war among women's activists and organizations (Benderly 1997; Kašić 2007; Cockburn 2007). Now they hoped to use the louder voice of regional networks to draw attention to their demands for greater inclusion in the various local, municipal and national assemblies that were being elected in Balkan countries throughout this period as well as in bodies more directly established by the UN and other international actors.

UNSCR 1325 gave the newly established regional women's organizations a tool to pressure the public, political parties and national governments into including more women in politics and policy-making through gender quotas, gender equity legislation and gender agencies. Displaying boomerang behavior, women's organizations attempted to use the moral and political authority of international acceptance to exert local pressure. UNSCR 1325 was adopted during what one parliamentary representative has called the 'golden age' of women's civic engagement in Bosnia-Herzegovina (Borić 2008). After organizing to introduce gender quotas, women's organizations and newly elected women politicians also successfully campaigned for the establishment of gender mechanisms at all levels of government including a Gender Equity Law in 2003, a Gender Agency in 2004 and a Law against Domestic Violence in 2005. Interviews with activists suggest that UNSCR 1325 was a valuable tool in these efforts (Žene Ženama 2005, 2007).

UNSCR 3125 proved an equally valuable tool in Kosovo, where the 'standards before status' policy   that Kosovo must achieve a certain standard of democratic governance before resolving its status in relation to Serbia   meant that appealing to international norms was a powerful discursive strategy for pressuring local elites. For example, the RWL argued:

> At the moment when the world is poised to hear a decision on Kosovo's status, and at the moment when all our countries are looking to build strong relationships with the European Union and NATO, a democratic parity of women with men in Kosovo's assembly would send an unmistakable message about Kosovo's readiness for a fresh start. (RWL 2007a)

Additional gender equity legislation followed with gender quotas adopted in the electoral laws in 2008.

Women's organizations skillfully employed the perceived carrot of recognition and legitimation by the international community in their efforts to pressure local governments into UNSCR 1325. At the same time, they clearly understood that international actors' compliance with UNSCR 1325 was the starting point for any meaningful implementation, given the immense authority they wielded over all aspects of post-conflict reconstruction in Kosovo and Bosnia-Herzegovina. In Bosnia-Herzegovina, the women's organization Žene Ženama led the effort to monitor international as well as national implementation of UNSCR 1325 (Žene Ženama 2007). 'Overall, the international community has failed to make a significant contribution to institutionalizing the promotion of a gender perspective into its activities and its own structures', the women's organization charged (Žene Ženama 2007: 5). Drawing upon the widespread popular perception that the international community 'talks about democracy but works behind closed doors', this appeal to international actors to follow their own norms concerning inclusiveness appears to have resonated with the populace. Following double boomerang logic, the women's organizations argued that 'greater international accountability to the population and to the responsibilities of international human rights treaties and legal agreements such as UNSCR 1325 would enhance the success and standing of international actions in BiH' (Žene Ženama 2007:

39). In other words, if the international community wished to gain legitimacy with the local population, it must abide by international norms.

Women's organizations took an even more public approach in Kosovo, organizing high profile public demonstrations to pressure the UN administration into complying with UNSCR 1325. KWN and the newly formed regional organizations were able to draw upon popular frustration with UNMIK to gain support for their own efforts to pressure it, through demonstrations, letter writing campaigns and other measures, to include women in the status negotiations and to implement UNSCR 1325. Meanwhile, WPC and RWL denounced the failure of international actors to comply with international norms, demanding that the 'failures by the United Nations to fulfill UNSCR 1325 ... be corrected in the future' (RWL 2007b).

Such efforts resulted in a measure of success, albeit limited. After three members of the RWL met with UN Secretary-General's Envoy for Kosovo, Martti Ahtisaari, in 2007, he inserted a direct call for the implementation of UNSCR 1325 in his proposed draft Security Council resolution on Kosovo. Although women were still excluded from the negotiating team, they were included in the various expert working groups that supported this team (UNIFEM 2009). Moreover, this strategy of drawing upon population frustration with the UN, at the very least, focused popular attention on UNSCR 1325 and, in some cases, also resulted in changes in the behavior of international actors.

REGIONAL AND HUMAN SECURITY

Women's organizations in the Balkans and elsewhere have stressed that a human security perspective is essential to achieving gender equality in post-conflict settings. International actors, similarly, have touted human security as an important focus of their efforts in the Balkans (Arifagić and Sabović 2007; Djurdjević-Lukić 2007; Kstovicova et al. 2007). In contrast to traditional security concerns, human security situates the locus of protection on the individual rather than on the state. Based on a bottom-up approach that relies on input and participation from civil society, it includes a regional focus that emphasizes cooperation across 'soft borders' in achieving human rights and transitional justice rather than protection of hard borders (Mostov 2010). Reflecting this position, UNSCR 1325 calls upon international actors to adopt a gender perspective that focuses on 'the special needs of women and girls during ... post-conflict reconstruction' as well as expanding the 'role of women in field based operations especially among military observers, civilian police, human rights and humanitarian personnel' (United Nations Security Council 2000).

Although women's organizations in the Balkans may emphasize different issues, they are in agreement about the substance of human security in relation to UNSCR 1325. In October 2008, the RWL held a widely publicized conference in Pristina on the implementation of UNSCR 1325 and security in the Balkans 'to give a voice to women in the western Balkans and introduce strategic political and security leaders to a women's perspective of peace and security in the region . . .' (RWL 2008b). The concept of human security articulated in conference documents included the fight against organized crime, corruption and violence in the region as well as the commitment to address the 'role poverty plays in prolonging regional instability and insecurity' (RWL 2008c). Increased representation of women in the security and the political sectors and support for reproductive rights were also emphasized as important goals (Rasić 2007; Zajović 2007; RWL 2008d).

In attempting to promote human security through UNSCR 1325 and women's participation in security arrangements, women's organizations encountered considerable resistance by international actors. One serious human security challenge that brought women's organizations into direct conflict with some international actors involved sex trafficking. Women's organizations were instrumental in documenting and publicizing the complicity of peacekeeping forces and other international actors in human trafficking in the Balkans (Mendelson 2005; Žene Ženama 2005, 2007, 2009). They also documented and publicized the failures of international actors to bring their own personnel to account (Global Rights 2004; Žene Ženama 2007, 2009). Jurisdiction over such crimes falls to the host country and some are better than others in punishing offenders. In their extensive public education campaigns concerning sex trafficking, women's organizations repeatedly pointed out that such impunity from prosecution is unacceptable and insisted that the international community enforce anti-trafficking laws and punishments as stipulated by UNSCR 1325 and other international norms.

Such efforts resulted in a number of successes and concrete programs. For example, in 2007 KWN reached an agreement with the Multinational Taskforce to deliver information sessions on women and UNSCR 1325 to NATO forces throughout Kosovo. They also began collaborating with police forces, providing training on UNSCR 1325 including appropriate responses to violence against women (Halimi 2007). A similar program was launched in Bosnia-Herzegovina involving long-term cooperation between women's organizations and various security forces including the European Union Force (EUFOR) and European Union Police Mission (EUPM) that involved extensive training in women's human rights and gender equality. A recent assessment noted 'remarkable moves in gender sensibilization', reform processes in the security sector pertaining to the punishment of perpetrators of gender violence and 'greater participation of women in peacekeeping, humanitarian and reconstruction processes' (Žene Ženama 2009: 13). Former government official Lejla Somun similarly concluded that UNSCR 1325 had proved valuable in the security sector in bringing together the Defense and Interior Ministries, the police and women's organizations around concrete security tasks (Somun 2011). Nevertheless, according to one prominent activist in anti-trafficking efforts, UNSCR 1325 was of limited help in the fight against sex trafficking and other human security issues because it 'ghettoized' women's issues, allowing decision-makers to ignore them (Hadžihalilović 2011).

UNSCR 1325 has proved to be of at least limited usefulness in increasing attention to issues involving violence against women, but what about when it comes to more traditional security matters? Both the RWL and the WPC link human and regional security in their approach and emphasize that their voice must be heard not only on the 'soft issues' of development and human rights but the 'hard issues' of the status of Kosovo or constitutional reform in Bosnia-Herzegovina. Interestingly, while they claim the right to have their voice heard as women, their concerns are not framed in terms of specific gender issues. It is precisely in these more traditional security areas that these women's organizations have had to fight hardest with international authorities to have their voices heard. KWN leader Rogova describes this attitude in a meeting between KWN and a UNSC delegation:

> Women activists began by discussing issues related to Kosova's final political status. The UN ambassador interrupted, 'Status is an issue for political parties. Let's talk about women's issues. For example, let's talk about Resolution 1325'. Kosovo women were surprised at the ambassador's obvious lack of knowledge that according to UNSCR 1325, women should be involved in negotiating Kosovo's final political status. They asked, 'Don't you think that status is an issue that affects women? This is directly stated in Resolution 1325'. (Rogova 2007: 45)

When the RWL and WPC opposed the six-point plan on Kosovo reached between Serbia and UN Secretary General Ban Ki-Moon as a breach of democratic practices, the UNDP refused to allow KWN leader Rogova to speak at the 'International Conference on Women and Governance in Eastern Europe and CIS' unless she removed all references to the six-point plan from her speech (RWL 2008a: 1). Rogova pointed out the irony of her exclusion from a panel entitled 'The Enabling Environment for Women's Political Participation: Kosova Women on the Frontlines of Democracy Building'. In her public response, she also reminded the UNDP that, in accordance with UNSCR 1325, 'women have a right to make their voices heard' (Kosova Women's Network 2008). After appealing to both national and global feminist constituencies and suspending all cooperation with the UNDP, Rogova received a public apology from head of the UNDP in Kosova, Fronde Mauring, and normal relations were restored (Kosova Women's Network 2008). Employing the double boomerang effect in this and other instances thus produced results.

TRANSITIONAL JUSTICE

Transitional justice is a third area in which regional women's organizations have used UNSCR 1325 as a tool of advocacy and organization. Truth commissions and transitional justice more generally have become staples of international diplomacy, and events in the Balkans have been central to this shift in international norms (Chetail 2009; Grodsky 2009). UNSCR 1325 calls upon all actors to adopt measures that support local women's peace initiatives and indigenous processes for conflict resolution. It also emphasizes the need to prosecute 'those responsible for genocide, crimes against humanity and war crimes, including those relating to sexual and other violence against women' (United Nations Security Council 2000). Both the RWL and especially the WPC have seen these as a central part of their work. With the establishment of regional women's organizations, support for a regional approach to this question has gained ground, despite considerable challenges. Along with other human rights and civil society actors, women's organizations have launched a significant initiative from below to pressure national governments and international actors to establish a regional truth commission.

The passage of UNSCR 1325 has provided women's organizations with a powerful tool to continue and to reconceptualize their previous work on transitional justice. During the 1990s, pressure from women's and other human rights groups, combined with other political exigencies, caused international organizations and foreign governments to establish the International Criminal Tribunal for the Former Yugoslavia (ICTY). Women's organizations played a pivotal role in gathering evidence of wartime crimes and in pushing for and defining the terms of the ICTY's mandate, particularly as it related to the prosecution of gender-based violence (Mertus 2004). Engaging in boomerang behavior, these organizations sought to use international pressure through the court to bring national governments as well as individuals to account.

After the recent wars in the Balkans ended in 1999, Women in Black Serbia (WBS) made transitional justice the main focus of its work (Zajović 2006a, 2006b, 2008). In 2005, WBS presented a resolution on women, peace and security to the Serbian Parliament, which demanded that the Serbian government admit its own complicity in initiating and perpetrating the violence of the 1990s. UNSCR 1325 has bolstered activists' subsequent work of monitoring war crimes trials in Serbia in the face of fierce resistance and even repression by the authorities as well as its regional efforts to promote reconciliation through the observance of the anniversary of the act of genocide at Srebrenica and other commemorations (Vuković 2007).

Nevertheless, despite their innovative work and the directive of UNSCR 1325 that women be included in transitional justice, women's organizations and leaders have not always felt they have received support from the UN. Indeed, the RWL and WPC have frequently expressed frustration at what they believe is a failure to consult women concerning the best methods of seeking transitional justice. Rather, many international organizations come to the region with their own plans and ideas, which do not include efforts already underway. As women's rights activist Nexhmije Fetahu explained, 'one of the biggest barriers civil society faced was international organizations that came to Kosovo with set plans and an "ultimatum" for "reconciliation" between people of different "ethnicities"' which left local women's organizations and other civil society groups out of the planning (Fetahu 2007: 26). Zajović echoed this sense of frustration with UNMIK's lack of progress on transitional justice, which she argued was caused by the 'militarization' of all its interactions and relationships (Zajović 2008). Responding to a perceived failure of internationally-run local projects and a lack of ownership in the ICTY process, women's organizations have attempted to hold the international community accountable to the transitional justice provisions of UNSCR 1325 and to advocate for a more grassroots approach to transitional justice (Solioz 2006; Gaffney and Alic 2008).

In 2006, two civil society groups led by Nataša Kandić of the Humanitarian Law Center in Belgrade and Vesna Terselić of Dokumenta in Zagreb held the first meeting of the Regional Truth Commission for the Former Yugoslavia RECOM, an initiative to establish a regional truth commission among countries of the former Yugoslavia. According to Kandić, the commission will focus on the victims' experience and establish the facts concerning all victims of the war (RECOM 2009). Coalition members, which in 2011 numbered more than one thousand organizations and individuals, focused their efforts during the first phase of activism on gathering signatures in support of a regional truth commission. At a recent meeting, held in Sarajevo in June 2011, which this author attended, RECOM leaders decided to move to the second phase of pre-senting national governments in the region with the petition (despite the fact that the original goal of one million signatures was not met); these govern-ments will then make a final decision about the establishment of the truth commission. Despite the initial skepticism of national and international actors alike, RECOM has gathered steam and has been endorsed by the EU, the ICTY and various regional officials.

As key actors in civil society operating at the regional level, women's organ-izations have been important to the RECOM process and they have used UNSCR 1325 in their efforts to gain international support for the grassroots effort. The RWL called for the establishment of a regional truth commission in accordance with UNSCR 1325 in its presentation to the UNSC in 2008. Women's organizations are heavily represented among the RECOM members (RECOM 2011). Valdeta Idrizi, a women's rights activist in the divided city of Mitrovica in northern Kosovo, was initially skeptical of attending a regional RECOM consultation, stating that 'I never would have gone if it had not been sponsored by these [women's] organizations, which I knew and respected' (Idrizi 2008). Nevertheless, several women's organizations have felt that gender concerns have not been adequately reflected in the RECOM process, and they recently decided to focus on their own grassroots initiative to convene a 'women's court' (Zvizdić 2011). Although the process is on-going, it appears that women's organizations are using UNSCR 1325, with some success through the double boomerang effect, to mobilize local support in order to pressure international and national actors to adopt regional mechan-isms of transitional justice.

CONCLUSION: THE POSSIBILITIES AND LIMITATIONS OF UNSCR 1325

This recent celebration of the tenth anniversary of UNSCR 1325 has provided an opportunity to assess its usefulness in creating enduring change concerning the role of women in conflict and post-conflict reconstruction. The conflicts in the Balkans were central to the formation and adoption of UNSCR 1325, which was put to the test almost immediately in the UN administered areas of Kosovo and Bosnia-Herzegovina. What lessons can we learn from the experience of women's organizations there?

The first lesson is that UNSCR 1325 has provided a useful, though limited, tool of empowerment and advocacy. Women's organizations have used UNSCR 1325 with some success to agitate for inclusion in all aspects of making and implementing peace agreements as well as representative bodies more generally. UNSCR 1325 has also provided a useful tool for organizing and advocating on behalf of not only the soft issues of human security, such as curbing human trafficking and training police and military forces to respond to violence against women more generally, but also the hard issues of state formation and international recognition. Finally, women's organizations have used UNSCR 1325 to gain support for regional truth commissions and other projects relating to transitional justice in which women's voices and experiences are central.

The second lesson to be learned from the Balkan experience is that UNSCR 1325 provides a framework for promoting a regional approach to post-conflict reconstruction. Human rights and other conflict and post-conflict issues are rarely confined to national borders, but almost always involve neighboring ethnic groups and states. Women's organizations often constitute effective cross-border partners. In organizing regionally to promote and monitor the implementation of UNSCR 1325 in the Balkans, women's organizations enhanced regional perspectives and cooperation, as well as strengthened women's role in shaping the post-conflict political order.

A third lesson involves local women's organizations' use of a double boomerang strategy in attempting to achieve their goals. While Keck and Sikkink's boomerang mechanism can explain important dynamics of activists' strategies as well as a key element of their success, the experience of women's organizations in the Balkans suggests the need for a more nuanced and complex understanding of strategies employed in promoting gender equality. In post-conflict situations, where international intervention authorities usually play a major role, the simple boomerang mechanism of appealing to international norms and authorities to pressure the state and local authorities may prove inadequate for at least two reasons: first, because international authorities often act like the state and in place of the state; and second, because international authorities when they are acting like a de facto state, are often reluctant to enforce international norms. In such cases, women's organizations may employ what I have called a double boomerang strategy, sometimes appealing to international norms and authorities to pressure national and local authorities and sometimes appealing to local and national constituencies to pressure international authorities.

Finally, despite some apparent successes, numerous challenges remain in attempting to use UNSCR 1325 as a tool to promote enduring change and gender equality. While a full discussion of this topic remains outside the purview of this article, using UNSCR 1325 appears to result in both main-streaming, which has bureaucratized and diluted feminist goals, and side-streaming, which has isolated gender from other post-conflict concerns. Moreover, while some women's organizations have repeatedly challenged the 'militarization of all relationships in society' as a result of intervention, they have not been able to challenge, let alone rewrite, the rules of the inter-vention game. Finally, although the women's organizations have called atten-tion to the issue of poverty through promoting a human security perspective, there has been little substantial challenge to post-conflict, neo-liberal models of development. Women's movements worldwide have been least successful in tackling economic bases of inequality, and women's organizations and activists in post-conflict situations appear to be no exception (Basu 2010). UNSCR 1325 has thus far failed to provide a robust tool to this end.

In conclusion, the experience of women's organizations and activists in the Balkans illustrates both the tendency of the United Nations and international actors to engage with women's issues selectively and instrumentally and the ability of local women's organizations to challenge this approach. While UNSCR 1325 will undoubtedly prove a useful tool for pressuring national governments, it may also serve as a valuable, though limited, tool for women's organizations to shape the actions of international actors. In conflict areas, where such international actors are likely to have a prolonged and profound presence, mobilizing popular support to compel international actors to observe UNSCR 1325 may prove an effective strategy. In such cases, the boomerang must travel out not once but twice.

Acknowledgements

I would like to thank Amrita Basu, Jill Benderly, Bob Donia, Andrew Halterman, Carol Lilly, Patrice McMahon, Julie Mostov and two anonymous reviewers for their valuable comments on earlier drafts of this article. I would also like to thank the National Council for Eurasian and East European Research for partial funding for this research.

Notes on contributor

Jill A. Irvine is President's Associates Presidential Professor and Director of Women's and Gender Studies at the University of Oklahoma. She is author of *The Croat Question, Partisan Politics in the Formation of the Yugoslav Socialist State* and co-editor of *State–Society Relations in Yugoslavia 1945–1991* and *Natalija: Life in the Balkan Powderkeg 1880–1956.* She has written numerous articles, book chapters and government reports about democratic transformations in the Balkans. She is currently working on a book on women, war, and political transformation in the Balkans funded by the International Research and Exchanges Board and the National Council for Eurasian and East European Research.

References

Anderlini, S. N. 2007. *Women Building Peace: What They Do, Why It Matters.* Boulder, CO: Lynne Rienner Publishers.

Anderlini, S. N. 2010. 'What the Women Say, Participation and UNSCR 1325', *MIT Center for International Studies.* Available at http://web.mit.edu/cis/pdf/WomenReport_10_2010.pdf (accessed 3 October 2010).

Arifagić, E. and Sabović, S. 2007. 'A Human Security Assessment of EU Engagement in Kosovo', *Sudosteuropa Mitteilungen* 47 (1): 35–49.

Basu, A. (ed.). 2010. *Women's Movements in the Global Era: The Power of Local Feminisms.* Boulder, CO: Westview Press.

Benderly, J. 1997. 'Rape, Feminism, and Nationalism in the War in Yugoslav Successor States', in West, L. (ed.) *Feminist Nationalism*, pp. 59–72. New York and London: Routledge.

Borić, B. 2004. 'Application of Quotas: Legal Reforms and Implementation in Bosnia & Herzegovina'. Paper presented at International Institute for Democracy and Electoral Assistance (IDEA) CEE Network for Gender Issues Conference, Budapest, Hungary, October 22–23.

Borić, B. 2008. Interview with author, 4 July.

Charlesworth, H. 2005. 'Not Waving but Drowning: Gender Mainstreaming and Human Rights in the United Nations', *Harvard Human Rights Journal* 18: 1–18.

Chetail, V. 2009. *Post-Conflict Peacekeeping.* Oxford: Oxford University Press.

Cockburn, C. 2007. *From Where We Stand: War, Women's Activism and Feminist Analysis.* London: Zed Books.

Cohn, C., Kinsella, H. and Gibbings, S. 2004. 'Women, Peace and Security Council Resolution 1325', *International Feminist Journal of Politics* 6 (1): 130–140.

Djurdjević-Lukić, S. 2007. 'Security Sector Reform and the Role of Civil Society in the Western Balkans', *Sudosteuropa Mitteilungen* 47 (1): 50–61.

Fetahu, N. 2007. 'Transitional Justice: The Role of Civil Society, Difficulties and Challenges', in Farnsworth, N. (ed.) *Through Women's Solidarity to a Just Peace: A*

Report Based on the Women's Peace Coalition Second Annual Conference, pp. 25–8. Belgrade: Women's Peace Coalition.

Gaffney, C. and Alic, A. 2008. 'First Regional Truth Commission Runs into Doubts', *Balkan Insight*, 5 August. Available at http://www.balkaninsight.com/en/article/first-regional-truth-commission-runs-into-doubts (accessed 14 January 2010).

Global Rights. 2004. *Shadow Report on the Implementation of CEDAW and Women's Human Rights in Bosnia and Herzegovina*. Available at http://www.iwraw-ap.org/resources/pdf/Bosnia&Herzegovina_SR.pdf (accessed 6 December 2011).

Grodsky, B. 2009. 'International Prosecutions and Domestic Politics: The Use of Truth Commissions as Compromise Justice in Serbia and Croatia', *International Studies Review* 11 (4): 687–706.

Hadžihalilović, S. 2011. Interview with author, 29 June.

Halimi, S. 2007. *Monitoring Security in Kosovo from a Gender Perspective*. Pristina: Kosovar Center for Gender Studies.

Idrizi, V. 2008. Interview with author, 28 June.

Irvine, J. A. 2007. 'Women's Organizations and Critical Elections in Croatia', *Politics and Gender* 3 (1): 7–32.

Kašić, B. 2007. 'Feminist Movements, Time Lags, Innovations: A Case Study of Feminism(s) in Croatia', in Saurer, E., Lanzinger, M. and Frysak, E. (eds) *Women's Movement, Networks and Debates in Post-communist Countries in the 19th and 20th Centuries*, pp. 213–22. Koln: Bohlau Verlag.

Keating, T. and Knight, W. A. (eds). 2004. *Building Sustainable Peace*. New York: The United Nations University Press; and Edmonton, AB: The University of Alberta Press.

Keck, M. E. and Sikkink, K. 1998. *Activists Beyond Borders: Advocacy Networks in International Politics*. Ithaca, NY: Cornell University Press.

Korac, M. 1998. 'Linking Arms: Women and War in Post-Yugoslav States', Uppsala Life and Peace Institute. Available at http://www.life-peace.org/default2.asp?xid=409

Kosova Women's Network. 2008. 'Statement on UNDP's Prevention of Kosovar Women's Participation in Politics and Violation of UNSCR 1325', 4 December 2008. Email from KWN listserve.

Kosova Women's Network. 2009. *Monitoring Implementation of United Nations Security Council Resolution 1325 in Kosova*, 2nd ed. Prishtina: Kosova Women's Network.

Kstovicova, D., Bojičić-Dželilović, V. and Martin, M. 2007. 'Civil Society's Role in Advancing Human Security: European Union Policies in the Western Balkans', *Sudosteuropa Mitteilungen* 47 (1): 20–33.

Kumar, K. 2001. *Women and Civil War, Impact, Organizations and Action*. Boulder, CO: Lynne Rienner Publishers.

Lithander, A. (ed.). 2000. *Engendering the Peace Process: A Gender Approach to Dayton and Beyond*. Halmstad: Kvinna til Kvinna.

Mazurana, D., Raven-Roberts, A. and Parpart, J. 2005. *Gender, Conflict, and Peacekeeping*. Plymouth: Rowman & Littlefield Publishers.

Mendelson, S. E. 2005. 'Barrack and Brothels, Peacekeepers and Human Trafficking in the Balkans', *Center for Strategic and International Studies*. Available at http://csis. org/files/media/csis/pubs/0502_barracksbrothels.pdf (accessed 13 October 2010).

Mertus, J. 2004. *Women's Participation in the International Tribunal for the Former Yugoslavia (ICTY): Transitional Justice for Bosnia and Herzegovina*. Washington, DC: Hunt Alternatives Fund.

Mostov, J. 2010. 'UNSCR 1325 and Regional Security: Networking for Peace and Security'. Paper presented at the International Studies Association Annual Convention, New Orleans, LA, 18 February. Available at http://citation. allacademic.com/meta/p_mla_apa_research_citation/4/1/6/9/2/pages416923/p41 6923-1.php (accessed 6 December 2011).

NGO Working Group on Women. 2005. *From Local to Global, Making Peace Work for Women, Security Council Resolution 1325 Five Years On Report*. Available at http://www.womenpeacesecurity.org/media/pdf-fiveyearson.pdf (accessed 9 October 2009).

Orford, A. 2002. 'Feminism, Imperialism and the Mission of International Law', *Nordic Journal of International Law* 71: 275–96.

Otto, D. 2009. 'The Exile of Inclusion: Reflections on Gender Issues in International Law over the Last Decade', *Melbourne Journal of International Law* 10 (1): 11–26.

Porter, E. 2007. *Peacebuilding: Women in International Perspective*. London: Routledge.

Rasić, M. 2007. 'Women, Peace and Security', in Farnsworth, N. (ed.) *Through Women's Solidarity to a Just Peace. A Report Based on the Women's Peace Coalition Second Annual Conference*, pp. 44–5. Belgrade: Women's Peace Coalition.

RECOM. 2009. *Report About the Consultative Process on Instruments of Truth-Seeking About War Crimes and Other Serious Violations of Human Rights in Post Yugoslav Countries: May 2006 June 2009*. Belgrade: Humanitarian Law Center.

RECOM. 2011. 'Koalicija za REKOM'. Available at http://zarekom.org/Koalicija-za-Rekom.sr.html (accessed 14 December 2011).

Rogova, I. 2007. 'Women, Peace and Security: Kosovo Women's Activists' Efforts to Implement UNSCR 1325', in Farnsworth, N. (ed.) *Through Women's Solidarity to a Just Peace. A Report Based on the Women's Peace Coalition Second Annual Conference*, pp. 45–9. Belgrade: Women's Peace Coalition.

Rogova, I. 2008. Interview with author, 1 July.

RWL. 2007a. 'Message from Members of the Regional Women's Lobby for Peace, Security and Justice in South-East Europe on upcoming Elections in Kosovo'. Available at http://www.rwlsee.org/images/stories/pressrelease/7112007.pdf (accessed 6 December 2011).

RWL. 2007b. 'Regional Women's Lobby Letter to UNSC'. Available at http://www. womensnetwork.org/images/pdf/al/Regional%20Womens%20Lobby%20Letter% 20to%20UNSC.pdf (accessed 6 December 2011).

RWL. 2008a. 'RWL Opposes Six Point Plan on Kosovo Reached between Serbia and UN Secretary-General', 18 November. Available at http://www.rwlsee.org/index.php? option=com_content&view=article&id=26%3Arwl-opposes-six-point-plan-on-kosovo-reached-between-serbia-and-un-secretary-general&catid=3%3Apress-release&Itemid=15&lang=en (accessed 22 October 2009).

RWL. 2008b. 'A Secure Future for Our Region: What Does It Take? Women Leaders Speak Out', Conference Concept Note. Pristina, Kosovo, 27 October. Available at http://www.rwlsee.org/images/stories/common/concnote.pdf (accessed 6 December 2011).

RWL. 2008c. 'A Secure Future for Our Region: What Does It Take? Women Leaders Speak Out', Conference Press Release. Pristina, Kosovo, 27 October. Available at http://www.rwlsee.org/images/stories/common/confpress.pdf (accessed 6 December 2011).

RWL. 2008d. 'A Secure Future for Our Region: What Does It Take? Women Leaders Speak Out', Conference Report. Pristina, Kosovo, 27 October. Available at http://www.rwlsee.org/images/stories/common/report.pdf (accessed 6 December 2011).

Shepherd, L. J. 2008. *Gender, Violence and Security*. New York: Zed Books.

Solioz, C. 2006. 'Strengths and Weaknesses of Civil Society in the Balkans: Continuities from Conflict to Peace'. Paper presented at World Movement for Democracy, Fourth Assembly: Istanbul, Turkey, 5 April.

Somun, L. 2011. Interview with author, 21 June.

UNIFEM. 2009. 'Implementing UN Security Council Resolution 1325 on Women, Peace and Security in South East Europe, Phase I and Phase II'. Available at http://www.peacewomen.org/assets/file/Resources/NGO/1325_Monitoring1325SEEurope_June2009.pdf (accessed 10 October 2009).

United Nations Security Council. 2000. 'Resolution 1325'. Available at http://www.un.org/events/res_1325e.pdf (accessed 6 December 2011).

Vuković, J. 2007. 'Security, the Activities of Women in Black, and UN Security Council Resolution 1325', in Zavojić, S., Perković, M. and Urošević, M. (eds) *Women for Peace*, pp. 182–6. Belgrade: Women in Black.

Zajović, S. 2006a. 'Conference Proceedings. Women, Peace, Security', 1–3 September, Struga, Macedonia. Available at http://www.zeneucrnom.org (accessed 21 October 2009).

Zajović, S. 2006b. 'Report: Women, Peace, Security, Fieldwork experiences workshops, interactive lectures, campaigns', Available at http://www.zeneucrnom.org/index.php?option=com_content&task=view&id=199&Itemid=54&lang=en (accessed 14 October 2009).

Zajović, S. 2007. 'Peace and Security from a Feminist-Pacifist Perspective', in Zavojić, S., Perković, M. and Urošević, M. (eds) *Women for Peace*, pp. 168–81. Belgrade: Women in Black.

Zajović, S. 2008. Interview with author, 24 June.

Žene Ženama. 2005. *Annual Report*. Sarajevo: Žene Ženama.

Žene Ženama. 2007. *Monitoring Implementation of UNSCR 1325 in Bosnia and Herzegovina. Final Report*. Bratislava: UNIFEM.

Žene Ženama. 2009. 'Ucestovanje javnosti u mirovnim procesima – Rezolucija Savjeta bezbednosti Ujedinjenih nacija 1325'. Available at http://www.zenezenama.org/zene/images/dokumenti/publikacije/obuka_trenera.pdf (accessed 3 September 2010).

Zvizdić, N. 2011. Interview with author, 25 June.

Index

For Product Safety Concerns and Information please contact our EU
representative GPSR@taylorandfrancis.com
Taylor & Francis Verlag GmbH, Kaufingerstraße 24, 80331 München, Germany

www.ingramcontent.com/pod-product-compliance
Lightning Source LLC
Chambersburg PA
CBHW070428270326
41926CB00014B/2991

9 7 8 1 1 3 8 3 8 3 2 9 6